LET US

Worship

LET US
Worship

by

JUDSON CORNWALL

Bridge-Logos
Gainesville, Florida 32614

Bridge-Logos

Gainesville, FL 32614 USA

Let Us Praise / Let Us Worship
by Judson Cornwall

Library of Congress Catalog Card Number: 2005936843
International Standard Book Number 0-88270-134-7

Unless otherwise identified. Scriptures quotations are from the *King James Version* of the Bible.

Scripture quotations identified AMPLIFIED are from the Amplified Bible. Copyright© The Lockman Foundation 1954-58, and are used by permission.

Scripture quotations identified NEB are from the New English Bible. Copyright © The Delegates of the Oxford University Press and Syndics of the Cambridge University Press 1961, 1970. Reprinted by permission.

Scripture quotations identified PHILLIPS are from the New Testament in Modern English Revised edition, J.B. Phillips, translator. Copyright © J.B.Phillips 1958, 1960, 1972. Used by permission of Macmillan Publishing Company Inc.

Scripture quotations identified RSV are from the Revised Standard Version of the Bible. Copyright © Division of Christian Education of the National Council of the Churches of Christ in the United States of America 1946, 1952 ® 1971 and 1973.

Scripture quotations identified TEV are from the Good News Bible - Old Testament: Copyright © American Bible Society 1976; New Testament: Copyright© American Bible Society 1966, 1971, 1976.

Verses marked TLB are taken from the Living Bible, Copyright ® 1971 by Tyndale House Publishers, Wheaton, Ill. Used by permission.

G1.316x.N.m604.35220

CONTENTS

Let Us Worship

To Charlotte Baker

a fellow-worshipper of God, a co-laborer in the ministry, an innovator of fresh ways to worship the Lord, and a long-time personal friend.

Acknowledgments

Since this is my thirteenth book, my wife has long ago become accustomed to the separation and subtle changes in my behavior when I accept the challenge of "just one more book." I, however, do not want to take for granted her graceful acceptance of these things. I thank my wife, Eleanor, for her encouragement to me during the seven years that I have carried this book unwritten in my spirit, and during the months that I have sought to reduce my thoughts to printed words.

I have never had less personal involvement in the mechanical end of writing a book than this book, for the very week that I began writing *Let Us Worship*, Pat Parrish came to Fountain Gate as my personal secretary. Since I was on a conference tour at the time, it fell her lot to learn on her own our office routine and the idiosyncrasies of my word processor. Then chapter after chapter of this book began to arrive by mail. She edited them, entered them into the computer, and had them ready for my rewrite on my short visits home. She has done an admirable job with great cheerfulness. Her arrival was surely timed of the Lord. It appears that God has joined a team together for the writing of many books to come.

Preface

It has been over ten years since a forceful prophetic word over me declared that God had called me to be a worshipper. Since that life-changing experience in a camp meeting in Seattle, I have been used of God to bring many hundreds of people into praise. But this has never seemed to satisfy my deep inner craving after God. As my own responses Godward deepened and matured, I began to minister more on worship than on praise, and the publishing house that released my first book, *Let Us Praise*, urged me to write a book on worship. I agreed with great joy, but every time I would begin the chore, the Spirit within me would either say that I was not ready to write such a book or that the Body of Christ was not yet ready to receive a book on worship.

For seven years I carried this yearning inside of me. I gathered material from many sources. I wrote magazine articles on worship for a variety of Christian publications, and I toured the world preaching exclusively on worship. It was not until the summer of 1982 that the Holy Spirit released me to put into book form the truths that had been burning deep within me for so long.

While awaiting the release for writing this book, I was challenged to write ten other books that I can see, in retrospect, laid the groundwork necessary to prepare hearts to embrace this book on worship.

When the Spirit released me to write this book, I felt that He was instructing me to use the style of writing that I had used for an earlier book, that is, short chapters written so that they can be read on their own, not only as part of the book. I trust that this is as pleasing to the readers of this book as it seemed to be to those who have read *Unfeigned Faith*.

I have not attempted to do a thorough exposition of all Bible passages that deal with worship. I have instead sought to inspire, direct, and channel the responses of the reader into worship, and to share from my experiences and observations over the past few years. If this book succeeds in inspiring worship in even a few persons, it will have been worth the enjoyable time I have spent in writing it.

1

The Call to Worship

It was one of those gorgeous fall days with a clear blue sky and crisp clean air that makes the New England states such a delightful place to visit. A Christian friend was driving me from the hospitality of his home in the foothills of Maryland into Washington, D.C., where I was to speak at a conference. Sitting in the back seat and enjoying the morning scenery, I was startled to see what appeared to be a large turkey farm in a corn field. As I was about to remark on it, I realized that what I was seeing were not turkeys, but hundreds of Canadian geese.

My host explained to me that modern methods of harvesting leave much grain in the fields and these Canadian honkers had stopped by on their migration south to take advantage of a free feast.

Seeing this field almost blackened with feeding geese reminded me of the many times I had stood gazing into the heavens watching the giant "V" formations of geese responding to an inner urge to fly south in the fall and north in the spring. For those who scoff at miracles, let them explain, if they can, what mysterious, unseen force of nature triggers twice a year the migratory instinct in thousands of these geese. For the young gosling it is a call to a totally new adventure into a vast, uncharted expanse of sky. For the mature goose it is another exhausting flight of thousands of miles fraught with hazards and hunger. Still, each goose must answer this unseen, unheard and, so far, unexplained call.

Similarly, there are times when Christians sense an invisible yet indisputable calling to draw near to God in worship. For the uninitiated, it is as threatening and challenging as the first migration is to the gosling. The intimate, personal, one-to-one relationship with God is a vast unknown to millions of people in today's generation, and yet the urge to attain it is beginning to surge through Christendom. Though latent and undefined, it is unmistakably there.

For many believers these are days of unrest. In spite of all that God has done in our generation, there is in some an underlying dissatisfaction which is really an anxious anticipation of something new on the horizon. God is moving by His Spirit and we are anxious to know what will happen next. This has created an ideal atmosphere for the religious opportunists. False prophets have arisen amassing millions into their cults. Because of this unrest and craving for the unrevealed, proponents of these so-called "new doctrines" have found eager, gullible audiences. Others, who have insisted that new forms and structure are the only hope for the Church, have had little difficulty in getting adherents. Those who have joined cults, especially young people, have been duped into raising huge sums of money, often at great personal cost, as a substitute satisfaction for an inner craving.

These inner stirrings are so real that they cannot be ignored, yet most of our attempts to satisfy them are futile. Consequently, frustration replaces inspiration and seeking replaces rest. We simply do not recognize that God is causing this unrest. He is drawing us unto Himself.

As a boy I enjoyed playing with a horseshoe magnet from a model "T" magneto and using its invisible power on a plate filled with metal filings. These tiny pieces of steel would shiver and quake as the magnet was lowered; then they would crawl over one another as though alive in response to the magnetic attraction. As I would gently move the magnet closer to the plate, the filings would make a chain reaching upward until finally the chain bridged the gap between the filings and the magnet. Upon contact, all of the small pieces would come together by the power of the magnet, and each particle became as magnetic as the magnet itself.

Isn't this descriptive of the Church's present condition? God is drawing His people closer, very much like a magnet. The unrest and uneasiness we feel are merely the response of our spirit to God's presence. Our dissatisfaction with the present status quo is merely a byproduct of the attraction of God's nearness. It is not ingratitude that is motivating us to abandon our present positions; it is the magnetism of His person that is precipitating change. The pull is upward and we are powerless to resist.

Some people are greatly threatened by the divine surge that moves upon them; others are excited but confused, while a great many totally misunderstand this drawing power of God and misread it as a craving of their body or soul. But such has been man's problem from antiquity.

Jacob

Didn't Jacob totally misread his encounter with God? Genesis chapter twenty-eight records his awakening dream in which he saw angels ascending and descending upon a ladder stretched from heaven to earth. He also heard the voice of God speaking directly to him. Upon awakening and dedicating the spot as "Bethel" ("House of God") he immediately pledged:

"of all that Thou shalt give me I will surely give the tenth to Thee" (Genesis 28:22). From that day forward Jacob gave himself to the pursuit of material things. Having stolen his brother's birthright and then manipulating his father-in-law's property to his own advantage, he returns to his own land a very wealthy man. With a drive that would be a credit to any corporation president, Jacob had pursued materialism and won.

But God's second intervention into his affairs proved just how wrong he had been. After Jacob wrestled all night with the Angel of the Lord (Genesis 32:24) there was a decided change in him. Physically he was crippled, emotionally he was exhausted, but spiritually he was transformed. He was even given a new name, "Israel," or "the God-ruled man." God's initial revelation had stirred Jacob, but he misread it as a drive to "get ahead." Not until he had ultimately succeeded did he realize that *things* cannot satisfy a longing after God. His spirit had been stirred to worship but his will had directed that conferred energy into the pursuit of "the good life." Yet such pursuit has never satisfied any man, while the pursuit of God ultimately makes "all things" available to the worshipper, for Jesus said, "If ye abide in Me, and My words abide in you, ye shall ask what ye will, and it shall be done unto you" (John 15:7). The principle of "... Seek ye first the kingdom of God, and His righteousness; and all these things shall be added unto you" (Matthew 6:33) was a divine law long before Jesus proclaimed it.

Moses

Moses was another man who had experienced an encounter with God, although he was far too young to understand it. His preservation from death was ordained of God, as was his being received into the palace of Pharaoh to be raised the son of the king's daughter. This awakened spirit within Moses sent him on a pursuit of social action. He was indignantly resentful of the treatment the Hebrews received and sensed himself to be their deliverer. However, God had not called him to pursue social equality but the divine presence. It was not until Moses took matters into his own hands by murdering an Egyptian oppressor, (Exodus 2:12) thereby necessitating his fleeing for his own life for an additional forty years on the desert, that God could call him unto Himself through the divine appearance at the burning bush (Exodus 3). After this heavenly revelation Moses dedicated himself to the pursuit of God and subsequently became the world's greatest example of a deliverer until Jesus Christ came into the world. Has any one man done more to put down social injustice or to raise his people from slavery to a nation of free men? Yet this was unachievable as long as he pursued it as a substitute for answering the craving of his spirit for fellowship with God. The pull of the magnet was to lift him upward, not to extend him outward. Yet once contact with God was achieved, he affected the life of everyone with whom he came in contact. Through him, God moved upon more than four million people. They were liberated because he was lifted by God's presence. Moses' time in God's presence became Israel's ticket to freedom, but he almost lost it all by misreading the calling of God unto Himself as the calling of his soul for social equality.

Israel

One would think that having this powerful object lesson in front of them day by day would cause the Israelites to yearn to be worshippers. In addition to Moses' life, they had also seen the mighty power of God demonstrated in the plagues upon Egypt and the parting of the Red Sea. Their daily water supply and provision of food was a supernatural miracle, as was their guidance through the wilderness.

Nevertheless, when God finally revealed Himself to them on Mt. Sinai and offered them a personal relationship, they requested that He not speak to them again, and in return pledged to do anything that He requested (Deuteronomy 5:24-27). They traded relationship for law and worship for works. As professional slaves they felt qualified to do but unworthy to *be*. They would do His work but not become His worshippers. So God gave them the Law, the Testament, and the Ordinances. He had them construct a tabernacle and form a priesthood. He kept them busy, but it didn't satisfy them. Repeatedly they murmured and complained. They rebelled at God's leaders and fearfully refused to enter the promised land. Their encounter with God had awakened their spirits to worship, but they misinterpreted it as a cry for good works, and only Moses and the Elders enjoyed the presence of God (Exodus 24:1, 9, 10). The rest of that generation was buried in the sands where they had insisted on being slaves instead of sons.

Idolatry

At the urging of Israel, Moses approached God on the fiery mountain and presented their petition that they be allowed to exchange relationship for service. During the forty days that God was giving Moses the Law and the Commandments the Israelites in the camp reacted to the absence of Moses as though they had totally lost God; they asked Aaron, Moses' brother, to make a visual representation of God for them so that they wouldn't feel so forsaken. Rather than point out that God had not forsaken them but that they had rejected God, Aaron yielded to their pressure and made a golden calf for them to worship (Exodus 32:1-6), and then he proclaimed a feast day for worship. Unfortunately their worship was given to this costly idol instead of to the true and living God. They correctly interpreted their drive to worship, but they prostituted it by giving that worship to something that was not God.

While God was grieved at Moses' involvement in social action as an attempt to satisfy the crying of his spirit, and put up for many years with Jacob's substitution of materialism for worship, and even accepted Israel's trade of service for sonship, God was stirred to a hot anger at Israel's prostitution of worship. Jacob and Moses could be brought to worship, but idolaters are already worshipping. The tragedy is that all of their adoration is going to something or someone other than God. This provokes God to wrath, and when "... the great day of His wrath is come ... who shall be able to stand?" (Revelation 6:17).

James and John

Men and women of the Old Testament were not the only ones to misunderstand God's call to worship; the New Testament plentifully abounds in similar individuals. For instance, James and John, the sons of Zebedee, enlisted the help of their mother to appeal to Jesus for them to be allowed to sit on His right and left hand in the new kingdom (Matthew 20:20 and Mark 10:35-37). All of their relationship with Jesus had stirred an inner desire which they interpreted as a yearning for power and authority. They felt that governmental control was the ultimate for them while completely overlooking the fact that they had been ordained to "be with Him" (Mark 3:14), not do with Him. They had been called to relationship not rulership; to love Him, not lead Him.

Samaritans

Similarly the eighth chapter of Acts tells us that during the revival in Samaria one of the outstanding converts was Simon the sorcerer. Hearing of this great stir in Samaria the apostles in Jerusalem sent Peter and John to assist in conserving the harvest and in maturing believers. Under the ministry of these two disciples the Holy Spirit was conferred to believers through the laying on of hands, and this so excited Simon that he offered the men money if they would give him this power to confer the Holy Spirit upon others (vss. 18-19). Although he had met Christ in conversion, he was unaware of the need for his spirit to worship. Therefore, he thought his greatest need was to do the miraculous. He lusted for power instead of loving the person of Christ.

Likewise the woman of Samaria, confronted by Jesus at Jacob's well, gives us a classic example of misinterpreting the divine call to worship. In John chapter four, Jesus told her that she had gone through five marriages and was living with the sixth man without the sanctity of marriage.

Christ did not condemn her for her many marriages or for her open involvement in adultery. Once she confessed it He ignored it and began to teach her to worship. It is as though He were saying, "You've tried to satisfy the craving of your spirit by your relationships with men, but it is not your soul crying, 'I want a man.' It is your spirit screaming, 'I want God.' The itch in your spirit cannot be scratched in your soul."

Isn't this what Paul was saying when he wrote: "Be not drunk with wine, wherein is excess; but be filled with the Spirit?" Doesn't this suggest that the same thing that drives one man to drink drives another man to God? One translates it as a cry of the appetite while another correctly interprets it as a craving of his spirit after God.

Some years ago while pastoring in Eugene, Oregon where we were involved in a building program, I had a rare evening off. Seated alone in my front room after having a delicious meal, I became aware of a deep longing or a craving for something. Rationalizing that I had not taken time to listen to music for many weeks I put some classical music on the stereo and sat back to relax and enjoy its soothing sounds. But the music only increased my edginess. Thinking that it was the wrong type of music for my mood I changed to gospel music, but its effect upon me was no better. I switched the music off and began to read, assuming that my intellect needed feeding because my involvement in the building program had consumed my reading time. Nevertheless, I couldn't find any type of literature that satisfied me.

Almost absentmindedly, thinking that my craving was for food, I wandered into the kitchen and prepared myself a large sandwich. But inasmuch as I had already stuffed myself on my wife's cooking less than an hour before, I soon realized that my craving was not physical. Finally, I had to admit that my need was not physical, emotional, or intellectual. This left only my spirit; so I got onto my knees to pray and began to touch the presence of God. Total satisfaction swept through my being. All along it had been my spirit yearning to contact God's Spirit, and I had misread it as a craving in my soul or my body. For the rest of the evening any music and any literature was enjoyable, for the deep crying of my spirit had been satisfied in God's presence.

How common this is to all of us. When God draws near to us, His presence begins to affect us as a giant magnet, but we frequently find it difficult to understand. Like Moses, we often get involved in social action, trying to better the lot of others or, like Jacob, we try to satisfy the new drive by amassing "things." We become materialistic in our pursuit instead of letting our spirits pursue God.

Sometimes we're like the Israelites who substituted service for relationship with God. No one can serve like a frustrated Christian who is trying to respond to the callings of God through activity, programs, ministry, or Christian service. The more pronounced the crying of the spirit the more they work, although they should know it won't satisfy their craving.

Occasionally we respond to the callings of God as Aaron helped Israel to respond—in idolatry. We pour out love, adoration, adulation, and a low form of worship on our pastors, our programs, our doctrines, our denominations, or whatever. It isn't satisfying because it isn't God, and our spirit is longing for a fuller relationship with the Spirit of God.

Tragically enough there are always those who turn to inordinate passion and illicit sex in their attempts to satisfy this inner drive for something more. Just how many lives and ministries have been ruined through this searching for love outside of God and His provisions only God in heaven knows.

While the sin of idolatry and the error of adultery may be obvious to all except those involved in it, the craving for position and authority can hide behind a mask of holy zeal. James and John were not the last beings who yearned for governmental authority more than they yearned for intimate relationship with God. The politics of the Church on earth are too widely known to require explanation. Titles are heady wine to some men and, for them, position is worth any price. But even when they graduate to the top office, their spirits are totally unsatisfied.

Perhaps the most insidious substitute we can make for worship is a lusting for divine power. Like Simon the sorcerer we want to confer spiritual power at will upon the needy or the petitioner. Somehow we feel that displaying His power is the zenith of Christian maturity. All too frequently we draw attention to ourselves rather than draw others to the true source of power. Church history has disclosed that many who have moved in the demonstration of power have also moved away from the divine presence.

Or, is it possible that we fall into the trap that had almost destroyed the woman of Samaria wherein we seek to find in human relationships what can only be found in God. No man can meet a woman's spiritual needs, and the woman has not been born who can meet a man's spiritual needs. Our spirit belongs to God and can only find fulfillment and complete satisfaction in Him.

Sadly enough, all of these substitutes for worship come from misunderstanding or misinterpreting the craving that God produces in man's spirit when He draws near. The spirit within us seeks release from captivity to soar into the presence of God as surely as the goose seems compelled to respond to the call to migrate. Perhaps since geese do not have the confusing signals of a spirit, soul and body combination as man does, they are freer to merely respond to the call so that their migration is inerrant. But man, in his complexity, often overlooks the reality of his spirit and the entire spirit world and gets terribly confused when God interposes Himself upon mankind. But that's what is happening at this time. God is drawing near to men intending to draw them near to Himself. Jesus Himself stated: "And I, if I be lifted up from the earth, will draw all men unto Me" (John 12:32). The Holy Spirit's move of the past years has certainly lifted up and exalted Jesus in a fresh, new way. The outcome of seeing Jesus anew will be determined by each individual's ability to recognize the accompanying call to worship.

But it will take more than mere recognition of a call to worship to make us worshippers, for although the desire may be inherent, the ability to perform what we desire was lost in Adam's fall.

Has God unkindly left an instinct for which there can be no satisfaction, or has God, who issued the call, also made provision for us to answer that call?

2

The Provision of Worship

The first time I met Eleanor Louise Eaton was when she was assigned as the pianist for my preaching team in my freshman year of Bible college in Southern California. That music was her life was evident from the very first service, for when she played the piano she sparkled and flowed vivaciously, obviously enjoying every minute of it. As these assignments continued, our relationship was enhanced by our mutual love for music, and when that relationship matured to my proposal of marriage I assured her that she would have a piano in the home at all times. The drive for musical expression is sometimes so strong in her that nothing else matters, and when that drive cannot be satisfied, as is so often the case when she travels with me, she becomes somewhat disoriented and even physically ill. This strong musical drive in her needs reasonable access to a piano, guitar, violin, organ, or mandolin, and I have consistently sought to have all of them available to her; not because she demands it, but because she really needs them.

God similarly deals with us! He has never created an inner drive for which He failed to provide a channel of fulfillment.

The drive of hunger, for example, is balanced with appetite and the enjoyment we receive by eating. Our sex drives are meant to find fulfillment and satisfaction in marriage, and our need for rest is fulfilled in a night's sleep. God instills a need, and then provides for the satisfaction of that need.

If the call to worship, that seems almost to be an instinct in every human spirit, is God created and has been divinely implanted within us, then we can rightly expect God to also provide an outlet for that urge to worship. At Jacob's well Jesus said: "...The hour cometh, and now is, when the true worshippers *shall worship* the Father in spirit and in truth ..." (John 4:23, italics added). This is not so much a command as it is a commitment. It is a promise of Jesus and a provision of the Father. That we are commanded to praise the Lord is quite clear in the Scriptures, but since worship is fundamentally love responding to love it cannot function out of command; it must be a willing response to a spiritual stimulus. But Jesus assures us that the love that we feel, and the flow of the Holy Spirit that we experience will not frustrate us, but will find their fulfillment when we release them back to God in worship.

"The hour cometh," Jesus said, "when the true worshippers SHALL worship." All other emphases will be set aside for worship. Mere ritual will give way for meaningful worship. This promise follows the earlier pledge that "... the water that I shall give him shall be in him a well of water springing up into everlasting life" (John 4:14). J.B. Phillips translates this: "For my gift will become a spring in the man himself, welling up into eternal life." Later in this Gospel John defines this spring, or river, as the gift of the Holy Spirit who would flow out of a person like "rivers of living water" (John 7:38). Jesus promised an inflow into the believer that would become an outflow back to its source, and when the Spirit flows through us back to God it is worship at a priceless level.

Later in this Gospel of John, Jesus expanded this promise in saying: "Howbeit when He, the Spirit of truth, is come, He will guide you into all truth: for He shall not speak of Himself, but whatsoever He shall hear, that shall He speak: and He will shew you things to come. *He shall glorify me*" (John 16:13,14, italics added). The *Merriam Webster Dictionary* defines *glorify* as: "to praise to celestial glory ... to give glory as (in worship)." So Jesus affirmed that the Holy Spirit in the life of the Christian would, indeed, glorify or worship Jesus through us. This is a divine promise with an accompanying provision.

But this is not only a promise of the Son, it is also a provision of the Father, for everything that Jesus promised the Father had to provide—even the very Spirit that would become the key to our worshipping. We cannot lose sight of the fact that in all of life in order for the lesser to bless the greater (worship), the permission of the greater is needed. As in Queen Esther's experience, unless the sceptre is extended we dare not approach the throne.

In the Book of Revelation, praise and worship of God stand second only to the revelation of Jesus Himself. It starts with the worship of the four mighty creatures who are joined by the twenty-four elders and, later, "many angels" (and John's parenthesis suggests that there were about 100 million angels), then a group so large that no one could number them united with them only to be joined later by "all the angels." Promenading through the streets of heaven and ascending higher and higher into the presence of God, praising with a "loud voice," they finally reached the throne room and saw God seated upon His throne. As soon as they saw God this shouting, singing throng lost their speech. The majesty, the glory, the power, and the radiant energy of holiness that emits from God is enough to cause anyone to fall silent in awe. But, "... A voice came out of the throne, saying, Praise our God, all ye His servants, and ye that fear Him, both small and great"

(Revelation 19:5). Is this a command? No, not really. It is a consent. They had been praising and worshipping until they saw God. God simply said, *Don't stop now, children. That's fine; I grant you sovereign permission to worship Me.*

When permission to bless was granted, John records that the expressed worship reached such high decibel levels that he was unable to measure or describe it. He just likened it to the sound of many waters, or the voice of many thunders. By simply granting permission, God provided His people with the right to express wonder and adoration in worship, and they responded enthusiastically.

This incident in the final book of the Bible does not stand alone in granting us permission to worship God, for the words "worship," "worshipped" and "worshippers" are recorded over 270 times in the Scriptures. Worship is the *main theme* of the Bible. All of God's creation has been called to worship Him. "… Let all the angels of God worship Him," Hebrews 1:6 declares. "All nations whom Thou hast made shall come and worship before Thee, O Lord; and shall glorify Thy name" (Psalm 86:9), the Psalmist declares. God's provision for man to worship Him is consistently expressed throughout the Old Testament as "Exalt ye the Lord our God, and worship at His footstool; for He is holy" (Psalm 99:5). Again, it is less a command than it is a provision for a deep-seated human drive that can only be fully satisfied in worship.

The provision God has made that allows man, the lesser, to worship God, the greater, could never be implemented by man if God had not made a further provision that would lift mankind from the dregs of sin and restore him to fellowship with a Holy God, for only the forgiven one can step from dread and fear of God to worship and adoration of Him. True worship is possible only on the basis of the divine atonement that was provided by God at Calvary. Through the self-offering of God in the Son, the believer now stands in a personal relation of sonship to

God on the basis of a new birth. Prayer, then, ceases being merely a pleading for mercy and becomes the praising of our merciful God. Through His High Priestly office, Christ enables men to offer acceptable worship unto God. Our restoration becomes the basis of our rejoicing, and Christ's finished work becomes the foundation of our worship. As the *Zondervan Pictorial Encyclopedia* reminds us, "The roots of Biblical worship are to be found, not in human emotions, but in the divinely established relationship of God to man." This does not deny that human emotions and reactions are involved in worship, but they are not the controlling factors.

The emotions of man do not constitute the true essence of worship. Rather, it is the renewed relationship with God that forms the basis of our loving response to God. No longer is our reaction to God's presence, "depart from me; for I am a sinful man, O Lord" (Luke 5:8), but like the Shulamite maiden we cry, "draw me, we will run after Thee" (Song of Solomon 1:4).

The true essence of worship is when His Spirit bears witness with our spirit, triggering the human spirit to respond in love and adoration to God Almighty. But, hallelujah, He has made that provision.

It becomes obvious to a maturing Christian that the Christian life is designed for worship. God made us with a desire and a need to worship, and in our new birth He made us able to perform that worship, for when we were born again we received the *life* of Christ that enables us to stand before God.

Paul declared, "Therefore if any man be in Christ, he is a new creature: old things are passed away; behold, all things are become new. And all things are of God, who hath reconciled us to Himself by Jesus Christ ..." (2 Corinthians 5:17,18). When we are made new we are also reconciled to God, and out of this glorious reunion comes the challenge and capacity to worship God in spirit and in truth.

Not only have we received this life of Christ, we have received the *mind* of Christ which enables us to both know and to worship God. Our carnal, natural minds neither know God or the ways of God, "but we have the mind of Christ" (1 Corinthians 2:16).

Furthermore, we receive the Spirit of Christ who enables us to contact God. "The Spirit itself beareth witness with our spirit, that we are the children of God" (Romans 8:16), Paul declares. Worship is fundamentally God's Spirit within us contacting the Spirit in the Godhead. God has made a marvelous provision for worship in sending His own Spirit to dwell in our hearts by faith. This indwelling Spirit shares some of the character of God with us in ripening the fruits of love, joy, peace, long-suffering, gentleness, goodness, faith, meekness, and temperance (see Galatians 5:22, 23) so that we can worship in a manner that is more consistent with the way God is worshipped in heaven.

This same indwelling Spirit of God also aids our worship through the operation of the Gifts of the Spirit. In his first Corinthian letter, Paul lists nine special "charismas," as the theologians like to call them, or "special abilities," as Ken Taylor translates the Greek word *pneumatica* in The Living Bible. These nine *gifts* logically divide themselves into three groups of three each enabling us to supernaturally know, do, and say. By action of the gifts of the word of wisdom, the word of knowledge, and the discerning of spirits we can understand things that relate to God and the spirit world where worship transpires. Through the manifestation of the gifts of faith, healings, and miracles the believer is divinely enabled to be an active participant in the works of God, and nothing enhances fellowship quite like doing things together. The last "special ability" in Paul's list (see 1 Corinthians 12:8-10) has to do with speech: prophecy, interpretation, and tongues. Fundamentally, tongues is man's communication with God under divine enablement, while prophecy is God's communication with man under the Spirit's anointing. These gifts become beautiful assets to worship in the life of the believer, for through them we can think with God's thoughts, function in His power, and speak and understand heavenly languages. Little wonder, then, that we are challenged to worship in the Spirit.

Throughout the Bible the beginning of worship lies in the object of worship rather than in the subject: that is, God is both the object and inspiration of our worship. He initiates it, and He enables us to perform it. Any believer can worship, because he can come to the Father in the name of the Son since that Name has been given to all believers. He can worship because the Spirit of God that provides worship is in that believer's life, and his worship is further enhanced because Jesus, seated in the heavens, enables man to offer worship that is acceptable unto God. Christ even made provision for mixing heaven's incense with our incense of worship so that it will have the right fragrance when it gets to the nostrils of the Father (see Revelation 8:3). As the *Zondervan Pictorial Encyclopedia* reminds us, "If worship is a response, it is the response of man to the living God who has made Himself known to man in His words and works." Worship issues from God, is a work of God, and flows through us to God.

Just as I have made provision for the satisfying of my wife's musical drive, so God has more than sufficiently provided all things necessary for fulfilling the implanted need to worship. That provision is in His Word, and that very Word becomes a channel for releasing our worship. He has also provided for worship through the atonement, and helps us release our worship by His Holy Spirit that resides in us.

Out of our new relationship with God our inner drive and desire to worship God can be completely satisfied. But for all this divine provision, men seldom become worshippers until they have had a confrontation with God, a confrontation that rarely occurs where, when or how it is expected.

3

Confrontation and Worship

All Christians intend to worship; that's the stuff of which heaven is made. But most Christians put off getting involved in worship unless, or until, they are confronted by the object of their worship and gently led into a response.

Like a boy in love, circling his jalopy around the block his girlfriend lives on, God seeks an opportunity to confront us with His presence to see if we will flee *from* Him in fear, or *to* Him in faith. The confrontation is His; the conduct is ours. How graphically this is portrayed in the drama of the woman at the well in the fourth chapter of the Gospel of John!

She wasn't much to look at, for life had dealt quite harshly with her, and it showed. The beauty of youth that had made her so attractive to men had long ago been spent, and now she was having to live ostracized from the society of the women of Samaria because of the reputation she had acquired in that spending of her life. She had to come to the well at mid-morning, long after the other women had drawn their households' daily supply of water. Hers was a lonely life, but since she could not change the causes of her social ostracism, it was equally impossible to alter the effects; she simply had to cope with it.

The sight of a weary, solitary, young man seated on the edge of the well was unusual for noontime. His tunic indicated that he was a Jew, and the obvious exhaustion etched on His face, plus the dust on His robe, suggested that He had been traveling for quite some time. As she lowered her bucket on the long rope kept coiled by the well, the stranger softly asked for a drink of water.

Surprisingly, her reaction was instantly defensive. Yet the request was a common one. Very common. She had drawn water for countless travelers, children, and even for thirsty animals. Why, then, did this request so disturb her? Why did she hear herself so challengingly respond, "What! You, a Jew, ask a drink of me, a Samaritan woman?" (John 4:9, NEB). Surely He should know that Jews have no dealings with Samaritans!

Was it His gentleness that threatened her? She didn't meet much gentleness in the course of a day. Or was it those piercing eyes that seemed to look right through her? What was there about this man that made her so uncomfortable? She knew men, and how to respond to them, but in all of her life she couldn't remember having been so challenged by a man whose only request was so simple and uncomplicated.

Jesus' response to the woman of Samaria only heightened her frustration with Him. "If only you knew what God gives," he said, "and who it is that is asking you for a drink, you would have asked Him, and He would have given you living water" (John 4:10, NEB).

Even a casual reading of this fourth chapter of John, in any translation, will reveal that Christ had deliberately set up this confrontation to ultimately change this woman. The subsequent revelation of who He really was prepared this woman to deal with what she had become and to inspire her to accept change.

Haven't we all discovered that Christ still waits at some busy spot in our life intending to reveal Himself to us? It may not be during our morning devotions, or at evensong. It could well be at high noon, when our mind is totally concerned with natural things, that Christ invades our consciousness with a sense of His presence. It is very natural for us to live the majority of our life without an awareness of God, for we are earthbound creatures, locked in a time-space dimension, who live most of our lives attuned to our five senses. Somehow, God and the spiritual realm do not fit into sensory comprehension and awareness, unless there comes a stimulus from outside of ourselves.

Sometime ago, while waiting for my flight out of Will Rogers Airport in Oklahoma City, Oklahoma, I glanced through the local newspaper and saw this *Prayer for Today* on the editorial page:

I can never tell, O God, when suddenly Thou wilt break into my life. Just when I think I am safest, there's a sunset-touch, a flower-bell, someone's death, and there Thou art, looking deep within my soul. For Thy faithfulness I give thanks. Amen.

Sometimes God's confrontations are comforting, especially during periods of loneliness or great sorrow. But more frequently, His sudden invasion into our tiny world creates deep inner conflicts. Even an infinitesimally small amount of His nature that is manifested in a confrontation acts like a full-length mirror reflecting the tremendous imperfections of our nature. Who wants to be around total perfection? What woman ever wants to go to a party where America's most beautiful woman is the guest of honor? Or what man wants to walk the beach side by side with Mr. Muscleman, U.S.A.?

It is the comparison of our nature with Christ's that so ruthlessly reveals our flaws. It isn't always what He says, but the attitude He manifests that silently, but completely, reveals our attitudes for what they are. The selfishness that motivates us most of the time is completely unmasked in the light of His selfgiving. No wonder we squirm so uncomfortably while His purity amplifies our impurity and His attitudes condemn ours! The contrast is never complimentary to us. We always end up looking like "the bad guy."

Even Isaiah, the most spiritual man of his generation, was shocked at seeing himself in the light of God's presence. "...Woe is me!" he cried, "for I am undone; because I am a man of unclean lips, ... for mine eyes have seen the King, the Lord of hosts" (Isaiah 6:5). Later in his book he wrote: "But we are all as an unclean thing, and all our righteousnesses are as filthy rags" (Isaiah 64:6).

Unfortunately, few of us can so meekly admit our condition. Rather than confession, Divine confrontation usually invokes conflict. We tend to become defensive trying to turn the attention away from ourselves. This is evident in the four separate defensive responses of the woman of Samaria to Jesus.

First, in verse seven of John, chapter four, Jesus merely asked for a drink of water, but rather than provide it, or deny the request, the woman asked for a racial adjustment in saying, "... the Jews have no dealings with the Samaritans" (verse 9). Next, in verse ten, Jesus offered her "living water," but she retorted with an argument about the size and origin of the well, In verse fourteen, Jesus obviously wanted to meet her spiritual needs but she countered by suggesting that her natural needs should be met (verse 15). Further, in verse six, Jesus discussed her marriage, but she wanted to discuss His prophetic office (verse 19). No matter what Jesus said, she countered it, attempting either to confuse or totally reject the issue. So do we! But it does not stop the confrontation, for master interrogator that He is, Christ just continues to probe with questions until we see the truth about ourselves.

Her greatest problem seemed to be that she was out of relationship with God, her marriage, and others, and until she could confess this it would have been impossible to make a worshipper out of her, for worship, seat of man's relationship to God, cannot ascend much higher than his relationship with his fellowman. John clearly establishes this in his first epistle: "If a man say, I love God, and hateth his brother, he is a liar: for he that loveth not his brother whom he hath seen, how can he love God whom he hath not seen? And this commandment have we from Him, That he who loveth God love his brother also" (1 John 4:20, 21).

Undoubtedly, this is why a fundamental theme of the Holy Spirit is proper relationships. When Paul urged the church at Ephesus to "be filled with the Spirit" (Ephesians 5:18), he immediately taught them to use this new charisma to strengthen and purify their relationships with one another. In verse nineteen he exhorted them to express the overflow of the infilling of the Spirit one to another in melody and song; then, in verse twenty-one, he entreated them to submit one to another. Verse twenty-two called for wives to submit to their husbands, while verse twenty-five asked husbands to submit to Christ, and chapter six directed children to submit to parents, laborers to submit to employers, and for the employers to be rightly related to their employees. All of this is an outgrowth of being "filled with the Spirit."

Is this enjoyable? Do we automatically respond? Of course not! It is as distasteful and difficult for us as it was for the woman at the well of Samaria, or the saints at Ephesus. But it is a Divine imperative. Because the "living water" comes to produce worshippers, and since worship demands a warm, close relationship with God, the Holy Spirit first involves Himself with our improper relationships on a horizontal plane to prepare us for adjustment on the vertical plane. The Spirit will first confront us, then convict us of inequities in all of our interpersonal relationships. If we will confess instead of contest, we will be changed, for that is His ultimate goal.

When God confronts us—when He begins to approach us to be worshippers—there is a tremendous resistance that rises up within us. But this would cease if we could only realize that God does not challenge to produce chaos, but to effect a change. He doesn't come to us to destroy but to build; wise master-builder that He is, He excavates before He lays the foundation. He is not interested in a temporary work, and He takes no short-cuts. Since worship will be the main occupation of the saints throughout all of eternity, He is building for eternity.

Perhaps there are some individuals who reach out and up to God in worship without having to be arrested with a Divine confrontation, but many of the men and women of the Bible had to be confronted by God before they became worshippers of God. Consider the case of Abraham who very likely was as idolatrous as the other inhabitants of Ur of the Chaldees. If God had not spoken to him and called him out of that land, would he ever have been a worshipper of the true and living God?

Moses is another example of a man who had to be confronted before he would become a worshipper. His experience at the burning bush changed Moses for life.

But the burning bush experience was not the result of Moses seeking God; it was God confronting Moses on the backside of the desert.

Perhaps the patriarch Jacob could stand as a prime example of the need for a Divine confrontation. His cheating, tricky nature got and kept him in trouble throughout much of his life. Still, God confronted him at Bethel with the vision of angels ascending and descending upon a ladder that stretched from earth to heaven, and later an angel wrestled with Jacob all night long. It took two confrontations and the better part of a lifetime to make a worshipper out of Jacob, but God succeeded.

Anyone can praise, but he who would be a worshipper needs his own voice from heaven, his own burning bush, wrestling angel, or well-side encounter with Jesus, for confrontation is a necessary prelude to worship. The letter to the Hebrews declares "for he that cometh to God must believe that He is, and that He is a rewarder of them that diligently seek Him" (Hebrews 11:6). Intellectual knowledge is not sufficient belief that "He is." It must be a faith that comes out of a vital experience with God. After the experience at the burning bush, Moses never doubted the existence of God, nor did the Samaritan woman need to use theological proof of the existence of God to bring her countrymen to Jesus. One intimate contact with God makes a lifetime believer out of skeptics.

Since worship is the interpersonal relationship between man and God, one of the two must initiate the experience. As we have seen, it is generally God who approaches man, as He did Adam in the garden of Eden. Out of this confrontation will come a new faith in God and a change in the individual who met with God, for when confrontation is responded to rather than resisted, we become more God-like, and this affects our relationship with others, and with our God.

This confrontation will be the initial step that lifts us out of our self-centeredness into a God-consciousness, freeing us from the inhibitions that sin had imposed upon us, thereby releasing us to a rejoicing response to our saving God.

If all of this sounds a bit confusing, be of good cheer, for confusion is the natural by-product of divine confrontation. Just ask the woman at the well.

4

Confusion and Worship

When God confronts us with His presence it often induces confusion, for things are not always as we had imagined them to be. "Confusion is a work of the devil," some respond, while others affirm that confusion cannot be associated with God since the Scripture affirms that ". . God is not the author of confusion . . ." (1 Corinthians 14:33). That verse is absolutely accurate, for God is not the author of confusion; He's the revealer of our confusion. Let me illustrate this.

In many of the conferences in which I have ministered I have been approached by one or more individuals whose opening remarks have been: "Brother Cornwall, I just want to tell you—," and then they pause while looking me right in the eye and ask, "You *are* Brother Cornwall, aren't you?" When I assure them that I am, indeed, Judson Cornwall on a full-time basis they have often responded by saying, "Well, you sound like him, but to be perfectly honest with you, you don't look like you're supposed to look, and I find it very confusing."

If I ask them what I'm supposed to look like I have been told that they thought I was African American, or bald, or tall, or very much older than I appear to be.

Am I the author of the confusion or merely the revealer of it? For a period of time that may have extended over several years as these people had listened to cassettes of my preaching, or they had read my books, they formed a mental image of what they thought I looked like. That image became so real to them that when they were confronted with the real person it so violated their preconceived image as to confuse them.

Isn't this the basis of the confusion that stems from confrontation with God? All of us have preconceptions of what God is like. Much of it we have learned from the hymnbook, some of it came from our Sunday school teachers and pastors, and some ideas we've picked up from religious art and poetry. It is very likely that when we actually meet the Lord in our well-side experience we will find that we have imagined Him to be far different than He really is. God can only be known through His self-revelation. The testimony of a third party may assist, or it may ultimately confuse, but no matter what we may think about God, He is who He has revealed Himself to be in His Word.

It is unlikely that dealing with religion will confuse anyone since it functions within the boundaries of codified doctrine and ritual that can easily be learned by enrolling in a catechism course, but when we begin to deal directly with God confusion is to be expected because, as Isaiah puts it, "... My thoughts are not your thoughts, neither are your ways my ways, saith the Lord. For as the heavens are higher than the earth, so are my ways higher than your ways, and my thoughts than your thoughts" (Isaiah 55:8,9).

When I was in grammar school still struggling with fractions and equations, illness of my math teacher necessitated a substitute teacher who happened to be a recent graduate from college. In retrospect, I think he probably wanted to motivate us to a higher appreciation of mathematics, but what he actually did devastated us. In his very first class he propounded a problem in calculus on the front blackboard, and then he began to show us how it could be solved. His calculations filled the entire front blackboard; then he began to fill the blackboard on the side wall. The more he wrote his computations the more confused I became, until I fled from the classroom, book in hand, and ran home in tears to tell my parents that I would never go to school again as long as I lived, because I was a stupid idiot who didn't even know what the teacher was talking about. Yet a few years later, during my high school days, I probably could have stood alongside him and helped him in the computation.

The problem back in grammar school was that the realm of mathematics that the teacher was sharing with me was as high above my head as the heavens are above the earth. He was talking about a world to which I had never been introduced.

God is *not* the author of confusion, but when He talks to us, even in spiritual baby talk, it is so far above our understanding as to produce confusion. Even a prophetic word tends to be above our comprehension, and the many and varied interpretations we have on the Bible indicate that there is very often a mental confusion as to what it means. Even a thorough knowledge of the original languages of the Bible does not always unlock the hidden meanings, for those who knew Greek and Hebrew the best are the ones who crucified Jesus. It is never by the natural mind that we understand God, for ". . . the carnal mind is enmity against God: for it is not subject to the law of God, neither indeed can be" (Romans 8:7); actually, our natural mind gets greatly confused when confronted with the things of God for divine truth can only be spiritually discerned.

Because this is true, God has more difficulty communicating with us than we have in talking to our dog. Humans are mentally qualified, or at least educationally trained, to acquire knowledge by proceeding from the known to the unknown. What we know becomes a platform from which we progress to new knowledge. But what is there in our world that is comparable to heaven?

We lack an innate spiritual platform from which we may proceed into spiritual knowledge, since we lack the basis of comparison which is a standard learning tool.

Please remember that confusion is not the enemy of faith, it is a by-product of faith. Until we begin to deal with God on a personal level we will probably not experience confusion, but God, His realm, and even His dealings in our lives can be very confusing to the soulish nature of all of us. Fortunately, it is only our intellect that gets confused; our spirit seems to respond favorably to God's Spirit, even though the communication at that spirit level oftentimes has difficulty filtering down into the intellectual level of our lives.

However, we can take courage that this kind of confusion is ample evidence that we must be dealing with God.

True worship will always demand that our vision rise from the earthly to the heavenlies; that our will be in perfect accord with God's will, and that His thoughts replace our thoughts. The more this becomes true in our lives, the less confusion we will have when we are in the presence of God.

After Jesus confronted the Samaritan woman at Jacob's well, she, too, became confused and she evidenced her confusion in at least three areas. Since I will be dealing with these in separate chapters, we'll merely look at them at this point.

That worship is the theme of the confrontation between Jesus and this woman is evidenced by the fact that worship is mentioned ten times in verses 20 through 24. The purpose of the confrontation was to produce worship, but confusion began to reign almost immediately in this woman's mind. Her first confusion concerned the *place of worship*, for she said, "Our fathers worshipped in this mountain; and ye say, that in Jerusalem is the place where men ought to worship" (John 4:20). God in human form was talking to her, and she could only think about a proper place for worship.

She also evidenced confusion as to the *concept of worship*, for she immediately began to plead the historicity of "our fathers," but the way worship was conducted in past generations has little bearing on worship in the present. Certainly Abraham worshipped God, but God was now manifesting Himself to this woman. She, like we, failed to realize that methodology is quite unimportant to God. Motivation is what God looks for, and if our desire is to release our spirit into the presence of God to love and adore Him, our worship will be accepted since worship is that interpersonal involvement of a man or a woman with God. We needn't get confused with the trappings or seek to imitate the proficient worshippers. We should merely find the way that our spirit can pour out unrestrained love to the Father.

Some of us demand full knowledge about worship before we ever begin responding to God. It reminds me of the young man who wanted to read the entire marriage manual before he went out on his first date. He was so over-informed that he became confused and merely muddled his way through the evening, unable to enjoy the company of his companion.

Worship is best learned by worshipping. We learn by associating with the object of our worship, for He is an excellent teacher.

This woman at the well further evidenced confusion as to the *person of Christ*. He had chosen to reveal Himself to her as the Messiah, but she chose to see Him as one of the prophets. She, as we, lowered Christ's revelation of Himself to something she could accommodate at her level of experience. She preferred to think of Jesus in terms with which she was comfortable rather than to accommodate a new revelation.

Not too unlike her, we can easily prefer to respond to a historic rather than a present person, for we're more comfortable with the impersonal than the intimate Christ. We prefer distance from God to closeness to Him, for the closer to Him we get the greater our initial confusion seems to be.

Not too long ago, I decided it was time for me to progress from a typewriter to a word processing system for my writing ministry. I was strongly advised to purchase a home computer with software for word processing, so I began my search. Initially I was embarrassed to talk with the salespersons because I didn't understand their vocabulary. I tried to smile and say "yes" in the right places, but one salesman put me in my place very quickly by saying that he could tell by the glaze in my eyes that I didn't understand a thing he was telling me. Eventually I worked my way through the confusion and purchased the needed equipment. It took me several months of studying the instruction books and actually working with the equipment before the mystery began to fade and the confusion gave way to understanding. Listening to others only heightened my confusion, but "hands-on" experience brought me out of my confusion.

Similarly, hearing sermons about worshipping, or even reading about worship cannot settle the inner confusion that results from our initial divine confrontation. Only spending time in the presence of the object of our worship can replace confusion with confession.

When Saul of Tarsus was headed for Damascus, intent upon killing the Christians of that city, he was confronted by God in a blinding, bright light, and Saul's initial response was, characteristically, confusion. "Who art thou, Lord?" he asked. God sent him to a private room in the city and left him blinded for a season so that Saul could get to know God through an extended confrontation. Out of this and subsequent times in the presence of God, Paul was able to trade his confusion for a vital confidence that Jesus was the Christ, the Son of the living God. By the time he began writing the epistles of the New Testament, all confusion had vanished and his faith laid hold upon that which he still did not understand, but he was no longer devastated by the unknown in God.

Confusion is more evident in beginners of worship than those who are experienced. Perhaps we would be more accurate in referring to this as *pre-worship confusion*, for once we begin to really worship, confusion is replaced with confidence.

When I finished my flight instruction I signed up with an FAA flight instructor who was authorized to give the flight test prior to the issuance of a private pilot's license. The day I was scheduled to take that flight exam was cloudy. We patiently waited for the clouds to lift, but when late afternoon came and the clouds were as low as ever, the instructor suggested that we make the flight above the clouds. Fifty feet after the plane left the runway we were enveloped in clouds and I was not to see the ground again for two hours. At 2,000 feet we broke through the clouds, so I took my entire flight test with billowy white clouds beneath the plane rather than the earth, with which I had developed a warm familiarity during my flight training.

Twenty minutes into the flight, my instructor asked me if I had any idea where we were. I had carefully plotted the proposed flight, but, since I didn't have visual contact with landmarks, I was using time/speed calculations to try to keep track of our flight on the map on my lap. Hesitantly pointing to the spot on the map over which I thought we were flying I said, "right here."

"Well, that's where you're supposed to be," he said, "but how do you know where you really are?"

I started to explain my calculations to him. "Reverend," he interrupted, "we're not flying on instruments in the clouds; we're flying above the clouds on visual flight rules. Look outside the window and tell me where we are."

"But I can't see the ground, sir," I replied.

"You can see enough of it to plot your course," he said. "This area is mountainous, and the tops of the higher peaks are sticking out all around us. You've looked at them for several months of flying. Now identify them for me."

Looking around, I quickly identified the Twin Sisters and Mount Hood and realized that I had my north and east bearings clearly visible. Before long I was identifying other mountains and the sense of not knowing where I was gave place to a positive awareness of my location. I couldn't see all of the ground, but I could identify enough of the high elevations to know where I was over the ground, and from them I could keep my bearings.

Our coming into worship is not too unlike my flight examination. Initially we may find confusion hanging over us like low clouds, but if we will have faith in Christ to get us above those clouds we will find great mountain peaks of revelation that we have become comfortable with in the Scriptures that are sticking up far above our confusion level. We can set our course and determine our flight path by keeping these landmarks in constant view.

In confronting us, God will not reveal anything contrary to what we have learned in the Bible. He will merely make abstract truth become personal truth, and He will reveal Jesus as God's Truth personified, worthy of our worship.

Once our confusion gives way to courage we are faced with another potential problem in worship. What is the proper timing of worship?

5

The Timing of Worship

This year I was scheduled to spend the Easter season as the conference speaker in Norwich, England. I purchased my ticket a month in advance, sent my wife to visit her mother in California, and suggested that the pastor slip out of town for a change of pace the week before I was to leave. On Tuesday morning, after I had finished teaching a class at Fountain Gate Bible College, I took myself out for a leisurely lunch, shopped for some Easter cards, washed my car, and slowly made my way back to my office. Cleaning up some final details of my work load, I thought it might be profitable to begin packing my briefcase, so I took my airline tickets out of the file and casually glanced at them. I had already put them in the case before what I had read soaked into my consciousness. Six P.M. TODAY?!! Impossible! I had ordered my tickets for the following day, but a call to my travel agent confirmed that it had become necessary to fly me a day earlier than I had requested. Hadn't I been informed?

I had three hours to pack and get to the airport, which is an hour's drive away. I made it, but it was nervewrackingly close! I was prepared to fly to England, but my timing was off.

The best of plans are useless if they are not implemented on the right schedule. Solomon understood this, for he wrote:

To every thing there is a season, and a time to every purpose under the heaven: A time to be born, and a time to die; a time to plant, and a time to pluck up that which is planted, A time to kill, and a time to heal; a time to break down, and a time to build up; A time to weep, and a time to laugh; a time to mourn, and a time to dance; A time to cast away stones, and a time to gather stones together; a time to embrace, and a time to refrain from embracing; a time to get, and a time to lose; A time to keep, and a time to cast away; A time to rend, and a time to sew; a time to keep silence, and a time to speak; A time to love, and a time to hate; a time of war, and a time of peace (Ecclesiastes 3:1-8).

This principle is especially applicable to worship. Jesus said, "… the hour cometh, and now is, when the true worshippers shall worship the Father …" (John 4:23, italics added). The time for worship is NOW because the object of our worship is not locked into our time-space dimension; God dwells in an eternal *now*! All of His commandments are effective immediately.

But while we give mental assent to this fact we are habitually oriented to time divisions from years to minutes. Our entire lives are divided into time spans of years, months, days, and hours. Our activities, attitudes, and even our ambitions are cataloged and controlled by our memories of the past, our involvements in the present, and our hopes for the future. Since what we are carnally affects what we do spiritually, it is to be expected, then, that our worship responses will be divided into time segments.

Perhaps our strongest concepts of worship are rooted in the past. Each religious heritage can point historically to times of great worship. The Lutherans point to the days of Martin Luther as days of outstanding worship which became the foundation for their liturgy and litany. The Apostolics point to the great Welsh revival and the Methodists remind us of the days of Wesley. All religious heritages that were birthed in revival have experienced days and even years of vital, viable worship as these believers responded joyfully to the realized presence of a mighty God. While it may be necessary to seek out such history in a used book store, uncensored church history records singing, dancing, shouting, weeping, and even glossolalia as a normal part of the response of the founders of our Christian heritages.

Unfortunately, however, experiences cannot be transmitted genetically, nor can they be transferred historically. It takes similar personal encounters with God to produce like worship responses, and all too frequently it is the doctrine rather than the experience that is passed on to succeeding generations.

Although I have ministered in a great variety of religious heritages, I have yet to find one that lacked some form of worship. When I have asked for an explanation of why certain things were done I have always been referred to their past, although I was frequently told that the act was meaningless to today's generation. This embrace of the forms and ceremonies of the past without present vitality was condemned by Christ when He charged the religious leaders of His day with holding to the traditions of the elders rather than embracing the Word of God (See Matthew 15:6).

We may have an excellent memory of the past, and there is both safety and inspiration in this, but we cannot call this worship, for worship is always a NOW activity. It is a present involvement with God that inspires and releases fresh worship. What God *has* done for us may well inspire praise, but worship, as a response of love to love, functions only in the present.

Some genuinely born-again believers who refuse to lean upon a great heritage as a substitute for worship are so eschatalogically minded that their whole concept of worship is future-oriented. Their theme song could well be:

When we all get to heaven,

What a day of rejoicing that will be!

When we all see Jesus,

We'll sing and shout the victory. *

They long for heaven and its pearly gates, and they speak enthusiastically about joining the saints above in adoration of God, but in the here-and-now they are nonparticipants in true worship. Perhaps their story is revealed in a paraphrase of an old song: "To praise above with the saints we love, Oh, that will be glory. But to praise below with the saints we know, well, that's another story."

While few of us have difficulty with the concept of future joy and worship around the throne of God, we dare not ignore the statement of Jesus that "the hour ... now is when the true worshippers shall worship the Father ..." (John 4:23). Good intentions cannot substitute for godly worship any more than a promise can substitute for a performance. Anticipation of a future response may very well trigger a present response, but it cannot substitute for it.

If, then, worship cannot flow out of the past or be borrowed from the future, it follows that it must function wholly in the present. "Now is the accepted time ..." (2 Corinthians 6:2), today is the day for worship. We are no longer Old Testament covenant people who awaited the great feast days of Israel so that they could worship; we are New Testament saints and Christ, our lamb, has been sacrificed for us once and for all. Furthermore, Christ has become the great High Priest for all believers and "... He ever liveth to make intercession for us"

---

* (Note: no copyright info., E.E. Hewitt; taken from *Melodies of Praise*, Pub: 1957, Gospel Pub. House.)

(Hebrews 7:25). We need not await a designated day, a special season, or an inscribed invitation. We have been invited, inspired, and impelled to worship right here and now. While the ordinances of the church may assist our worship they are not prerequisites for it. Gothic arches, well-tuned pipe organs, and robed choirs may inspire awe, but true worship is a response to God and He is available everywhere, at all times, and with or without religious trappings. Therefore, worship should not be merely a Sunday activity; it should be a daily duty. God is no different on Tuesday than He is on Sunday; it is simply that we habitually have a greater awareness of God on Sunday, and worship demands such an awareness. Happy is the Christian who has learned to practice the presence of God, for that person is well on the way to being a *now* worshipper.

During the days of His pilgrimage, Jesus beautifully illustrated this principle of worshipping in the now. Although He had spent eternity with the Father and knew that He would return to the heavens in just a few short years, He maintained a current relationship with the Father. Repeatedly we read of His spending all night in prayer to the Father, not in petition, since He knew that all things had already been delivered into His hands, but in conversation and communion, which form the basis for true worship. His communion with the Father was so constant that at any moment He felt comfortable saying, "Father, I thank Thee that thou hast heard me ..." (John 11:41).

Similarly, Paul speaks of praying without ceasing, of rejoicing evermore, and of giving thanks in all things. Obviously, Paul did not feel that the Sabbath or the synagogue were necessary for worship. He worshipped on a sinking ship, in a stinking prison, and in a Sanhedrin court. Wherever Paul and God got together, worship followed.

While there is strength in corporate worship, individual worship is both taught and demonstrated throughout the Scriptures. Therefore, since worship is neither an ordinance of

the church that requires the services of a minister or the exclusive
ministry of the plural body of believers, a Christian can worship
morning, noon or night.

Worship that is one-on-one knows no restrictions of place
or means. Its only limitation is when, for worship must be
offered in the present. But it is human nature to procrastinate.
One of Satan's most powerful tools is the little word "someday,"
for with it he can prevent us from acting on our convictions.
Just as "someday" will likely keep a sinner forever separated
from God, so "someday" will keep a consecrated Christian from
becoming a worshipper of God. There is never the "more
convenient season" that Felix pled before Paul. If we will not
worship today, we will not worship tomorrow. If we cannot
rejoice in the midst of trial, it is improbable that we will rejoice
in the midst of triumph. If we await the right mood it is unlikely
that the right one will ever come along, for all moods have their
limitations. But what have convenient seasons, trials or
triumphs, or special moods to do with worship anyway? If God
is the object of and inspiration for our worship, then His very
unchangeableness should make worship a continuously present
function. Wasn't it Paul who asked us:

Who shall separate us from the love of Christ? shall
tribulation, or distress, or persecution, or famine, or nakedness,
or peril, or sword? ... I am persuaded that neither death, nor
life, nor angels, nor principalities, nor powers, nor things
present, nor things to come, nor height, nor depth, nor any
other creature, shall be able to separate us from the love of God,
which is in Christ Jesus our Lord (Romans 8:35, 38, 39).

If worship is love responding to love, and if nothing in
heaven, on earth, or in hell can separate us from God's love,
then surely nothing can separate us from responding to that
love. That response is worship.

It is possible to be as prepared to worship as I was prepared to go to England and still miss it unless we realize that worship is an activity for today rather than for tomorrow. Today is all that we have. Yesterday is gone forever, and tomorrow may never arrive, so today is the only proper time to worship.

But even if we accept the timing of worship, what do we mean when we say *worship*, for this word means different things to different people. What is the history of the word, and how is it used throughout Scripture?

6

The Etymology of Worship

Confrontation with Christ is not our only source of confusion. The use of the English language can also be confusing both to the speaker or writer and to the listener or the reader. Words are not only tools, they can be dangerous tools, for they are capable of concealing as well as revealing. How often I have thought that I had clearly said what was on my mind only to discover that the same series of words generated an entirely different train of thought in my hearers, and I wonder if I will ever get over the shock of an editor's note in the margin of my manuscript asking, "are you certain this is what you mean?" Usually a trip to the dictionary will reveal that I misunderstood the word I had used.

As a case in point, last year my secretary came into my study on Monday and asked me if I meant what I had preached on Sunday in saying that we Christians are running the gauntlet in these days. I assured her that I meant exactly that, so she challenged me to look the word up in the dictionary. To my chagrin, I discovered that for years I have been challenging Christians to run the glove. The word I should have been using was gamut; close, but not close enough to be correct.

I think that many Christians misuse the word *worship* simply because they do not know what it actually means; they have never traced the etymology of the word or even looked the word up in a dictionary. They have merely appended it to an attitude or action and felt that this sufficiently identified it. But communication demands that both speaker and hearer be in agreement on the meaning of the words that the speaker uses.

The English word *worship* comes from the old English word *weordhscipe* which was later shortened to *worthship*. It is concerned with the worthiness, dignity, or merit of a person or, as in the case of idolatry, a thing. In the English court it is still used as a noun in referring to a dignitary as "his worship." Worship, in the verb form, means the paying of homage or respect, and in the religious world the term is used for the reverent devotion, service, or honor, whether public or individual, paid to God.

When writers are choosing between words, striving to use the most descriptive one available, they rely heavily upon synonyms or words that are analogous for the word they are considering, for these unfold varying shades of meaning. Wouldn't the same action help us better understand this word *worship*? The *Merriam-Webster Dictionary* lists the following twelve words as either analogous words for worship or synonyms of worship: adore, admire, dote, esteem, exalt, love, magnify, regard, respect, revere, reverence, and venerate. This is what the English word *worship* means. It is the adoration, veneration, exaltation, and magnification of God. It is when we respect, esteem, love, admire, and even dote on God that we are worshipping Him. Quite obviously, *worship* is totally concerned with the worthiness of God, not the worthiness of the worshipper.

An American visiting England when the Queen rode through the streets of London in her ceremonial coach might be horrified to see thieves, prostitutes, and skidrow bums bowing and curtsying along with the lords and ladies of the land, but an Englishman would understand that it is the dignity of the Queen that is being responded to, not the dignity of the one who is paying the respect.

In establishing and developing language, words are chosen to represent articles, things, attitudes, or actions; hence the performance of worship antedates the word *worship*. Still, that word was used as a symbol of what was being performed at the time that the word was coined.

In the Old Testament the one Hebrew word that is consistently used for the worship of God is *shachah*. It occurs 172 times in the thirty-nine books of the Old Testament. The translators of the King James Version of the Bible have used nine different words or expressions in translating this word, *shachah*, the most frequent one being "worship." But it is also translated as: to bow down, make obeisance, do reverence, fall down, prostrate, stoop, crouch, and beseech humbly.

Quite obviously, then, worship is more than an attitude; it is an attitude expressed, and the magnitude of the attitude determines the measure of the actions. A lukewarm heart cannot perform boiling hot worship, nor can a rebellious life revere God with any depth of sincerity.

This Hebrew word *shachah* was used to describe Abraham's reverent prostration before the three angelic visitors who came as God's messengers to inform Abraham about the planned destruction of Sodom and Gomorrah. As these angels approached Abraham, he prostrated himself completely and then further ministered to their needs temporal and social. That is called worship (*shachah*) (see Genesis 18). Later when Abraham sent his servant, Eleazar, to find a bride for his son, the Scripture records, "he worshipped the Lord bowing himself to the earth" (Genesis 24:52), and again the Hebrew word is *shachah*.

This word is used to describe the action of the elders of Israel when Moses brought to them his first report that God was about to deliver them from the bondage of Egypt. We read, "and the people believed: ... then they bowed their heads and worshipped" (Exodus 4:31). Surely worship should be a natural response to a promise of deliverance from bondage that has totally controlled our lives. Have you ever observed the worship of a person who has been saved from the drug culture? It usually is uninhibited and filled with thanksgiving, for great deliverance often generates great worship!

Every use of the word *shachah* in the Old Testament indicates action. They were doing something as an expression of an inner attitude or feeling, and their body was helping to exhibit their emotions. They not only said something, they did something. They were not merely thankful (an attitude), but they expressed their thanksgiving (an action). They worshipped in a way that they, others, and God knew they were worshipping.

Since the New Testament was written in the Koine Greek used in commerce, rather than in the classical Greek of the scholars, we need not be surprised to find three separate words for worship. The Greek word *latreuo* is used four times, and Robert Young tells us that it means to worship publicly, while W.E. Vine says that it signifies to serve or to render religious service. It is the word that is used in secular literature to describe the service performed by the priests in the temple.

A second Greek word for worship is *sebomai*, which appears in our New Testament eight times. It comes from the root word *sebas* which means to fear, so *sebomai* signifies to fear or to hold in awe. None who has experienced the awesomeness of coming into the divine presence of God will deny the reaction of fear that gave way to reverence and a sense of awe and wonder.

But the most commonly used word for worship in our New Testament is *proskuneo* which is used at least 59 times. It is actually a combination of two separate Greek words: *pros*, which means towards and *kuneo*, which means to kiss. Literally, then, *proskuneo* means "to kiss towards." Some scholars say it means to kiss the hand in admiration, while others say it would better signify to kiss the feet in homage, but didn't the Shulamite maiden find a more kissable place on the body when she cried, "Let him kiss me with the kisses of his mouth, for thy love is better than wine" (Song of Solomon 1:2)?

The word *proskuneo* is far more descriptive than the Hebrew word *shachah*, for to the bowing is added kissing, and this requires close contact. We can bow at a great distance, but kissing requires contact.

To the early church in Ephesus, with its mixture of Jews and Gentiles, Paul wrote, "But now in Christ Jesus ye who sometimes were far off are made nigh by the blood of Christ" (Ephesians 2:13). Unquestionably believers have been brought together, but just as genuinely, we New Testament believers have been brought close to Christ Jesus. If the Old Testament saints tended to gesture to God at a distance, the New Testament saints are beckoned to get close enough to embrace God, to love Him, to kiss Him, to pour out adoration unto Him intimately, and to touch God in deepseated worship with our senses, our emotions and our wills.

In the story of the Samaritan woman at the well the communication between her and Christ Jesus contains this Greek word *proskuneo* ten times. Every act and fact of worship recorded by John in the fourth chapter of his gospel is this "kiss toward" concept of worship. It is personal, full of feeling, and fulfilling. It pictures the interplay between two persons who have deep, committed, loving feelings for each other.

Occasionally, before a service, someone will say, "Oh, Brother Cornwall, I wish you could bring us to real worship tonight to where we'll all get out in the aisles and prostrate ourselves before the Lord."

I have no problem with taking a position of humility that brings us to a prone position before God, but isn't it limiting to think that we cannot worship until an entire congregation has assumed a specific bodily posture?

As we have seen, the Greek words for worship contain the element of reverence and respect, but they also contain the added sense of an inward attitude of drawn affection. This is seen in Jesus' response to the questions about worship by the Samaritan woman, who was drawn to Him by His forgiveness and kindness. In John 4, Jesus tells her that the time, place or method of worship is not the important thing, but rather the genuineness of worship. The kind of worship that the Father desires is worship that is done "in spirit and in truth" (John 4:24). In fact, there is only one place in the entire New Testament that refers to a specific outward display in worship in the Church, and that speaks of an act of repentance by a former unbeliever (see 1 Corinthians 14:25). Instead, it seems that for the New Testament believer, worship is the natural outflowing of an inward attitude of drawn affection. God's presence attracts us to Him, and our inner being flows back unto Him in a great variety of ways.

One pastor stated not long ago that his congregation was starving on a diet of Greek roots, and I agree that mere word study for the sake of word study can be less than edifying; still we must remember that the Bible was not written in English, and that translators are often pressed to find a word in English to accurately picture what was meant by the Hebrew or Greek word. Therefore, it generally enlarges our concepts to briefly study the variegated shades of meaning the Hebrew and Greek words convey. In this case, etymologically, worship is a bowing, prostrating, kissing the hands, feet, or lips, and a feeling of awe and devotion while serving the Lord with the whole heart.

The original words for worship in our Bible speak of an attitude being expressed with action. They infer depth of feeling, closeness of partners, and a covenant relationship. Worship is communicated affection between man and God. It involves both motion and emotion, but true worship is far deeper than either of these, and merely uses them as a channel of release for the depth of love and adoration that generates in the heart of the believer who is drawn into the presence of a loving God.

Worship, then, is far more than merely singing a song or clapping the hands. It is an expression of something—but let's leave that for the next chapter.

7

The Expression of Worship

The pastor's role is not always pleasant. From time to time over the years I have had to call one of the men of my congregation into my study to talk to him about his marriage. When I tell him that his wife seems to be absolutely convinced that he has ceased to love her it nearly devastates him. After the shock subsides what usually follows is a verbal protestation of love and an expression of bewilderment as to what could cause his wife to doubt his love for her. It usually boils down to his inability to express his love to her in a meaningful and understandable way. He knows that he is supposed to love his wife, for this is what marriage is all about according to the Bible. But his performance has not been very convincing.

Similarly, most Bible-believing Christians accept that God made man for a purpose, and that purpose is worship. Paul wrote, "... we should be to the praise of His glory" (Ephesians 1:12), and that "all things were created by Him, and for Him" (Colossians 1:16). Life's highest purpose is to be offered up to God in adoration and gratitude to be true worshippers of God.

What we Christians have difficulty admitting, however, is that most of us do not worship very well. So often our "worship" services consist of the preliminaries, a choral number and a sermon, and all too frequently our public worship degenerates into a formalism that is devoid of vitality and spiritual life, whereas Biblical worship is celebration of God. How long has it been since God was celebrated in your church? Is it a lack of love, or is it a lack of understanding of how to express our worship that keeps our Sunday worship so stilted and stifled?

Some of our frustration in trying to worship may be rooted in the inexplicability, the inexpressibility, and the intangibility of worship. Because it cannot be codified into law or ritual we feel insecure in performing worship. In his book, *An Expository Dictionary of New Testament Words*, W.E. Vine said, "The worship of God is nowhere defined in Scripture. A consideration of the Greek verbs shows that it is not confined to praise; broadly it may be regarded as the direct acknowledgment to God of His nature, attributes, ways and claims, whether by the outgoing of the heart in praise and thanksgiving or by deed done in such acknowledgment" (p. 236).

While we may lack a positive definition, we do gain some insight by researching the meaning of the verbs used to tell of worship. The *International Standard Bible Encyclopedia* says, "The total idea of worship, however, both in the Old Testament and New Testament, must be built up, not from the words specifically so translated, but also and chiefly from the whole body of description of worshipful feeling and action, whether of individuals singly and privately, or of larger bodies engaged in the public services of sanctuary, tabernacle, temple, synagogue, upper room or meeting place" (p. 3110).

Since we gain further understanding by looking at the way men worshipped in Bible times, let me review one such occasion. David was old and feeble, and already one of his sons had proclaimed himself as the King of Israel. God's faithful prophet, Nathan, came into David's presence to remind him that he had promised to crown his son, Solomon, as his successor. In response to the prophet's suggestion, for David always heeded the words of the prophets, David arranged to have Solomon proclaimed king. Shortly thereafter David died. Following the period of mourning, the nation gathered to anoint Solomon as their reigning king. In this national celebration there was a time of high worship, and the chronicler lists seven of the acts of worship that were performed by the people on that occasion: (1) they blessed the Lord God; (2) they bowed down their heads; (3) they worshipped (*shachah*); (4) they sacrificed sacrifices unto the Lord; (5) they offered burnt offerings unto the Lord; (6) they did eat and drink before the Lord; and (7) they did it all with great gladness. (See 1 Chronicles 29:20-22).

I used to be disturbed that the Bible does not give us a positive definition of worship, but I have come to believe that we would make an empty ritual of any definition that would have been given. Since the foundation of worship is love poured out it would be most difficult to define anyway, for the moment we encase loving behind a set of hard and fast rules, we ruin it. Spontaneity is vital to the expression of love, both in the natural and in the spiritual.

Perhaps as close a definition of worship as we can find in the Word comes from the lips of Jesus when He said, "… thou shalt love the Lord thy God with all thy heart, and with all thy soul, and with all thy mind, and with all thy strength: this is the first commandment. And the second is like, namely this, Thou shalt love thy neighbour as thyself. There is none other commandment greater than these" (Mark 12:30-31). Love that releases all of the heart's adoration, that expresses all of the soul's attitudes, that explains all of the mind's determination, and utilizes all of the strength of the worshipper's body is worship.

How weak and feeble our whispered praises are when measured by this standard.

Any Christian who really observed this *all* standard of worshipping God would be branded as a fanatic, and he would likely be banned from attending some churches. But those same actions at a football game would gain him the title of "fan." Celebration of a team's victory calls for a release of the heart, soul, mind and strength, but God is too frequently offered only the "leftovers."

I must admit, however, that the very process of trying to explain worship tends to cheapen it, even as trying to explain how to love generally puts more emphasis on the "make" than on the "love," thereby emphasizing the mechanical rather than the emotional and devotional aspects of loving.

Volumes could be written trying to explain worship but, like the endless volumes now available on loving, ultimately more is learned by doing than by reading.

Not only is there an inexplicability to worship, there is an equal inexpressibility of worship. Since worship is basically the outpouring of inner attitudes to God with a subsequent release of emotional and accompanying expressive body action and a commitment to obedience, we do, indeed, have difficulty expressing it.

There is a passage in the letter to the Romans that my religious heritage consistently interpreted as intercessory prayer, but I wonder if it is not far more involved with worship than intercession. Paul wrote, "... the Spirit also helpeth our infirmities: for we know not what we should pray for as we ought: but the Spirit itself maketh intercession for us with groanings which cannot be uttered" (Romans 8:26). It does not seem to me that we need as much help in framing our petitions to God as we do in expressing our deep inner feelings to Him. Furthermore, our greatest infirmities are spiritual, not physical, for we have lived so long in the limitation of our timespace dimension that we have great difficulty seeing into the spiritual world, and we are even quite unknowing about our own spirit. With the aid of the Holy Spirit, who resides in the spirit of the believers, the deep inner love and adoration that we seem humanly unable to release and express to God are poured out to Him "with groanings which cannot be uttered." Charles Spurgeon calls this "raptures of ecstasy." What we are unable to release, the Holy Spirit releases in rapturous waves of ecstasy. In this sense, then, we could say that worship is a subjective experience. Its force and flow come from within us.

Worship, of course, is a response to a relationship, therefore, it is not the performance that makes worship, but worship motivates the performance, just as it is not the hugs and kisses that produce the love I have for my darling wife, it is that love that has matured over these forty years that inspires the hugs and kisses.

Worship, I repeat, is love responding to love, so it is not the bowing, the dancing, the clapping and the singing that produce the worship, for at best they can only express that worship, but it is the worship that produces the jubilant responses. True worship may have its times of silence and sighing as well as its times of singing and shouting, but the method of expression does not of itself determine the intensity of the worship.

No matter what form of expression may be used, worship never fully expresses the inner glow we feel when we are drawn close to God. Each could wish that he was three people instead of a mere triunity so that he could express himself in a greater variety of ways. When we begin to worship we realize that our *mouths* are restricted by the vocabularies of our mind, and those vocabularies are limited in the words that adequately express depth of feeling. In worship we also discover that our *bodies* are restricted by existing physical strength and by conventional restraints. Just how long can we dance, or stand, or raise our hands unto the Lord?

Even our tears may be as much evidence of the deep frustration we experience in trying to express our love to God as they are an act of worship. Somehow we can never fully express our worship. Perhaps that is why corporate worship is so valuable. As many individuals express their worship in varying ways, all forms of worship expression can be released unto God at one time, and although no one person has worshipped God completely, the corporate group has completely worshipped God.

That there is an intangibility to worship becomes self-evident to both student and teacher. It is not as definable as the doctrine of salvation or as describable as water baptism, but it is desirable and delightful both to God and to man in spite of its indefiniteness. One thing about worship that is definite, however, is that since worship is a response to God, it requires being in God's presence to perform it. Praise can be taught and practiced as liturgy, but worship cannot. Prayer can be read from a book, but worship cannot. Religious service can be performed in a perfunctory manner, but not worship. Singing can be an acquired art, but worship is not even an art form.

Worship is an interpersonal action between an individual and his or her God when in the divine presence. It is quite intangible. It is unseen, undefined, unscored, and without script, but when it is happening the worshipper knows it, and so does God. Even public worship is merely many individuals responding to God's presence at the same time and in the same place, and often in the same manner, but true worship is always one-on-one: the person and his God.

Perhaps this is why there are far more praisers than there are worshippers. Praise is more tangible, is quickly demonstrable, and easily adapts to corporate situations. But praise is intended to bring us into God's presence while worship is what we do once we get there. We traverse God's courts with praise, but when we are drawn into the holy place with God, worship is the prescribed response.

None of us should allow the inexplicability, the inexpressibility, or the intangibility of worship to deter us from being active worshippers. Love is equally inexpressible, inexplicable, and intangible; yet we enjoy it, and we would find living without it devastating. Worship can be as fulfilling for the spiritual nature as love is for the carnal nature. We can exist without it, but we cannot live very well without it.

We dare not lose sight of the fact that God became man, lived among us, and died for us, not merely to rescue us from hell but to restore us to our Edenic relationship with God Himself. Therefore, the ultimate work of the cross is less an act of rescue and more a work of restoration. Calvary, and the subsequent work of the Spirit in the lives of Calvary's converts, enables us to come back and learn to do once more that which we were created to do in the first place—to worship the Lord in the beauty of holiness; to spend our time in awesome wonder and adoration of God, both feeling it and expressing it. Why have the American churches missed this? We immediately make a worker out of a new convert, while God wants to make a worshippper out of him. Perhaps we have paid too little attention to the words of Jesus in the hour of His temptation in the wilderness. When the devil took Jesus to an elevated spot and showed him the kingdoms of the world and all their glory, he said to Jesus, "All these things will I give Thee, if Thou wilt fall down and worship me" (Matthew 4:9). Jesus responded by saying, "Get thee hence, Satan: for it is written, Thou shalt worship the Lord thy God, and Him only shalt thou serve" (Matthew 4:10). The divine order, recorded in both the Old and New Testaments, is *worship* first, *service* second. "Thou shalt worship the Lord thy God, and Him only shalt thou serve.

"We dare not reverse this divine sequence, for service that substitutes for worship is unacceptable to God, since God never accepts a replacement for anything He has commanded. But service that is an outgrowth and an expression of worship is both accepted and blessed by God.

In suggesting at the beginning of this chapter that worship is celebration, I am not implying that we assemble to exchange emotional highs or to indulge in soulish tumult. But we cannot ignore the fact that the characteristic note of Old Testament worship is exhilaration. David testified, "I was glad when they said unto me, Let us go into the house of the Lord" (Psalm 122:1), and another psalmist exhorted, "Make a joyful noise unto the Lord, all ye lands. Serve the Lord with gladness: come before His presence with singing ... Enter into His gates with thanksgiving, and into His courts with praise ..." (Psalm 100: 1, 2, 4).

The visual representation of redemption that the sacrificial system afforded often induced a hilarious, joyful, and cheerful response. They watched their substitute die in their place, and when the blood was sprinkled upon them they were assured forgiveness of all their confessed sins. Little wonder, then, that they invoked one another, "O, come, let us sing unto the Lord: let us make a joyful noise to the rock of our salvation. Let us come before His presence with thanksgiving, and make a joyful noise unto Him with psalms" (Psalm 95:1, 2). They were involved with far more than mere liturgy; they were experiencing liberation, and they responded by celebrating God quite hilariously. Their minds were filled with God's truth and their spirit overflowed with God's joy. This is a sound basis for worship.

Worship occurs when our spirit contacts God's spirit. The way that we respond to that contact is partially dependent upon our basic nature, and partially controlled by our, environment at the moment. Sometimes our house gets very dry during the heat of the summer, producing an ideal situation for the build-up of static electricity. Occasionally when my wife walks across the carpet to greet me she builds up a very positive charge, and when she kisses me, SNAP! A spark of electricity jumps the gap between us. Worship is akin to that. In the midst of praising, something sparks between God and us and, SNAP! We're involved in a worship experience.

As an organist, I have accompanied many soloists through the years. Sometimes, however, I have ended up playing a solo rather than accompanying the singer because as the soloist began to sing unto the Lord, that mystical *snap!* occurred and she found herself in a worship experience right in front of everyone and singing gave place to tears or praise. I have had that happen to me while I was preaching. It seems that I took such a tiny step towards God and enjoyed that bridging spark that brought me together with my God. How easily we forget that God's kingdom isn't multiple light-years away; Jesus taught that the kingdom is here and now. Wherever the King is, the kingdom is also; so when the King is present, His kingdom is also here.

That worship is the total release of our spirit to God's Spirit is true. Perhaps the best way to understand that is to liken it to that mystical something that happens when two people who love each another get close enough to kiss. During his absence he wrote a letter, sent a telegram, wired flowers, and even bought a box of candy. He called to his love as he stepped off the airplane, and all of this was appreciated and received. But when he got close enough for a hug and a kiss, everything else was considered preliminary. This is the main event! Love is flowing; worship is transpiring.

The gifts functioned as elements for the expression of his love but it was the touch, the closeness, and the release of tenderness that made it a loving experience.

If, therefore, elements prepare the way for such a loving experience, are there also elements that prepare the way for worship and which may become the very channels through which worship is released?

8

The Elements of Worship

Hezekiah was only twenty-five years old when he took the reins of government after the death of his godless father, Ahaz. Reflecting the godly influence of his tutor, Isaiah, this new king opened the doors of the house of the Lord the very first month after his coronation. Under his father, all temple worship had ceased, and the temple had become a storage building for the king.

First Hezekiah regathered the priesthood and challenged them to reinstitute worship for all Israel and to clean out the house of the Lord. Second, he provided for the recasting of the vessels of the Lord that had been destroyed by Ahaz (see 2 Chronicles 29).

It was not until after all the elements of worship—the brazen altar, the laver of the outer court, the lampstand, the table of shewbread, and the altar of incense of the holy place—had been completely restored in the cleansed and repaired temple that Hezekiah called the congregation together to worship.

The chronicler records that:

... When the burnt offering began, the song of the Lord began also with the trumpets, and with the instruments ordained by David King of Israel. And all the congregation worshipped, and the singers sang, and the trumpeters sounded: and all this continued until the burnt offering was finished. And when they had made an end of offering, the king and all that were present with him bowed themselves, and worshipped. Moreover, Hezekiah the king and the princes commanded the Levites to sing praise unto the Lord with the words of David, and of Asaph the seer. And they sang praises with gladness, and they bowed their heads and worshipped (2 Chronicles 29:27-30).

Hezekiah restored jubilant worship to Israel. But he began by restoring the elements of worship, for he realized that without these channels of worship neither the priests nor the people would have a route of access to God or a means of expressing their worship to God. These elements were not mere rituals, they were channels for the communication of worship unto God. Elements of worship, then, are important.

To review, just what is worship? It is an attitude of heart, a reaching toward God, a pouring out of our total self in thanksgiving, praise, adoration, and love to the God who created us and to Whom we owe everything we have and are. But worship is even more than that.

The worshippers in the Old Testament gave tangible evidence of their heart attitude. They built altars, made offerings, slew animals and later became deeply involved with the elaborate ritual of the tabernacle worship. These saints translated their heart attitudes into *facts* of worship. Even the Magi who came to worship the child Jesus had tangible evidence of their heart attitude in the gifts they presented as they fell down before Him (see Matthew 2:11).

Has Christ's position as the sacrifice slain once and for all negated these acts that give tangible evidence of our heart's attitude? No! Only the sacrificial system was abolished in Him. Wise men still worship Him, and they will need some elements to help them express that worship. We are being reintroduced to some acts of worship such as clapping of the hands, raising our hands, dancing before the Lord, bowing on our knees, and using our voices to sing and shout His praises; but we have only scratched the surface. A broad dimension of worshipful expressions are just now beginning to resurface in our generation but, actually, they have been a part of worship from antiquity.

Those who have recently been released from extreme formalism and ritualistic worship usually decry the need for elements. "I want to be free to worship the Lord in my own way," they cry. "I don't want to go back into bondage." But it isn't long until they discover that they must either embrace old elements of worship or invent some new ones for, limited beings that we are, we all need something that will inspire us to worship and channel our desires into a true worship experience. The Bible has given us quite a variety of such elements and even Jesus did not condemn them. He did, however, condemn the exaggerated emphasis on ritual practice which was used as a substitute for genuine righteousness (see Mark 7:6).

In the very giving of the Lord's Prayer and the new ritual of the Lord's Supper, Jesus recognized that men need aids to worship. He consistently taught the need for commitment to God, for the expression of divine love back to God, and for purity of heart and mind which would normally find expression in acts of worship. It is the certainty of God within us that gives substance, reality, and power to any external motions used to translate heart attitudes into acts of worship.

God did not make us mystics. When we seek a mystical approach to God we tend to become hyper-spiritual and unduly emotional, trading substance for feeling. Often this approach is embraced for lack of proper understanding of the difference between supernatural and spiritual. Everything that God does is entirely natural to Him and His spiritual kingdom. It only seems supernatural to us because we view all spiritual acts from our natural world. If God never violates His nature in what He does, if all His acts are very natural to Him, then I would expect Him to appreciate worship that is consistent with our born-again nature and that is natural to us. True worship need not violate our God-given nature. It should express it. We need not be "spooky" to be spiritual. The most spiritual men of the Bible were very down-to-earth human beings who had learned how to come into God's presence and worship. Even their great spiritual power did not divest them of their humanity as Paul and Barnabas declared to the people of Lystra when they sought to make gods of the apostles after they healed the cripple who had never walked. Paul and Barnabas "ran in among the people, crying out, and saying, Sirs, why do ye these things? We also are men of like passions with you ..." (Acts 14:14, 15).

No, we're not mystics, we're men. We're not miniature gods; we're mere people who need to do something to successfully make the transition from our natural kingdom to God's spiritual kingdom.

Those things that we *do* to bridge this gap are elements that help give form and substance to our worship. The Gospels record such elements, Paul manifested them in his life, and the Epistles teach about them and command us to use them, for God has not left worship a total mystery; there are certain things that we can do that both bring us into worship and express that worship unto God.

Prayer is one such element. Jesus regularly used the prayer channel for times of fellowship with His Father, and Paul taught and practiced the use of prayer as a channel for worship. We need to communicate in order to come into communion, and prayer is essentially communication. If we can talk with God, then we can fellowship with Him and flow worship unto Him. Just as nothing strains a marriage faster than a breakdown of communication, nothing will disturb worship more than prayerlessness. How often have we bridged the gap between our world and His through the channel of prayer.

Prayer, in its simplest essence, is a communication from man's spirit to God's Spirit, while worship is communion between these two spirits, and communication greatly aids communion. It is safe to say that the prayerless saint is never a worshipper.

Praise, confession of sin, and confession of faith are also elements of worship. They will be considered in greater depth a little later in this book, but we can't ignore the fact that praise is very often the vocal end of worship, although it cannot become a substitute for it. Furthermore, the very confession of sin is a part of worship, for it is an acknowledgment of the finished work of Christ at Calvary and it is a positive application of divine grace. We dare not let sin keep us out of God's presence when confession of sin will help to bring us into His presence.

Even the confession of our faith can become an element of worship, for faith must be released to be effective, and faith is most normally released in our speech.

Reading the Scriptures can become another channel for worship, for private reading of the Bible for spiritual edification often elevates the reader into a worshipful atmosphere that makes contact with God simple and most natural. Even public reading of the Scriptures can become an element of worship, for this was part of the worship of the early New Testament church. (Private copies of the Word were unavailable to all but the very wealthy). If prayer and praise are fundamentally our communication with God, then reading the Scripture is basically God's communication with us. Since worship is like dialogue we must have movement in two directions: God comes to man and man goes to God. Like Jacob's ladder, there is an ascending and a descending. If worship is to meet God, we should expect to meet Him in His Word.

Sometime ago I was ministering in a small church in Virginia. That night the worship leader evidenced great exhaustion, and the song service was lifeless. I stepped to the pulpit and offered to take over. Opening my Bible I invited the congregation to turn with me to the first chapter of the book of Hebrews, assuring them that I was not going to preach; I merely wanted everyone to stand and read the chapter in unison with me. At first, every few verses I paused and helped them to realize what they had read, and then we would read on. By the time we had completed chapter 2 that congregation was so conscious of the presence of God that they had already begun to worship. The mere awareness of God's provision for us in Christ Jesus formed that "spark" that bridged the gap between earth and heaven. If the Old Testament priests could minister at the golden altar of incense only if the lampstand was lighted, then we, too, need illumination to aid our worship. Proverbs 6:23 says, "For the commandment is a lamp; and the law is light ... ," and the Psalmist declares, "The entrance of Thy words giveth light ..." (Psalm 119:130).

Preaching is also an element of worship. The New Testament makes great provision for preaching, for it proclaims God's Word, it declares God's work, and it enlightens, informs, and inspires God's people to respond to Him. Every prophesying and exhortation are elements of worship since they, too, declare the words and works of God and magnify His offices.

Anointed, Bible-centered preaching should be a part of the worship of the church but it should not be a substitute for worship. One notable thing about a New Testament church service must have been that almost everyone came feeling he had the privilege of contributing something to it. Paul wrote, "To sum up, my friends: when you meet for worship each of you contributes a hymn, some instruction, a revelation, an ecstatic utterance or the interpretation of such an utterance" (2 Corinthians 14:26, NEB). Preaching, then, is not the end; it is a means to an end. Worship is the end to be sought in all our church services. Everything should contribute to worship or have no place in our gatherings.

The Lord's Supper was instituted as an element of worship. "This do ye, as oft as ye drink it, in remembrance of me," Jesus said (1 Corinthians 11:25). This element of worship replaced not only the Passover but the temple offerings. This is probably why there is so much sacrificial language associated with this sacrament. "This is my body which is broken for you," and "this is my shed blood" all speak of the death of the lamb slain for the sins of the people.

The great beauty of the Lord's Supper is that it is Christological rather than liturgical in the narrower Old Testament sense.

It is not the mere serving of the Communion that becomes an element of worship, but it is the remembering of the covenant we have entered into because of this shed blood, and the memory of Christ Jesus Himself. I have participated in observances of the Lord's Supper that were more funeral services than times of worship. Conversely, I have enjoyed some very bright periods of worship during the serving of the Communion. The difference lies in the concept being presented at the time. When it is Christ-centered there is a great potential for worship, but when it is ceremony-centered, it often becomes a substitute for worship.

Certainly these examples do not exhaust the many elements of worship made available to us throughout the Bible. Space does not permit our discussion of song, Christian fellowship, church construction, testimony, baptism, pageantry, choral presentations, etc., as aids to our worship experience, but we are somewhat familiar with them by virtue of personal experience.

I feel constrained, however, to admit that there can be negatives to the employment of these elements of worship. Each may be a part of worship but any and all are vehicles for worship that can give guidance to worship and can become expressions of worship, *but in themselves* they are not worship.

Just as we can have a Communion service without it becoming a worship service, we can pray seven times a day and still not worship. It is even possible for the one who preaches the sermon to fail to worship, since ritual, for ritual's sake, will never produce worship. While it is true that worship does not require vestments, cathedrals or pipe organs, these may be elements that help to bring the saints to worship. Jesus continually emphasized that worship was a one-to-one relationship that was not dependent upon locale or trappings, while all the time refusing to condemn the liturgy of His day. I embrace the statement made in the *International Standard Bible Encyclopedia*, "Anything that really stimulates and expresses the worshipful spirit is a legitimate aid to worship, but never a substitute for it, and is harmful if it displaces it."

Our Quaker brothers and sisters leaned to the mystical approach in worshipping God; so they came together in total silence awaiting the worship experience, but the way into worship is not silence; it is expression. It is not in doing nothing, but in doing something that will stimulate, direct, and then channel our worship unto God. The goal of our life should be to get into the divine presence rather than to find and follow a prescribed ritual. Whatever we find that brings us into that divine presence should be continued until we flow into a full worship experience.

Although varied rituals may help bring us to the place of worship, it will be the expression of correct attitudes that enables us to step from ceremony to Communion. But just what are the correct attitudes of worship and what will be the attitudes of those who observe that worship? And, even more important, what will be the attitude of the One who is being worshipped?

9

The Attitude of Worship

The Bible does not even give us her name, but she performed a most beautiful act of worship in the house of Simon the Pharisee. Because what she did in worshipping Jesus parallels what Mary, the sister of Lazarus, did to Jesus in the home of Simon the Leper, some believe that this is the same incident. Whether or not there were two separate but similiar incidents, or merely one that has been reported differently by two writers, is unimportant at the moment. Luke merely identifies this woman as "a sinner" who brought an alabaster box of ointment, "and stood at His [Jesus'] feet behind Him weeping, and began to wash His feet with tears, and did wipe them with the hairs of her head, and kissed His feet, and anointed them with the ointment" (Luke 7:38).

In this simple story, Luke deals very strongly with the attitudes involved and released in worship: those expressed and released by the worshipper, those expressed and inferred by the spectators, and the expressed attitudes of Jesus who was so lavishly worshipped on this occasion. These, or similiar, attitudes will usually be present when worship is being released to God in an earnest and truthful manner. Whether they produce the worship or are a by-product of the worship may be difficult to determine, but they are active in worship.

The first attitude that seemed to impress Luke was this woman's brokenness, for he records that she "stood at His feet behind Him weeping, and began to wash His feet with tears" (Luke 7-38). Brokenness is a good beginning attitude in worship, for tears have a way of cleansing the soul. When we, with all of our imperfections, stand in the presence of the completely perfect Christ, the very contrast is enough to break our hearts.

David understood the place of brokenness in worship, for he wrote, "the sacrifices of God are a broken spirit: a broken and a contrite heart, O God, thou wilt not despise" (Psalm 51:17). In referring to a broken spirit, David uses the Hebrew word *shabor* which means to shiver, to break to pieces, or to reduce. A spirit that trembles in God's presence, or has been broken into multiple pieces, is classified as an acceptable sacrifice in worshipping God. He does not indicate whether the spirit may have been broken by God, by the worshipper, or by the harsh realities of life; he just indicates that no matter what has broken us, that brokenness can be brought to God in sweet surrender, and it is accepted as an attitude of worship.

When David spoke of "a broken heart," however, he used an entirely different Hebrew word, *dakah*, which means to crumble, to beat to pieces, to bruise, to crush, or to humble. To this he adds the expression "a contrite heart." "Contrite" is a word that is used to describe the process of

making talcum powder. In days gone by some brands of talcum came in containers on which were printed the words, "this is stone that has been contrited." It simply means that what was once part of a mountain has been ground and pounded so fine that it will float on water. It now has taken an entirely different form. Did the prophet have this in mind when he wrote, "Is not My word ... like a hammer that breaketh the rock in pieces" (Jeremiah 23:29).

Worship requires being broken! Most of us have built such protective walls around our emotions that we cannot release tenderness, love and adoration. We're more like the alabaster box than the ointment that was poured out. Until something breaks that rock-hard attitude there can be no love poured out on Christ.

But tears are not only an evidence of being broken and contrited; tears are also an expression of full emotion. Jesus told us, "... thou shalt love the Lord thy God with all thy heart, and with all thy soul, and with all thy mind, and with all thy strength ..." (Mark 12:30). Usually this much concentration and exertion will build such a wave of emotion that it can only be released in tears. As the tension of a beauty pageant reaches the climactic moment when the winner is about to be announced the atmosphere becomes electrifying, and when the winner is announced she generally bursts into a flood of tears as a release of the pent-up emotions that had been building.

Should worship be any different for us? If we, too, have set all of our heart, soul, mind, and strength to come into God's presence, when that climactic moment occurs tears should be a natural expression of the release of joy and happiness. Tears are nothing to be ashamed of, for even great athletes have been seen joyfully weeping after winning an event. Since tears are such a part of our release of high level emotion—and airports, where I spend so much time, are a good place to witness tears as friends and loved ones meet in joyful embrace we should expect to burst out crying like this worshipping woman, for we have finally come into the presence of a loving God.

A second worshipful attitude that this unknown sinful woman displayed was humility. Luke remembered that she "began to wash His feet with tears, and did wipe them with the hairs of her head ..." (Luke 7:38). Paul reminded the Corinthian believers that "if a woman have long hair, it is a glory to her: for her hair is given her for a covering" (1 Corinthians 11:15), which suggests two reasons why this act of wiping the feet of Christ was a display of humility. First, in the days of Jesus the women wore a covering over their hair as an outer symbol that they were under the authority or covering of a man. It was not too unlike our custom of wearing a wedding ring. When this unnamed worshipper loosened her long hair allowing it to fall freely around her, she had the attention of every man in the room, for this was an act done only by a wife in the privacy of her bedroom, or by a prostitute as she attempted to turn a trick. The fact that Simon was so amazed that Jesus, with His prophetic insight, would even let this class of woman touch Him (see Luke 7:39) suggests that Simon either knew her reputation from past experience, or what she was doing was so classified as part of her trade that all the men were horrified. This woman put her reputation on the line in order to worship Jesus in the manner that she felt He should be worshipped, and so must we. Peer pressure has kept far too many saints from releasing their affection to Christ. There must come a time when the question "what will others think of me" gives place to "what will Jesus think of me?"

Furthermore, I see humility in this act of wiping the dusty feet of Jesus now made muddy with the nearly endless tears that have fallen on them, because Paul declared that a woman's hair is her glory, and this worshipping woman took her glory to wipe up the mess.

Her act indicates her attitude. Absolutely nothing she had was too good for Jesus!

When God was speaking through the prophet Isaiah, He declared, "For thus saith the high and lofty One that inhabiteth eternity, whose name is Holy: I dwell in the high and holy place, with him also that is of a *contrite and humble spirit*, to revive the spirit of the *humble*, and to revive the heart of the *contrite ones*" (Isaiah 57:15, italics added). God declares that He not only dwells with the angels in heaven, but He also dwells with the contrite and humble spirit here on earth. Brokenness and humility form a dwelling place for the Almighty God, and God's presence is a necessary prerequisite to worship.

Even the New Testament tells us that "... God resisteth the proud, and giveth grace to the humble. Humble yourselves therefore under the mighty hand of God, that He may exalt you in due time" (1 Peter 5:5). Pride and humility are not too unlike the positive and negative poles of a magnet. If you attempt to put two magnets together, positive to positive or negative to negative, the combined energies of the magnets will repel and push the magnets away from each other. If, however, you reverse the polarity of one of the magnets and bring the negative pole of one magnet to the positive pole of the other, the combined force in the two magnets will attract each other until it becomes difficult to separate them after they have joined.

If we approach God in the pride of our being, accomplishment, or station in life, we are pushing away from the divine presence. But if we approach God in true humility He draws us unto Himself and none can separate us from the love of God that is in Christ Jesus our Lord. Worship without humility is like love without commitment; it is shallow, emotional and fleeting.

A third attitude of worship that is exemplified in this story is *love*. It was not merely that she felt the love of Jesus or even felt love for Him, but she expressed what she felt. She poured love out in an unashamed, nonsexual manner. She evidenced that love in kissing Christ's feet. Unloving worship is worse than an uncaring stepmother, for love must become the heart of all worship.

Still a fourth attitude that was displayed in this act of worship is *giving*, for she poured out the contents of the alabaster box on the feet of Jesus. That the ointment was precious and costly is indicated by the fact that it was contained in alabaster. Very likely this represented her savings account, for widows and unmarried women rarely trusted their funds to the bankers of their day. Gold coins and costly spices were stored as their savings. In Mark's account of Mary anointing the head of Jesus, the value of the spikenard that she poured out was calculated as a full year's salary. Just how valuable this particular ointment may have been is purely a matter of speculation, for Luke didn't even identify the nature of the ointment. But whatever its value, this woman poured it out on Christ's feet as an act of worship. She gave Him the best that she had. She did not confine herself merely to expressing her emotions; she also gave tangible evidence of her love, devotion and adoration.

I have already stated that one of the characteristics of Old Testament worship was jubilation and joy, but another major facet of Israelite worship was gift-giving. Three times God discussed the compulsory feasts that His covenant people were to attend, and all three times God commanded that "they shall not appear before the Lord empty" (Exodus 23 :15, 34:20, and Deuteronomy 16:16). No worshipper could approach God with empty hands, for Old Testament worship involved sacrifices, gifts, and offerings, all of which were brought by the people themselves. No gift, no worship! God made no provision for freeloaders in His economy. They could, if forced by poverty, trap a sparrow or bring a turtledove, but they could not worship empty-handed.

Should New Testament saints do less? The very psalter which formed the hymn book of the early church exhorted the believers:

O sing unto the Lord a new song ... bless His name ... Declare His glory ... Give unto the Lord ... give unto the Lord glory and strength ... Give unto the Lord the glory due unto His name: bring an offering, and come into his courts. O worship the Lord in the beauty of holiness: fear before Him, all the earth (Psalm 96:1-9).

After telling the saints in Corinth about the gifts of the Spirit, the power of love, and the surety of the resurrection, Paul concluded his letter by writing, "Now concerning the collection for the saints, as I have given order to the churches of Galatia, even so do ye. Upon the first day of the week let every one of you lay by him in store, as God hath prospered him, that there be no gatherings when I come" (1 Corinthians 16:1, 2). Nowhere in the New Testament is worship discussed more fully than in this letter, and in the midst of that discussion Paul, too, says we should not come empty-handed.

It certainly is not that heaven is short of funds and needs the meager gifts that we can bring; it is simply that our worship needs an attitude of surrender in giving. We, too, need to pour out our "ointment" upon Christ to release a greater depth of worship upon our God.

Whenever our expressed attitudes of worship are observed by non-worshippers, we can expect them to react with attitudes of criticism. Like Simon the Pharisee, they will criticize Jesus for allowing such lavish worship to come from such sinful people and they will criticize the worshipper for wasting on Jesus what might well have been given to the poor, as the disciples did when Mary anointed Jesus' head. But if the attitudes of the non-worshippers can keep us from worshipping we will never become worshippers, for they have always outnumbered us greatly.

Simon's criticism expressed an attitude of self-righteousness when he said, "If He knew what kind of person she was ... ," inferring that Simon very well knew. The self-righteous always project that they know something that no one else knows, but the worshipper is only concerned with responding properly to the person he has come to know.

Throughout life, expressed attitudes involve responsive attitudes. Love extended generally induces a love response, while anger vented often stirs an angry retaliation. When this unnamed woman poured out her brokenness, humility, love, and sacrificial giving upon Jesus, He, in turn, released His attitudes toward her. The first such attitude was forgiveness. Jesus said, "Her sins, which are many, are forgiven; for she loved much ... " (Luke 7:47). Simon had told Jesus that in his opinion the person who had been forgiven the most would love the most, but Jesus reversed it and said it is the love that produces the forgiveness. Salvation is more than a sinner forsaking his sins, it is a sinner responding to God's love!

The next three attitudes Jesus demonstrated to her are given by Luke in the last verse of this chapter, "And He said to the woman, thy *faith* hath *saved* thee; go in peace (Luke 7:50, italics added)". Faith, deliverance, and peace all have their origins in Christ Jesus. None of us can generate them, but all of us can receive them. They are reciprocal responses to our expressed attitudes of worship.

There is no greater place to receive faith than while worshipping at the feet of Jesus. Furthermore, no matter what we may need to be saved from (the Greek word Luke used is *sozo* which means "deliver, protect, heal, preserve, be whole, do well, save"), our complete salvation is vested in the Savior, and when we are worshipping Him our salvation is assured. Similarly, there is no peace like the peace a worshipper finds when he has completely poured out himself upon his Lord.

Attitudes are vitally important in all of us, for they color and control our actions. True worship will flow out of proper attitudes, but what is our attitude about the object of our worship? Just who is to receive worship? Is it but a name, or a person? Does our attitude towards who He is affect the way we respond to Him?

10

The Object of Worship

In my travels throughout the world, I have watched persons of many different cultures bow until their foreheads almost touched the ground; kneel, or fully prostrate themselves for long periods before their god, while others crossed a cobblestone courtyard crawling on their hands and knees to do obeisance to their god. I've seen baskets of fruit presented to an idol, and have watched while sacrifices have been burned on a flaming altar. I've been a spectator as the worshippers marched in great ceremony, parading their idols through the streets of the city, singing, dancing and playing instruments in honor of their god. I've also observed obviously poor people drop coins into collection boxes or place money directly into the hands of their priest in return for some assistance in performing their worship. These sincere people sacrifice to pour out their adoration upon their gods, but it is all in vain, for they have chosen the wrong object of worship. In two separate psalms the futility of this worship is expressed in identical words:

The idols of the heathen are silver and gold, the work of men's hands. They have mouths, but they speak not; eyes have they, but they see not; they have ears, but they hear not; neither is there any breath in their mouths. They that make them are like unto them: so is everyone that trusteth in them (Psalm 115:4-8, 135:15-18).

How can worship offered to an inanimate object be efficacious?

"To worship or not to worship" has never been the question, for all of God's created beings are inherently worshippers. No matter how vociferously he may deny it, each person on earth is instinctively a worshipper. It is in his genetic strain! The issue has never been, shall we worship or not? It is more consistently a question of *whom* we will worship.

The object of our worship is always the greatest point of controversy in worship. This controversy did not begin with man here on earth. According to Isaiah 14, Lucifer's fall was the result of high-level pride that caused him to express a desire to become the object of Heaven's worship. He has never lost this aspiration. From his temptation of Eve in Eden to the temptation of Christ in the wilderness, Satan consistently recruited worshippers from among earth's inhabitants, and he still does.

All fundamental Bible-believing Christians agree with Jesus that God is the only acceptable object of worship. They know of God's expressed hatred of idol worship, and they have read in the Old Testament of God's repeated punishment of those who worshipped anything besides the true and living God. They accept, intellectually at least, God's demand that He alone should be worshipped.

Most of these same Christians have also memorized Christ's pointed statement on worship from John 4:23. "The hour cometh and now is when the true worshippers shall worship the Father in spirit and in truth." And yet, for all of their mental acquiescence to God's exclusive rights to their worship, even a casual observer will discover fundamental Christians offering worship to lesser gods in their lives.

If we will accept the dictionary's definition of worship as, "to adore, to revere, to exalt, to magnify, to dote, to admire or to esteem," then it becomes quite obvious that many Christians worship, to a lesser, extent perhaps, many things that are beneath the image of God.

Some exalt their denomination in a manner that at least borders on worship. Others dote dangerously on their pastor, while still others magnify a doctrinal truth almost to the place of God Himself. Furthermore, we've all seen people, even God-fearing saints, so love possessions as to become worshippers of them, and others have disgusted us as they become worshippers of themselves.

Not that anyone intends for his affections to get so out of control as to direct his worship to something less than God, but still it happens all too frequently, for what we love soon becomes what we worship. Perhaps this is why the Bible so clearly commands us: "Love not the world, neither the things that are in the world. If any man love the world, the love of the Father is not in him" (1 John 2:15).

So the key to maintaining the divine monopoly in worship is to "... Love the Lord thy God with all thy heart, and with all thy soul, and with all thy mind, and with all thy strength ..." (Mark 12:30). When everything within us loves God fully, He alone will be the object of our worship. Otherwise, we will be as vacillating in our worship as we are in our loving.

Unfortunately the propensity to idolatry is inherent in each of us. Worshipping something short of God seems more natural to us than worshipping God Himself, since we find it easier to relate to the tangible than to the intangible and to respond to the seen rather than to the unseen. Yet God is the only truly acceptable object of our worship.

Jesus told the woman of Samaria that the true worshippers would "worship the Father" (John 4:24), but few of us have a good concept of God the Father. At Mt. Sinai when God revealed Himself in fire, smoke, thunder, and lightning, and then spoke directly to Israel, the people were so terrified that they asked God to never do that again. So God sought to reveal Himself through the law as a God of law and order who was approachable through ordinances, means, and the mediacy of the priesthood, but the people found themselves unable to keep His laws and, furthermore, they preferred to let the priesthood become their substitute rather than their mediator in worship. If God revealed Himself in angelic form the people expected to drop dead, so at Bethlehem God revealed Himself as the God-man. He became a person like us in order to lead us to the person of God. As a baby He was non-threatening to all but Herod, and as a man He was understandable, lovable, and comfortable to men, women and children.

Jesus came not only to redeem us from sin but to reveal to us the Father. The Scripture says, "In many and various ways God spoke of old to our fathers by the prophets; but in these last days He has spoken to us by a Son, whom He appointed the heir of all things, through whom also He created the world. He reflects the glory of God and bears the very stamp of His nature, upholding the universe by His word of power" (Hebrews 2:1-3, RSV).

If you listen to Jesus speak you'll hear the voice of the Father, for Jesus said, "I have not spoken on my authority; the Father who sent Me has Himself given Me commandments what to say and what to speak" (John 12:49 RSV). Look at Christ's marvelous works and see the Father at work, for Jesus also said, "The Son can do nothing by Himself. He does only what He sees the Father doing, and in the same way. For the Father loves the Son, and tells him everything He is doing" (John 5:19, 20 TLB). Everything about Jesus reveals the Father to us, and in becoming like us, Christ caused us to lose our fear of the Father. Through Christ, we've come to know, trust, and love the Father; therefore, we can worship Him.

Christ Jesus is not only a revelation of the Father to us, He is also our access to the Father. Everything in the Tabernacle in the wilderness is a type of Jesus. He is as much our means of approach unto the Father now as He was then. Paul declares this in saying, "For *through* Him we both have access *by* one Spirit *unto* the Father" (Ephesians 2:18, italics added).

Diagrammed, this verse would look like this:

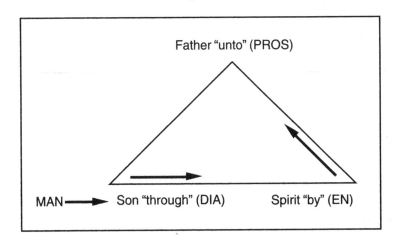

Jesus said virtually the same thing when He affirmed, "I am the way, the truth, and the life: no man cometh unto the Father, but by Me" (John 14:6). At His ascension, Christ returned to heaven as our interceding High Priest (see Hebrews 7:25), not to assure our salvation, for Calvary assured that, but to secure a permanent access to the Father so that we might be worshippers.

And so, dear brothers, now we may walk right into the very Holy of Holies where God is, because of the blood of

Jesus. This is the fresh, new, life-giving way which Christ has opened up for us by tearing the curtain—His human body to let us into the holy presence of God. And since this great High Priest of ours rules over God 's household, let us go right in to God Himself, with true hearts fully sprinkled with Christ's blood to make us clean, and because we have been washed with the pure water. " (Hebrews 10:19-22, TLB)

Certainly "the hour ... now is when the true worshippers shall worship the Father ... " (John 4:23). Christ has both assured this and made it available to us.

But Christ is not only our access to worshipping the Father; He is a proper object of our worship Himself, for Jesus is in the Father. He taught us, "Believe me that I am in the Father, and the Father in Me ... " (John 14:11).

Christ Jesus receives worship in His own right, for men on earth worshipped Him. His birth was marked by the worship of the Magi, the shepherds, Simeon the prophet, and Anna the prophetess. During His ministry, Jesus received worship from a leper, a ruler, the Syro-Phoenician woman, the two Marys after the resurrection, His disciples, and many others. Surely Jesus would not have allowed men to worship Him if He was not worthy to receive it. In accepting worship Jesus Christ was admitting and declaring Himself to be very God; therefore, He is totally worthy of all worship.

Even the angels are instructed to worship Jesus (see Hebrews 1:6), and Matthew records the antiphonal chanting of worship by the angels at the birth of Jesus. In Heaven the Elders and the living creatures worship Jesus (see Revelation 4:9-11), and the Word declares that everyone shall worship Him (see Revelation 15:4 and Philippians 2:10-22).

Furthermore, most of our expressions of worship are either unto Jesus or in His name, for prayer is directed unto Him and in His name, and praise is generally concerned with Him and

His works. Even our thanksgiving is directed to Him, as Paul did in saying, "... I thank Christ Jesus our Lord, who hath enabled me ..." (1 Timothy 1:12), and the rituals we observe are commemorative of Jesus.

However, whether we worship the Father through the Son or worship the Son in the Father, the level of our worship will be determined by our concept of the One we are worshipping and many of us are confused about Christ Jesus as was the woman at the well.

Jesus had revealed Himself to her as the Messiah, but she chose to see Him as a prophet (compare John 4:25, 29 with 19). The concept of the man at the well actually being the Messiah was too lofty for her; there had never been a Messiah, but there had been prophets and she could relate to that, so she, like we, lowered a divine revelation until it fit her past theology.

Every new move of God tends to be dragged down to the level of a prior move of God, and every fresh revelation God gives of Himself is apt to be diminished to a prior revelation with which we are already comfortably related. What it amounts to is that we never allow our concepts of God to enlarge. The majority of our singing, testifying, and talking about Jesus refers to Him as our Healer, Savior, Comforter, Blesser, Baptizer, Lover, and so forth. These are *roles* that He fills in His relationships with us, but they only illustrate a small facet of who He really is. To the sinner, Christ fills the role of a Savior; to the seeker, He becomes the Baptizer; to the sick, Jesus functions as the Healer; and to the sorrowful, Jesus becomes the Comforter. But the New Testament does not declare that He is any of these things. Consistently the New Testament declares that Jesus Christ is *Lord*.

Our initial introduction to Jesus was as one who met our needs, and many never allow Him to reveal anything else about Himself. But worship requires that we respond to someone higher than the Jesus of our discovery, or the Jesus who meets our needs. We need to worship the Christ of divine revelation; the Christ who is the Almighty God.

Perhaps this can best be understood by looking at the responses of John the Beloved Disciple. For over three years this young man lived and ministered with Jesus. It appears that he had a more intimate relation to Jesus than the other disciples, for he was with Jesus on the mount of transfiguration, in the garden, in the judgment hall, at the whipping post, and stood and watched the crucifixion. It was to this John that Jesus entrusted the care of His earthly mother. Yet we never once read of John worshipping Jesus during these days. It was not until many years later, when banished to the Isle of Patmos and receiving a vision of Jesus as the Ancient of Days, that John fell at His feet and worshipped Him (see Revelation 1). This, too, was the experience of Isaiah in the Old Testament. Until these great men began to see Jesus as more than God's provided means for meeting men's needs they did not worship, but when they saw Him as God, worship was an inevitable response. Just as a substitute vision will produce a substitute response, a shallow concept will produce shallow worship.

Quite frequently over the years I have been with groups where God so honored the preaching of the Word that His presence sovereignly enveloped the congregation. When I have turned the service back to the leader, he has often responded by saying, "I don't know when I have ever sensed the presence of the Lord Jesus Christ like I do in this service tonight. Let's everyone bow his head ..."

What is said following that is predetermined by that leader's concept of and orientation to Christ Jesus. If he is evangelistically inclined, he will say, "... I want all those who need to accept Jesus as Savior to come to the front right now." People come and get saved.

If he is a leader with a compassion for the sick his call will be, "... all who are suffering with pain, stand right where you are and we'll pray for you." They stand, and often they are healed.

While I believe in and practice altar calls upon occasion, I am often saddened that when the Lord actually makes His presence known we seek to work Him rather than worship Him. Knowing Him only as a meeter of our needs never inspires any higher worship than praise.

Much of the time that I travel my wife stays at home. When the tour is over, I look forward to having her meet me at the airport. I am so thankful to God that my delightful wife does not greet me at the airport with a quick hug and kiss and then begin immediately to tell me, "Honey, the furnace broke down, the roof is leaking, and we've got trouble with the car again. I'm so glad that my fix-it man is home again."

No, that's not how I am received back home after a period of absence. I'm welcomed, loved, fed, rested, and then she helps me find the list of things that need repairing. I am her fix-it man, and she knows that I will have everything fixed before I leave on my next tour. But she did not marry a repairman, she married a person; she relates to me for whom I am, not merely for what I can do for her. Until we see Christ Jesus as He is, not merely for the roles that He fills, we will never be able to worship Him.

Our challenge is to worship the Father, but God has revealed Himself as love, light and a consuming fire. We could not worship such concepts, so God became man, and they called His name Jesus. This Jesus is the express image of the Father, and comes both as a demonstration of the Father and as a revelation of Him. If we restrict our concept of Jesus to being the one who meets all of our human needs, we will also restrict our revelation of the Father, and, furthermore, we'll severely limit our worship responses.

It's this very confusion that makes it so imperative that a worshipper have the assistance of the Holy Spirit. The Spirit actually knows God the Father and God the Son, and as a member of that Godhead He dwells within the life of the believer. Worship without the aid of the Holy Spirit is probably impossible.

11

The Holy Spirit and Worship

I stood on the platform at a conference some years ago as the congregation released themselves to worship God in a way with which I was uncomfortable. I watched for a few moments and soon realized that they had come into a depth of sincerity and expression beyond my experience levels and I could not honestly reject it. Nonetheless, I could not participate in it from my inner being; I could only conform to their outer actions.

"I don't know how to worship!" I cried to the Lord.

"But I do," the Holy Spirit seemed to respond within me, "And I'll teach you, if you'll let Me."

I must confess that I didn't learn to worship their way during that one service, for I found that learning is a progressive work of the Holy Spirit. Patient teacher that He is, He leads us progressively from where we are to where we should be in our worship. Throughout the months that followed, I would rise to a level of worship and find some invisible force hindering me from entering a higher level. I would see into the things of the Lord, and my heart would want to respond in adoration, but somehow I couldn't get the words out of my mouth; I just couldn't release my emotions. There was something between me and the God I deeply desired to respond to. Having already confessed any known sin in my life and not being aware of any wrong attitudes, I stood facing this invisible barrier completely stymied.

I was, and still am, convinced that anytime there is something between me and God in the time of worship, that that hindrance will never be on God's side, for there is absolutely nothing in God that prevents our worshipping Him. Nothing! That meant that the barrier was within me and I did not know what it was.

Sharing this with others has convinced me that my experience is not unique; they, too, have faced this invisible barrier to worship. Is not this the reason that God put His own Spirit within our hearts, to enable us to cry, "Abba, Father?" God knows what changes are necessary on man's side, rather than on His side, to make worshippers out of us, so by living within man's spirit, God is able to help us to overcome the barriers to worship that may be sin-generated, culturally-induced, or religiously ingrained in us. Our training in life and religion have predetermined our responses to God, and our spirit has set up an automatic veto in our memory circuits so that the moment we seek to go beyond that ban our minds flash "does not compute" back to us. The Holy Spirit, working from within, begins to reprogram our conscious and subconscious minds to release us to worship God in fresh new ways.

It is to be expected, then, that Jesus would tell the woman at the well that the worshippers "... shall worship the Father in spirit and in truth ... God is a Spirit: and they that worship him must worship him in spirit and in truth" (John 4:23, 24). For while praise can be the product of the human spirit, worship is impossible without the aid of the Holy Spirit of God.

Oh yes, "Holy Spirit of God" is a correct title, for He is called this at least twenty-seven times in the Scriptures.

He is also called the "Spirit of the Lord" some thirty times, and the "Spirit of Christ" on repeated occasions. The Holy Spirit is an integral part of the Triune Godhead, for He is as united with the Father as is Jesus Christ. He is presented in the Bible as the promise of the Father and the gift of Christ and, in a way that is easier stated than explained, God's Spirit establishes residence in the lives of individual believers, for Paul says, "Know ye not that ye are the temple of God, and that the Spirit of God dwelleth in you?" (1 Corinthians 3:16). It is this indwelling Spirit of God that becomes the channel for God's graces and self-revelation to come to be effectual in the lives of Christians, "... because the love of God is shed abroad in our hearts by the Holy Ghost which is given unto us" (Romans 5:5).

In the *International Standard Bible Encyclopedia* Phillip Wendell Crannel is quoted as saying, "Worship ... is the response of God's Spirit in us to that Spirit in Him, whereby we answer, 'Abba, Father,' deep calling unto deep" (page 3112). Worship of the Father, then, is not merely man's spirit on earth responding to God's Spirit in Heaven; rather it is God's Spirit in man responding to God's Spirit in God. It is the Holy Spirit worshipping through us, and how much more capable He is at this than we are.

True worship has always been both spiritual and in the Spirit, so when we worship God through Jesus Christ in the power of the Holy Spirit our worship will be both "in Spirit and in truth."

New Testament worship has two essentials in it that are lacking in the Old Testament. First, it is Christological in its orientation. Whereas the Old Testament worshipper approached God through the rituals and sacrifices of the temple, the New Testament worshipper stands in a personal relation of sonship to God on the basis of adoption in Christ Jesus. He is more than a suppliant; he is a son. He approaches God not through the services of an earthly mediator, but through the mediation of Christ Himself. Today's believer need not approach God through means of structure only, he has the resident Spirit of God to channel his worship directly into the Holy of Holies.

God, come in flesh to fulfill His work of grace in men, has given worship a depth and a content which was totally lacking in the Old Testament. Surely, then, our worship should not be less enthusiastic, joyful, or expressive than theirs, should it?

The second essential to be found in New Testament worship that was not obvious in the worship of the Old Testament saints is that the ministry of the Holy Spirit is now available to all believers, whereas it seemed to be restricted to selected leaders in the Old Testament. This is evidenced in the early work of the Spirit in an individual's life as the Spirit guides him into a conversion experience. Before conversion we were spiritually dead, and the Psalmist declares that, "The dead praise not the Lord" (Psalm 115:17). Prior to conversion we were "children of darkness," so terrified by the light of God's countenance that we dared not come into His presence. But since our conversion we are "light in the Lord." This converting work of the Spirit, whereby former children of the devil become children of God who are partakers of the divine nature, makes it easy for us to worship God in praise, song, prayer, and in ordinances.

A further work of the Holy Spirit that is available to the New Testament believer is the infilling of the Spirit, or, as some prefer to call it, the baptism of the Spirit. It is the experience that the disciples received on the day of Pentecost, and to which Paul alluded when he inquired of the saints in Ephesus, "Have ye received the Holy Ghost since ye believed" (Acts 19:2). When they replied that they had not so much as heard about the Holy Spirit, Paul laid his hands upon them, and ". . . the Holy Ghost came on them; and they spake with tongues, and prophesied" (Acts 19:6). Later when Paul wrote a letter to this church he admonished them, "And be not drunk with wine, wherein is excess; but be filled with the Spirit; speaking to yourselves in psalms and hymns and spiritual songs, singing and making melody in your heart to the Lord" (Ephesians 5:18,19), thereby linking this infilling of the Spirit to worshipping God.

But this indwelling Spirit of God not only gives us a melodious worship response to God, He also bears the *fruit* of the spirit within our lives. This effectively replaces much of our carnal nature with God's divine nature, for after listing the horrendous works of the flesh, Paul writes, "But the fruit of the Spirit is love, joy, peace, longsuffering, gentleness, goodness, faith, meekness, temperance ..." (Galatians 5:22, 23). As a corrective instruction Paul challenged the Christians in Galatia to "walk in the Spirit, and ye shall not fulfill the lust of the flesh" (Galatians 5:16). Since the greatest hindrances to worship are inherent in our natural lives, this work of the indwelling Spirit in freeing us from the works of the flesh breaks the bondages that prohibit, or greatly restrict, our worship by the very fruit of His presence, for our unloving nature is replaced with His fruit of love, and our inner turmoil is superseded by His peace, while His gentleness overrides our harshness. When we are able to worship God with the character of the Holy Spirit, our worship is accepted.

Furthermore, this indwelling Spirit helps the believer in his worship through the operation of the *gifts* of the Spirit, as we saw in Chapter 2.

These spiritual energies that enable us to know things about which we could have no knowledge apart from the Spirit's impartation make worship a knowing experience as well as an emotional experience. The word of wisdom, word of knowledge, and discerning of spirits, as they are listed in 1 Corinthians 12:8-10, is God sharing what He knows with His unknowing saints, and this knowing aids, abets, and accommodates our worship.

The three spiritual gifts that enable us to perform wonders in the spiritual, faith, gifts of healing, and the working of miracles (see 1 Corinthians 12:9, 10) bridge the gap between earth and heaven by demonstrating the availability of spiritual might and authority in our time. These are, of course, powerful evangelistic tools, but they also inspire worship in the lives of Christian believers as well.

Probably the most prevalent of these gifts during times of worship are the vocal gifts which Paul lists as "prophecy, divers kinds of tongues, and interpretation of tongues" (see 1 Corinthians 12:10). In the fourteenth chapter of 1 Corinthians, where Paul gives some instruction in the proper use of these giftings in the public assembly, he says that the tongues are a communication from man's spirit to God, and where this is interpreted we can all join the speaker in glorifying God, while the expression of prophecy is God's communication to man through man. All are concerned with spiritually enabling us to participate freely in the two-way communication that characterizes true worship. It is communication of our spirit that is aided by the Holy Spirit.

The use of the tongue in worship is explained by Paul when he says, "... he that speaketh in an unknown tongue speaketh not unto men, but unto God: for no man understandeth him; howbeit in the spirit he speaketh mysteries" (1 Corinthians 14:2). I would understand this to suggest that by using a language unknown to the speaker, the Holy Spirit is able to by-pass the censorship of the conscious mind and to worship God at a much higher level than would otherwise be possible, for all of our communication with God is regulated by our concepts of God plus our faith levels. This often limits our worship drastically, but when the Holy Spirit can worship through us according to His concepts, and at His faith level, our worship indeed "speaketh mysteries." When a believer submits to the work of the Spirit in sharing God's character through the *fruit*, and in sharing the charismata of God through the operation of the gifts of the Spirit, he is already a long way toward being a true worshipper.

But this is not the only way the New Testament believer has the advantage of the Holy Spirit to help in worshipping. All of the elements of worship that we discussed in Chapter 8 are greatly assisted by the Holy Spirit. For instance, prayer, so essential to worship, comes with the assistance of the Spirit. Paul, who was known for his prayer ministry, declared, "I will pray with my spirit by the Holy Spirit that is within me; but I will also pray intelligently—with my mind and understanding" (1 Corinthians 14:15, Amplified). Prayer without the help of the Spirit can be a laborious and unfruitful task.

Praise, which is often the vocal end of worship is, fundamentally, a rejoicing of the Spirit as Paul declared to the church in Philippi, "For we (Christians) are the true circumcision, who worship God in spirit and by the Spirit of God, and exult and glory and pride ourselves in Jesus Christ ..." (Philippians 3:3, Amplified).

Furthermore, the confession of sins and confession of faith is both a conviction of and a confession by the Holy Spirit, for Paul declared, "No one can (really) say Jesus is (my) Lord, except by and under the power and influence of the Holy Spirit" (1 Corinthians 12:3. TAB).

Even the reading of the Scripture as worship must be illuminated by the Spirit, and preaching, which God has chosen to be a part of worship, must be in the power and the demonstration of the Spirit; otherwise it is not part of, nor will it produce, worship.

Worship is not a performable act without the help of the Spirit, whether we choose to worship through means of the sacraments or a more free form of expression to God. We don't know how to worship, so we must be guided in each worship experience. The way we worshipped yesterday may not be the way the Spirit would lead to worship today, and the only way we will really know the route into God's presence for the present moment is to maintain a sweet communion with the Holy Spirit so that He can lead us into the Holy Place of communion with God.

When I was in South Africa I was given a copy of *New Vision*, a magazine which is published by Vision Publications as a part of the ministry of the Christian Interdenominational Fellowship of South Africa. In this Volume 3, #6 issue they had an interview with the Rev. Brian Bird of St. Nicholas, an Anglican Parish in Port Elizabeth. In answer to the question "You mentioned the Holy Spirit giving life to the Body?" the Rev. Bird answered: "Yes! The Holy Spirit prevents our worship from becoming stereotyped and dull. The glorious thing is that the Spirit blows where He wills and He is always fresh, never dull or routine. In a sense, we have to 'open the windows' at the beginning of a service and ask Him to blow upon us and lead us. It is obviously risky if we don't like drafts and sometimes we keep the windows tightly closed! If we fall into the trap of saying: 'This is how it worked last week, let's try and do the same thing today,' we will be 'making it work' and we will lose the freshness, the life of the Spirit. Therefore we use the elements of the liturgy without following it precisely if the Spirit leads us elsewhere. There is a responsibility to be open to the Spirit and aware of where He is taking us. The Holy Spirit wants to glorify Jesus and we most certainly do; so the result must be worship, and that worship will be different each time."

To become worshippers "in spirit and in truth" we must learn to follow the gentle nudgings of the Spirit; to move with the Spirit. He is a person, you know, and He has varying moods. Whatever mood He may indicate we would do well to stop everything else and follow it. If He is present in a rejoicing disposition, we should give ourselves to enthusiastic rejoicing.

If the Spirit seems to be in a giving mood, we would wisely give an offering to God. Whatever He is doing, we must do it with Him, for that will bring us into genuine worship.

Worship is always a *now* act. But doesn't this present problems when we are separated from the sacraments and the church structure? Where is the proper place of worship for the Spirit-inspired believer?

12

The Place of Worship

For the second time in ten years, and for a full eighteen months, the army of Nebuchadnezzar, King of Babylon, maintained a tight siege around the city of Jerusalem. Zedekiah, uncle to Nebuchadnezzar, had been appointed as a caretaker king after the first fall of Jerusalem. But he rebelled against the king of Babylon and now he found his kingdom under a second siege. With starvation taking its toll inside the city, Zedekiah tried to sneak away in the middle of the night but he was captured. Then he was forced to watch while his sons were slain, after which his captors put out his eyes, bound him with fetters of brass, and carried him to Babylon.

At the first capture of Jerusalem, the Babylonian army had stripped the house of the Lord of all its treasures. This time they completely destroyed both the temple and the city of Jerusalem, and marched the surviving residents to Babylon to become slaves, leaving only the poor of the land to "be vinedressers and husbandmen" (see 2 Kings 25).

The people who remained in the land of necessity intermarried with the populace in the surrounding areas and formed the group that was later identified as the Samaritans. Having neither city or temple, these Samaritans were forced to worship on the mountain, patterning their religion after the Jewish tradition but without the benefit of the Levitical priesthood. Because they did not suffer the rigors of the captivity and since they did not keep their Jewish lines pure, when the dispersed Jews returned to rebuild the city and temple under Ezra and Nehemiah, these Samaritans were despised by the repatriated Jews. They refused to have any dealings with them, thus forcing the Samaritans to continue in the form of religion they had developed during their caretaking years: their worshipping on the mountain.

This formed the basis of the argument of the woman at the well when Jesus spoke to her about worship. "Our fathers worshipped in this mountain; and ye say, that in Jerusalem is the place where men ought to worship," the woman told Jesus. "Jesus saith unto her, Woman, believe me, the hour cometh when ye shall neither in the mountain, nor yet at Jerusalem, worship the Father" (see John 4:20, 21).

To this woman the issue of worship was all tied up in your way or our way; your place or our place; your rituals or our rituals; your heritage or our heritage, on the mountain or in the city? She is not, however, to be condemned, for we have the same questions when the matter of worship is discussed, only we phrase them differently. We want to know whether worship is best performed with sacraments and ritual, or in a more free-form style. Some are convinced that we cannot worship in organized religion, using liturgical forms and practices, feeling that this is spiritual Babylon, so they associate exclusively with para-church groups.

Most Protestants are convinced that none can worship in a Catholic setting, while many Catholics have asked me if Protestants ever worship, for they have only seen them work at their religion. Still others get greatly disturbed over whether the worship is in the soul or spirit; the emotions or the will.

While there may be something to be said in each of these arguments, Jesus chose to bypass these fundamental hedges to worship and go to the real core of the issue. "But the hour cometh," He said, "and now is, when the true worshippers shall worship the Father in spirit and in truth" (John 4:23). Ignoring the mountain/city based argument, Jesus stated quite simply that true worship occurs in the spirit. The Greek word He used is *pneuma* which is translatable as "breath" or "spirit," and is used for God's Spirit, man's spirit, and demon spirits. Whether this refers to worship in the Holy Spirit, which would be theologically accurate, or to worship in the human spirit, which is equally correct, may depend upon our understanding of the context. In the King James Version the translators consistently use a capital "S" when they feel that the context indicates that it is the Holy Spirit, and here they have used the lower case. I checked over thirty other translations of the New Testament and found only two of them who disagreed with the King James, and these are not translations now in popular use. The context here would seem to indicate that Jesus is referring to the human spirit and simply saying that worship does not take place in shrines or cities, but in the spirit of the worshipper.

This in no way violates the teaching of Ephesians 2:18 which we have already discovered tells us that we worship by means of the Holy Spirit. The Spirit of God, is, indeed, the *means* of worship, but man's spirit is the *place* where worship occurs.

Man was created a tripartite being, for he was made in the image of the Triune God Who is Father, Son and Holy Spirit (see Genesis 1:26). In his tripartite being, man is spirit with an active will and an implanted God-consciousness; man is *soul* with an intellect and emotions; and man is *body* with its self-consciousness and world-consciousness. In God's specific creation man's spirit dominated and directed man, but sin inverted this creation, giving fundamental control of the life to man's body. It takes the regenerative work of Christ in God to restore man to God's original plan wherein he can be directed from his spirit. Diagrammed in pyramid format the contrast would appear as:

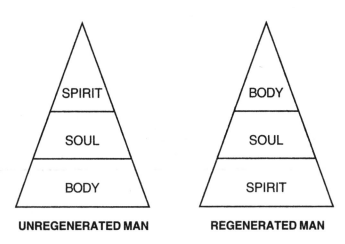

UNREGENERATED MAN   **REGENERATED MAN**

Because what is uppermost in a person's life controls the rest of his life it is obvious that the unregenerate must respond Godward ("worship") from their physical nature. It is interesting that most people who come to God for salvation come because of an extreme personal need in their physical life. As has been wisely stated, "Few persons come to God because they want Him; they come to Him because they need Him."

While the unconverted must respond Godward from their physical nature the Christian may do so, too, and far too many Christians attempt to worship in the physical area of their lives without ever learning how to worship God in their inner, eternal, spirit.

It should be obvious that religious ritual can be performed in any of the three areas of a person's life, for man ultimately responds Godward with all that he is: spirit, soul, and body.

Bodily reverence or respect toward God can be seen in lifting of the hands, standing, prostrating before the Lord, bowing, clapping the hands, waving the hands, kneeling, dancing, singing, and so forth. These may be done as an expression of worship in response to the direction of man's spirit or they may be done as a religious exercise that never gets close to true worship.

Furthermore, there are people who involve their bodies in masochistic actions as acts of worship by maiming the body, wounding themselves, by undue fastings, or denying their bodies needed sleep or proper recreation. They feel the more miserable their body feels and looks the greater the level of their worship. It is sad that they cannot realize that their actions are marring a creation that was made in the image of God.

Still others, whose approach to God is primarily physical, depend upon special robes, special make-up or religious jewelry (which I call holy hardware) and consider that the wearing of them constitutes worship.

But for every person who attempts to worship God through purely physical actions, there must be a thousand who reach after God in soul devotion, for singing, shouting, praising, weeping, and emotional expressions may be channels of worship in the spirit, or they may be done as a substitute for worship.

Soulish worship is *feeling* motivated and depends upon external impetus rather than divine anointing. It can so duplicate true spiritual "feelings" as to pass for true worship, since we are limited to one set of emotions which are played upon by both our soul and our spirit. If a "worship service" requires emotional stories and psychological impetus to stir it into being, it is very likely soulish worship. So much of America's "evangelistic services" and "gospel music" are soulish both in origin and in result. That men's emotions are deeply touched is undeniable, but unless their spirits contact God there will be neither conversion or worship, for both are an action of the

Spirit of God upon the spirit of man, and soul is not spirit any more than body is spirit.

While fully knowing that religious ritual, which men called worship, was being performed in the physical and soulish realms, Jesus told the woman at the well that "... true worshippers shall worship the Father in spirit ..." (John 4:23). In saying this Jesus not only disassociated worship from physical and soulish actions performed in a specific place, but He said that worship would occur in the spirit of the worshipper. Actions of the body and soul may form a prelude to worship, or may become expressions of the worship, but the true worship takes place when a person's spirit contacts God's Spirit.

Throughout the Old Testament this place of contact was often associated with a physical location. Jacob had his Bethel, Moses had his Sinai, and the children of Israel had their tabernacle. But in each of these the key was not the location or the methodology employed to express their worship. The characteristic factor of worship in each place was that these men met God. That is still the hub of all worship experiences, and to meet God, man must come to God.

Probably the greatest cause of failure in worship is our attempt to perform it before we arrive in God's presence. It was because Jacob met God at Bethel on at least two occasions that he could worship, and it was because every time Moses climbed to the top of Sinai he found the presence of God that he was able to worship. Later, it was when the High Priest entered the Holy of Holies and shared in the Skekinah of God that he could worship beyond the mere performance of ritualistic acts. And so it will be with us.

But where is God in the New Testament economy? We are taught that, "Whosoever shall confess that Jesus is the Son of God, God dwelleth in him, and he in God," and "Hereby know we that we dwell in him, and He in us because he hath given us of His Spirit" (1 John 4:15,13). God dwells in men. But where in men has God taken up residence? Paul declared that "The Spirit itself beareth witness with our spirit that we are the children of God" (Romans 8:16). God's Spirit resides in man's spirit, not in his body or soul, hence it is imperative that worship be performed in man's spirit, for that is his contact point with God's Spirit.

But this concept is not to negate the teaching of the entire Bible that "... God is in heaven, and thou upon earth ..." (Ecclesiastes 5:2), and, "... our God is in the heavens: he hath done whatsoever he hath pleased" (Psalm 115:3). Because Christians worship where God is, they must have access and rights to heaven, which answers to the Holy of Holies of the tabernacle and the temple. Since at the death of Jesus at Calvary the thick veil in Herod's temple was torn from the top to the bottom indicating that the perfect sacrifice of God's Son had met all of God's holy claims, therefore, access into His presence could be extended to all in whom His Spirit had taken residence.

The writer to the Hebrews expressed it this way: "Having therefore, brethren, boldness to enter into the holiest by the blood of Jesus, by a new and living way, which he has consecrated for us, through the veil, that is to say, his flesh; and having an high priest over the house of God; let us draw near with a true heart in full assurance of faith ..." (Hebrews 10:19-22). Access to God in His heaven has been assured both to the individual believer and to the collective body of believers that form the Church. The priesthood of all believers is consistently taught throughout the Bible, and when believer-priests meet together in the name of the Lord Jesus Christ they, as a company of priests, can lay hold, by faith, upon God's promised right of entrance, and they may enter the Holy Place to worship Almighty God in the beauty of holiness.

Hence heaven cannot be too far away, for a group of saints can step from the church pews into the divine presence in but a moment of time. It is not so much a matter of heaven coming down, as with Jacob, as it is the reality of the believer-priests going up into the spiritual heavens where their great High Priest awaits to assist them in their worship of God.

Worship, then, is far more than the awe that beautiful architecture can produce, or the reverence that vestments may incite, or the sense of sacredness the sacraments can bring, or even the stirred emotions that music often produces; worship is the interaction of man's spirit with God in a loving response. It begins in the spirit of man and, with the aid of the Spirit of God, ascends into the very presence of God Himself in the Heaven of heavens.

This is why the issue of *where* we should worship can never be germane. True worship is not dependent on buildings or any external stimuli, for God is worshipped in man's heart and in God's Heaven. This can occur when that person is in the world's most beautiful cathedral or when he is milking the cows in a barn. Worship can take place with the aid of beautiful music or when surrounded by the insistent noise of everyday commerce. It requires neither privacy nor the public performance of God's appointed leaders in the church. A thousand things may assist a believer in his worship of God, but fundamentally that worship is an inner reaching out and up to God, so where it takes place on the face of this earth is totally irrelevant, for it must reach God in Heaven before it can become a full worship experience anyway, and that is where true worshippers worship.

In saying that the true worshippers will worship in the spirit, was Jesus merely separating the true from the false worshippers, or did He have something further in mind? Could He also have been referring to the use of truth in worship instead of deceit?

13

The Truth in Worship

In stating to the woman at the well that "the true worshippers shall worship the Father in spirit and in truth" (John 4:23), Jesus established at least three premises: first, that there can be true worshippers; second, that there is such a thing as true worship; and third, that there must be truth in worship.

Throughout the book we have been looking at true worshippers. Among the factors that separate true from false worshippers is their relationship to God, their motivation for worship, and their expression of that worship. The Greek word that Jesus used for "worshippers" is *proskunetes* which is the noun form of the verb *proskenien* that is translated as "worship" throughout John 4. But the noun form appears only here in the Bible. It indicates that a true worshipper is one who has such a love relationship with God that he has become a lover; he can "kiss towards," which is what the verb form means.

True worship must flow from a genuine relationship with God. A good relationship with a church may produce a good worker, but only a warm relationship with God can produce a true worshipper. As someone has said, "Worship is the upspring of a heart that has known the Father as a Giver, the Son as Savior, and the Holy Spirit as the Indwelling Guest." To this I would add that this knowing must be experiential and current. Warm spirits produce worshipping hearts!

Not only must a true worshipper have a vital relationship with God, he must also have correct motivations in his worship. His goal must be to give unto the Lord rather than to get from Him. Worship which attempts to "soften up" God so as to induce Him to do for us is improperly motivated and cannot be called true worship. The purest motivation for worship is love that bubbles out of the spirit of man like a spring of living water.

Furthermore, true worshippers will manifest accurate expressions of their worshipful feelings. Their love will be poured out in an unrestrained manner when they are in the presence of Christ. They will not allow themselves to be limited by the traditions of men, or bound by the worship ritual of their religious heritage. Neither will they embrace extra-biblical expressions, for they will choose to be Bible-directed in all of their responses.

In speaking of true worship, Jesus may well have been referring to the tremendous contrast between worshipping the true and living God and worshipping idols. While few Americans bow before carved images to worship them as gods, we are a nation of idol worshippers as certainly as any heathen country. It's just that our idols are more sophisticated than carved logs or molten metal. Some of religion's most beautiful rituals fall short of true worship, for they are not offered unto God but unto man. Others who worship are deeply involved in self-worship, and self is a very subtle idol, for it possesses that ability to intrude itself into our holiest moments. Paul warned us that, "… in the last days perilous times shall come. For men shall be lovers of their own selves … lovers of pleasures more than lovers of God" (2 Timothy 3: 1, 2, 4).

Love of self and self-indulgence go hand in hand, and the worship of material possessions is almost an obsession with many, for Americans have had a longstanding love affair with *things*. Our culture teaches us to love things and to use people to get them, while God teaches us to love people and to use things to bless them. Too frequently, cars, homes, boats, guns, and wardrobes are cherished, treasured, and idolized with emotions that should be poured out in worshipping God. The Psalmist told us, "... if riches increase, set not your heart upon them" (Psalm 62:10). We dare not Christianize the American dream and teach prosperity as indication of God's approval of our lives, lest we find ourselves worshipping what the world has unsuccessfully worshipped for generations.

Nothing could take us farther from true worship than demon worship. Behind most idols is a demonic power that accepts all of the worship ascribed to idols, whether they are stone or the sophisticated varieties.

America's obsession with the occult is nothing more or less than demon worship; some people now openly worship Satan himself. Even in our Christian churches some persons place such an undue emphasis on our authority over demons that it borders on demon worship. Some Christians talk more with demons than with God, while others know more demon names than divine names. Some believers have read more books on demons than on God, while still other Christians live in terrorizing fear of demons; fear is to the demonic what faith is to the divine. When we are controlled by our fears we become worshippers of the demonic in the sense that we submit to their fear-inspired commands rather than to God's divinely inspired Word.

The list of things short of God that are worshipped by people today would be nearly endless. Some so worship money that they have become "i-dollar-ters" while others worship business, pleasure, power and family.

Whether our veneration is for science, angels, nature, or service it obviously is not true worship, for it does not have the true God as its object. All worship not directed to the true God is *ipso facto idolatry.*

Besides all of this, Jesus said that a true worshipper would worship "in spirit and in *truth*"(John 4:23, italics added). Communion with God must be on His level. Since He is truth by nature, the one prerequisite for entry into God's realized presence is a true heart. "Let us all come forward and draw near with true (honest and sincere) hearts in unqualified assurance and absolute conviction engendered by faith" (Hebrews 10:22, TAB).

Not only must a worshipper be truthful in his approach and communion with God, but worshipping will reveal the truth to the worshipper. It will unfold to us truth about God, because we learn more about a person by being with Him for one day than by reading about Him for several months. Then we will learn the truth about ourselves as we see ourselves as God sees us.

In Matthew 15:21-28 we are told about a resident of Canaan, whom Mark calls a Syrophoenician, who seems to have heard that Jesus was going to visit the area of Tyre and Sidon. She practically met the boat at the shore, and the moment she saw Jesus she cried, "Have mercy on me, O Lord, thou son of David; my daughter is grievously vexed with a devil" (Matthew 15:22). She may have heard that blind Bartemeus was healed by yelling a similar cry or that two pairs of blind men, on widely separate occasions, had been restored to sight by crying this plea, for somehow this formula seemed to crop up repeatedly in the stories that had come out of Jerusalem. It had always seemed to work. Until now, that is. For no matter how earnestly, loudly, or passionately she cried this formula, Jesus "answered her not a word" (Matthew 15:23).

The actions of the disciples proved that she had been heard, for they pled with Jesus to send her away to get rid of the disturbance. But instead of complying with their request, Jesus replied: "I am not sent but unto the lost sheep of the house of Israel" (Matthew 15:24). In this one stage whisper, spoken loudly enough for the woman to plainly hear, Jesus unmasked the deceit and hypocrisy of her petitioning. She had been claiming a non existent relationship with Christ, for in imploring Him as the "Son of David" she was apparently claiming to be an Israelite, a daughter of David. This was untrue, since the Gospel writers clearly identify her as a Gentile. But because she did not feel that Gentiles had any claim upon Christ, she masqueraded as a daughter of Israel who had covenant claims on the "Son of David." All this pretense got for her was total silence.

When God gives us the silent treatment, it is usually because we, too, are claiming a nonexistent relationship. We, like her, pick up formulae that have worked beautifully for others and cry them religiously, whether they work or not. But unless we have the relationship that goes with the formula it will not work.

How many who have never been born again pray, "Our Father which art in Heaven?" Carnal Christians use the prayer language of the true bride, while the rebellious plead with God in their hour of trouble with the same expressions as the submitted saints. This will always be met by divine silence. God does not respond to hypocrisy, since He is truth by nature, hence we are instructed to "... draw near with a *true* heart ..." (Hebrews 10:22, italics added). Any form of deceit will deny us an audience with God. Someone has said, "Either live it or don't lip it."

Nevertheless, we go on giving lip service to the words that meant life to our fathers and to the founders of our denominations, often unaware that we have only the liturgy, not the life, of these men. We have expressed the words as fact for so long that we are unaware that they have become a fable, or we have claimed a nonexistent faith for so long that we cannot recognize our fraud. What can bring us out of our guile back into His grace? Worship in spirit and in truth!

Immediately after Jesus unmasked this imposter, she came "and worshipped him, saying, Lord, help me" (Matthew 15:25). Very likely, she prostrated herself before Him, perhaps even grabbing Him by the ankles and kissing His feet. She completely submitted herself to Him and poured out both her worship and her plea for help. And it worked. It always works! Worship is a door opener that gives the supplicant access to God. If we can claim no covenant that will afford us entrance to Christ, we can open the door to His presence with worship. When our faith has failed and we falter in our approach to God, we can always fall back on worship, for worship is a consistent door opener, to both the converted and unconverted alike, for all men have been invited to worship God. God declares, "shall all flesh come to worship before me, saith the Lord" (Isaiah 66:23). John saw a great company in Heaven singing the song of Moses and the song of the Lamb, ending it with these words: "... all nations shall come and worship before Thee" (Revelation 15:4). Worship will open the door to God for anyone.

It is only fair to point out, however, that this door opener to Christ automatically becomes an open door, allowing Him to get to us. Immediately after this daughter of Canaan began to worship Jesus, He began to probe into the depths of her heart. "It is not meet to take the children's bread," He said, "and to cast it to dogs" (Matthew 15:26). "You've claimed to be a daughter of Abraham, but in the eyes of Abraham's children you're nothing but a dog." These have always seemed like harsh words, but they were spoken by the world's most perfect gentleman. Christ was not condemning her, He was merely unveiling her to herself. He was causing her to not think more highly of herself than she ought to think (see Romans 12:3). J. B. Phillips translates this verse:

"Don't cherish exaggerated ideas of yourself or your importance, but try to have a sane estimate of your capabilities by the light of the faith that God has given to you all."

Our Lord was merely helping to adjust this woman's self-concept, and He did it while she was worshipping. As she was exalting Him in worship, He was exposing her worthlessness. While she spoke of His Majesty ("Lord"), He spoke of her hypocrisy. His goal was not to depreciate her, but to help her appreciate her true relationship to Himself, until she did, He could not respond to her without condoning her falsehood. But if she would accept His appraisal and respond accordingly, He could and would minister to her need. Truth can relate to truth.

Isn't it when we are worshipping that God reveals us to ourselves? It was so with Isaiah, for he, who was likely the most godly man of his generation, when caught up into God's presence cried out:

"Woe is me! for I am undone; because I am a man of unclean lips, and I dwell in the midst of a people of unclean lips: for mine eyes have seen the King, the Lord of hosts" (Isaiah 6:5).

Isaiah did not have this awareness when in the courts of earthly kings to whom he is reputed to have been a tutor, but when worship brought him into the presence of the heavenly King, he not only saw the Lord sitting upon a throne, "high and lifted up" (Isaiah 6:1), but he saw himself defiled and dirty. It is only when we are in the presence of heaven's Majestic King that we gain a true picture of ourselves. Compared with another, we may look great, but contrasted to Him, our artificial glory is revealed for what it really is.

So the Lord's response to the woman's worship was to call her a dog. How did she handle that? She said: "Truth, Lord" (Matthew 15:27). For until we acquiesce to His appraisal, communication with Him is ended. He has revealed our position and our condition; the next move is ours.

Admitting the truth that she was as separated from a covenant relationship with Christ as a dog is beneath his owner did not devastate this woman. She wisely changed her style of approach to match His estimate of her and gained everything she desired. She merely said, "yet the dogs eat of the crumbs which fall from their master's table" (Matthew 15:27). "If I am a dog, don't deny me a dog's privileges!" No greater principle can be learned than to approach Christ consistent with our true natures. If we're "a dog" and our natures have not been changed by a divine transformation, we can sit up, wag our tail, and lick the hand of the Master. If we're an infant in Christ, we can make pleasant "gooing" sounds and smile a lot. If we're a toddler, we can crawl to Him, pat Him, and say "da-da." But for a mature saint to do this would be ridiculous. Mature saints should approach Christ as a Christian adult.

We need not await a voice from heaven saying, "This is my beloved Son, in whom I am well pleased ..." (Matthew 17:5) before coming to God. We can come just as we are. He can cleanse us as surely as He cleansed Isaiah, and change us as completely as He changed Nebuchadnezzar or Saul of Tarsus. We merely need to respond to Him as we are and from where we are, and it is worship that opens the door for this revelation to come to us.

It is, indeed, worship that brings us into a right relationship with God and with ourselves, and this revealed truth about ourselves can help us to stop staring at what we were and to start seeing what we are becoming in Christ Jesus. This will enable us to trade condemnation for cleansing and introspection for acceptance. We can see ourselves as Sons of God, heirs of God, and joint heirs with Christ Jesus.

Truth is costly. "Buy the truth, and sell it not" (Proverbs 23:23) is wise admonition. The truth about ourselves can be especially costly, but worship that costs us nothing obviously has little or no value to us. What is a proper price tag to be put on worship?

14

The Price of Worship

In the Tabernacle in the wilderness, which is a pattern of things in heaven, worship was demonstrated in type at the Golden Altar of incense which was positioned in front of the veil that separated the Holy of Holies from the Holy Place, and midway between the Golden Candlestick and the Table of Shewbread. God had commanded that every time a priest came into the Holy Place he was to take a handful of the specially compounded incense and sprinkle it upon the living coals that perpetually glowed upon this altar. The resulting cloud of perfumed smoke filtered through the thin linen veil that separated God from the priests. It filled the priestly compartment with its fragrance and saturated the clothing, hair, and skin of the priest, himself thereby making the fragrance of God's presence available to the common man in the outer court.

This was a visual demonstration of worship that teaches the New Testament believer-priest to offer the worship of prayer, thanksgiving, worship, and adoration when he comes into the presence of the Lord so that the worshipper's spirit, soul, and body will be permeated with the fragrance of God. It only takes a handful of worship incense to create a cloud of

God's presence. But God wants that handful to be offered every time we go into the soul-spirit compartment of our lives.

For the priest to burn incense every time he went into the Holy Place, whether he entered to replace oil in the lamps, to trim the wicks of those lamps, to set the table of shewbread, or for whatever reason, was obviously a costly procedure, since we would suppose that there were many daily trips into this priestly compartment.

Furthermore, the incense itself was costly. It was composed of four ingredients that were blended in equal proportions, and none of these were commonly available to the Israelites. Stacte, onycha, galbanum, and frankincense had to be gathered from their respective sources and brought to the priests who then broke it into small pieces, beat it into powder, and blended it evenly so that it could be burned before the Lord. Whatever application one might choose to make of these four principal ingredients we must admit that our worship must come to a central place, be broken, beaten (contrited), and blended in order to be available for burning. This is costly in time, effort, emotion, and devotion, but worship always carries a price tag.

A further price that was attached to this incense was that it could be used for no other purpose than the worship of God. Any person caught using this same fragrance was to be stoned to death by the priests. There could be no "mass production" to bring the price down. God is very jealous of our worship and declares, ". . . Thou shalt worship the Lord thy God, and Him only shalt thou serve" (Matthew 4:10). Emotional enthusiasm, although easier to generate, cannot substitute for worship, nor can worship be used for anything or anyone but God. It is our "tree in the garden," the fruit of which belongs exclusively to God. We, like Adam, may not eat the fruit of it.

While I was writing this chapter I was the guest speaker at a breakfast gathering of Christians. The worship leader started by singing a chorus about the devil and, of course, our authority over him. The second chorus was directed to the devil himself, and the third chorus projected that we were an army that had the devil on the run. Only after that were we directed to sing about Jesus. The worship time was wasted and fell completely flat, for not only had we given Satan top billing by calling attention to him first, but we had mixed our worship in offering some to the demonic (for all public attention given to them is accepted by them as worship) and some to Jesus. It was not surprising, then, that one of the saints gave a pointed prophetic utterance saying that God didn't like sharing worship with anyone or anything else, and that we were to express our worship exclusively to God. The honor of worship belongs to God alone, and He will share this honor with none!

A handful of incense upon the coals every time the priest entered was God's minimum, for God's instruction to Moses was, "a perpetual incense before the Lord throughout your generations" (Exodus 30:8). God has chosen that there never be a time when worship is not being offered up before Him.

Where did these coals come from? Since God had kindled the original fire upon the Brazen Altar in the outer court He insisted that all fire used in the ceremonies of the tabernacle come from the Brazen Altar. God has specified, "And he shall take a censer full of burning coals of fire from off the altar before the Lord, and his hands full of sweet incense beaten small, and bring it within the veil: and he shall put the incense upon the fire before the Lord, that the cloud of the incense may cover the mercy seat that is upon the testimony, that he die not" (Leviticus 16:12, 13). The coals came from the altar of sacrifice indicating that the sweet spices had to be combined with the costly sacrifice before they became a cloud of incense. Has anyone yet calculated the price God paid at Calvary, our Brazen Altar in the New Testament?

Worship does, indeed, have a price tag on it. It requires fresh coals that must be produced in the fire that burns on the altar of sacrifice. In order to keep the coals hot enough to ignite the blended spices that comprise our worship incense, we must continue to offer unto God the sacrifices of praise, Bible study, meditation on the things of God, obedience to the will and Word of God, and faithfulness in Christian service. When a Christian's ardor grows cold no amount of spices will produce the incense of worship. We are challenged, "seeing ye have purified your souls in obeying the truth through the Spirit unto unfeigned love of the brethren, see that ye love one another with a pure heart fervently" (1 Peter 1:22), and the Greek word for "fervently" means red-hot. So unsavory is a lukewarm condition that God told the church at Laodicea, "So then because thou art lukewarm, and neither cold nor hot, I will spue thee out of My mouth" (Revelation 3:16). Worship will extract the price of maintaining a fire on the altar of sacrifice and a willingness to bring coals from that fire to the Golden Altar in our soul.

Has worship always had a price attached to it? The very first time that the word *worship* occurs in our Bible it has a very high price tag attached to it, for it is the occasion when God asked Abraham to offer his son, Isaac, as a burnt sacrifice. Abraham told his servants to await him while, "I and the lad will go yonder and worship" (Genesis 22:5). Abraham was prepared to pay the price of losing the son for whom he had waited many years, and for whom there could be no hope of replacement. That God provided a substitute at the very last possible moment does not detract from the fact that in Abraham's soul-spirit he had already paid the price demanded to worship the Lord his God.

Is Abraham the last saint who has been asked to lay his all on the altar in order to worship? Ask the missionaries who serve around the world. Ask the Christian businessmen who plow their profits into gospel ministry, and check with the prayer warriors who give up their recreation hours to bow before the Lord in humble prayer. Fundamentally, it is impossible to worship without paying a price. David knew this implicitly.

So serious was the crisis in David's life and administration that the Bible gives us a full account of this season in his life both in 2 Samuel 24 and 1 Chronicles 21.

In spite of God's prohibition, David had grievously sinned in numbering the people; so God had withdrawn His blessing and had replaced it with severe chastisement that was destroying people throughout the land. When God responded to David's repentance David was commanded to offer sacrifices in a specific manner in a specified place. However, the place God had chosen for this worship was already in use by its owner, Ornan, who was threshing wheat. David could not build an altar in the midst of the threshing operation; one or the other had to cease.

While this was being discussed, God allowed Ornan to see the destroying angel of the Lord standing with his drawn sword, and Ornan immediately offered to give the threshing floor to David for whatever atoning sacrifices could be offered. As a matter of fact, he also offered his oxen for the sacrifice and his threshing implements for the wood. Perhaps nothing inspires devotion more rapidly than the prospect of divine destruction.

At this point, David had to come to grips with whether God wanted *him*, the one who had sinned, to offer sacrifices, or whether it would be sufficient merely to have the sacrifices offered. Was it the sacrifice or the sacrificer that God was interested in? Ornan's offer gave David an excellent opportunity to reconcile self-interest with godliness, prudence with principle; of doing a good thing for nothing, for had David accepted the offer the offering would have lacked nothing that God had required as to place, manner, or sacrifice. The command would have been satisfied, and Ornan's offer was both expedient and inexpensive!

But worship must proceed out of the lives of the worshippers. These lives are already occupied with busy schedules that keep our minds and spirits threshing constantly. How tempting it is to let the pastor and church staff do the worshipping for us.

David resisted the temptation of doing a thing the least expensive way and insisted on purchasing both the floor and all the field around it. David felt that it was unworthy of his position and ability as king to freeload in worshipping God. He sensed that it would demean the greatness of God and his own relation and obligation to Him to offer God sacrifices that had cost David nothing. It was a costly transaction, but David valued his religion more than his wealth, so he paid full price for the place. He knew that if he accepted Ornan's offer it would have been Ornan's sacrifice, and that this would not have been an expression of David's spirit, for David was a giver and a true worshipper of God.

How easy it is to fall into the temptation of merely attending a worship service rather than paying the price to be a worshipper. To listen to the musicians play worshipfully is so much easier than to keep in practice on our own instrument so that we can participate. It is less costly to say the "amen" to a prayer than to actually be prayed-up before a service begins, just as it is easier to listen to a choir than to invest the hours necessary to be a participant with a praising choir. Ornan's offer is very pleasing to our flesh.

Real worship begins and is maintained at the cost of much thought, feeling, involvement, and prayer. If a person's prime feeling is of himself, he will take the easiest and most economical way to worship. But if a man's prime feeling is of God, he will pay whatever price is necessary to worship Him fully. In the first case, the person will seek the largest possible results from the least possible expenditure, while in the second case the expenditure will itself be an act of worship. Perhaps in worship there are two fundamental questions: How little may we do and how much can we do?

David paid the price to worship and offered sacrifices unto God, both burnt offerings, which were typical of the consecration of the worshipper's body, soul and spirit, and peace offerings, which were expressive of reconciliation and fellowship with God. We are told that divine fire came down upon the sacrifices and the judgment of God was stayed. So sacred was this acceptance of his worship that David designated this as the site for the future temple.

David summarized the whole of his attitude towards worshipping God when he responded to Ornan's offer of the free use of the threshing floor for the sacrifice with, "Nay; but I will surely buy it of thee at a price: neither will I offer burnt offerings unto the Lord my God of that which doth cost me nothing" (2 Samuel 24:24). Do we dare offer as worship that in which we have no investment?

Empty hearts, prayerless spirits, tired bodies, undisciplined minds, unopened Bibles, and careless attitudes have ruined far more worship services than all the demonic activity of hell. Satan is not our greatest hindrance to a true and full worship experience; we are our own greatest enemy when we seek to worship without having to pay a price. Still, even persons who would never consider attending a wedding shower or reception without a costly gift will consistently attend a worship service empty-handed. They have not come to give; they have come to receive, but worship is a two-way communication.

If the price of the performance of worship seems unduly high, just wait until we come into the realized presence of a Holy God in our worship experience. We will discover that holiness is not only the characteristic aspect of God's nature, but it is demanded of all who approach their Holy God. Worship and holiness are so closely interconnected that it is impossible to separate them.

15

Holiness and Worship

B etween God's promise to a shepherd lad and David's actual accession to the throne were years of struggle. Even after he was crowned king there were many enemy armies that had to be subdued before his kingdom was secure. Once this was behind him, David turned his attention to bringing the Ark, the symbol of God's presence, back to Jerusalem. When the Ark of the Covenant was finally resting in the tent that David had pitched for it, David handed Asaph, the chief musician, a psalm that had been written especially for this occasion. In the heart of this song David has scored, "Give unto the Lord the glory due unto His name ... *worship the Lord in the beauty of holiness* " (1 Chronicles 16:29, italics added). This plea is repeated at least twice in the Psalms (29:2, 96:9) as the writers realized that a holy God must be worshipped in holiness and that this holiness, far from being fearsome and dreadful, was beautiful, glorious, excellent, and honorable, as the Hebrew word for "beauty" (*hadarah*) would suggest.

There are at least three aspects of this imperative that the Spirit expressed through David and others. First, the One who is worshipped is holy. Second, the channel through which we worship is holy. Third, the worshipper must become holy in order to be involved in true worship.

That we have been called to worship a holy God is self-evident. Not only is God holy, but only God is absolutely holy; all other holiness is derivative. Some theologians define holiness as the pervading moral attribute of God's nature. Others insist that it is not one attribute among the other attributes, but that it is the innermost reality to which all other attributes are related. God is more holy than He is anything else. Whenever we get a glimpse into heaven and hear the mighty angelic beings praising God it is always "holy, holy, holy" that they chant, not "omnipotent" or "omniscient." The holiness of God is the consummate perfection, purity, and absolute sanctity of His nature. Hence we recognize that God is entirely separate from all that is evil and all that defiles, both in Himself and in relation to all His creatures. There is absolutely nothing unholy in Him at all; consequently there is nothing within Him that can be sympathetic with defilement and sin.

Others have defined holiness as "otherwiseness," that is, holiness is what we are not. It is the nature that God breathed into Adam that made him so completely different or "otherwise" from the rest of God's creation. God is so distinctly "otherwise" that we are hard-pressed to even find similes in life to help us describe Him. After the miraculous deliverance at the Red Sea Moses sang, "Who is like unto thee O Lord, among the gods? Who is like thee, glorious in holiness, fearful in praises, doing wonders?" (Exodus 15:11), and Hannah prayed, "There is none holy as the Lord: for there is none beside thee: neither is there any rock like our God" (1 Samuel 2:2).

Not only is God holy, the channel that enables us to worship God is called the Holy Spirit. In writing to the young church in Thessalonica Paul said, "For this is the will of God, even your sanctification ... For God hath not called us unto uncleanness, but unto holiness. He therefore that despiseth, despiseth not man, but God, who hath also given unto us His Holy Spirit" (1 Thessalonians 4:3, 7, 8). Paul clearly coupled God's call to holiness with the gift of the Holy Spirit, for while God has imputed His righteousness to the obedient ones and Jesus has conferred His justification upon the repentant ones, it is the Holy Spirit who has implanted His holiness in the consecrated ones by making His personal abode in their spirits. The Holy Spirit is the channel whereby God's holiness can be made available to us, and He is also the channel whereby we may worship a Holy God, as we have already seen in a preceding chapter.

It is the third aspect of the challenge to "worship the Lord in the beauty of holiness" that often raises barriers to our worship. A worshipper must become holy to continue worshipping a holy God, for holiness and unholiness cannot fellowship together, since one of the prime manifestations of holiness is a hatred of sin. When we approach worship, then, we have a holy God on one extreme and unholy men on the other. Unless God's Son had purchased holiness for men at Calvary and God's Spirit was effecting that holiness day by day in their lives, none of us could worship God.

As I wrote in my book, *Let Us Be Holy*:

"This matter of being holy, then, is far more than a deep religious feeling. It radically affects our life style. It is concerned with our attitudes, actions, associations, adorations, thoughts, love, and obedience level. Holiness is a governing principle of life to be manifested in every area of life as displayed inwardly and outwardly towards God, ourself, or others."

True worship is tremendously demanding upon holiness! The nominal Christian seems almost to get by merely adding God to his former way of life; but the Spirit-filled Christian finds that many of the old actions and attitudes have to be released in order to walk in the Spirit. Beyond this, the praising saint experiences inner workings of the Spirit that cleanse and change motives as well as manifestations. But the worshipping saint never comes to the end of these dealings of the Holy Spirit that change the person from a self-centeredness to a God-centeredness, for Christ did not come to repair, but to replace. He came to trade His life for ours; to bring our lives to the cross so that He can share His life from the resurrection side of the tomb.

The closer one gets to God the greater are the demands for godliness in the individual's life, for God is a holy God who cannot fellowship with or accept the unholy. He can and will share His holiness with anyone who strongly desires fellowship with Him, since God passionately yearns to have this kind of communion with man. He had it with Adam until sin separated the two of them, and He had it with Christ Jesus during the days He was here on the earth. Now, God desires to have it with the Christians of this twentieth century.

In a very real way, holiness is a divine energy that is completely destructive to all that is unholy. It is similar to light (another descriptive aspect of God's essential nature) which, whenever the two meet, cannot help but destroy darkness. Light can join light and actually intensify the measure of light, but light cannot join darkness. Just so, the holiness of God automatically destroys its opposite. The cry, "holiness, without which no man shall see the Lord" (Hebrews 12:14) is less a command and more a declaration of cause and effect.

When one attempts to approach God without holiness He mercifully hides Himself from the seeker, lest if the seeker should come into the divine presence, the holiness of God's inherent nature becomes a destructive laser beam to that worshipper.

Inasmuch as the ultimate level of worship is intimate fellowship with God, it is expected that we must rise to the nature of God before He and we can enjoy such a relationship.

While God condescends in grace to redeem us, He expects us to ascend in holiness to worship Him.

I do not mean to imply that one must become absolutely holy in order to have a worship experience with God, for the Bible abounds with illustrations of unholy men worshipping a holy God when His presence was made manifest. Balaam is a classic example of this. But I am saying that holiness is an absolute prerequisite in order to become a consistent worshipper. God invokes worship in the unholy in order to expose them to divine holiness, for until we have seen something of God's holiness we don't even know what true holiness is, nor are we motivated to pay the price necessary to have that holiness effected within us. Since God alone is the source of holiness, and only His Spirit can produce it in the life of a believer, there must be that initial confrontation with God to get the process started.

Holiness, however, is not intended to make life uncomfortable and unnatural. Actually, the opposite is true. Holy living involves life at its fullest, for true holiness brings us into a love, joy, and peace such as this world cannot know aside from Christ Jesus. This impartation makes worship possible at higher and higher levels, for it is a sharing of the very divine nature of God Himself.

The level to which our worship can rise is dependent upon at least two fundamental principles. The first is our concepts of God, which we have already examined earlier in the book, and the second is the level of holiness to which we have attained. We must know Him as He has revealed Himself in the Word, and we must become similar to that revelation.

In my book, *Let Us Get Together*, I remind us that:

"... life can only truly fellowship life of the same kind. A dog fellowships a dog, and a frog fellowships a frog, but it would be a stretch of the metaphor to suggest that a dog could fellowship a frog."

Along this pattern, God can only truly fellowship that which has His nature and His likeness; that's why He created man in His own image and likeness. That sin has marred man's similarity to God is well demonstrated, but the cross of Jesus Christ has provided restoration of man to the spiritual nature of God, thereby enabling men and women to rise to higher levels of association and companionship with Almighty God. Worship is the outpouring of a soul at rest in the presence of God, and this requires being a partaker of the divine nature.

When Isaiah was caught into the heavens and saw God sitting upon a throne high and lifted up and heard the seraphim chanting the holiness of God, he became totally involved with himself, crying out, "Woe is me! for I am undone; because I am a man of unclean lips, and I dwell in the midst of a people of unclean lips: for mine eyes have seen the King, the Lord of hosts" (Isaiah 6:5). It was not until after one of the seraphim purged his sin with a coal from off the altar that Isaiah could get involved with God. Isaiah's unholiness had to be replaced with God's holiness before he could worship God in any meaningful measure at all, and so must ours.

Since worship is the occupation of the heart, not with its needs or even its blessings, but with God Himself, the heart must be fixed fearlessly upon God and not be torn between introspection and devotion. All concept of self must be abandoned whether it be of self-negation or self-needs, so that the whole of our being can flow out to God in adoration, consecration, and affection. A.P. Gibbs, in his book, *Worship*, says, "Worship is the overflow of a grateful heart, under a sense of Divine favor." This requires such a measure of God's holy nature as to enable us to be relaxed in the presence of God, otherwise we will be so occupied with our unholiness that we cannot respond lovingly to His holiness. It is, obviously, impossible to be self-centered and to worship God. We must be God-conscious, not self-conscious, to be a true worshipper. Therefore the more God's nature is coursing through us, the greater our awareness of God will be and the less time we will spend involved with ourselves when we approach the throne of God.

In speaking of the Greek word that the New Testament writers used for "holiness," Dr. James Hastings, a scholar of the past century, wrote in *A Dictionary of the Bible*:

"*Hagios* is, above all things, a qualitative and ethical term. It refers chiefly to character, and lays emphasis upon the demands that that which is sacred in the highest sense makes upon conduct ... *Hagios* expresses something higher than sacred; higher than outwardly associated with God; higher than reverent, pious, worthy, honourable, pure, or even free from defilement. *Hagios* is more positive, more comprehensive, more elevated, more purely ethical and spiritual. It is characteristically Godlikeness, and in the Christian system Godlikeness signifies completeness of life. (v. 2, p. 399)"

Godlikeness, then, is a prerequisite to worship, but how much like God must we become before we can be worshippers? Perhaps a clue to this can be found in Zechariah's strange vision where the prophet saw "... Joshua the high priest standing before the angel of the Lord ..." (Zechariah 3:1). The amazing part of the vision is the fact that "... Joshua was clothed with filthy garments, and stood before the angel" (Zechariah 3:3). No high priest would knowingly come into the Holy of Holies defiled. Before entering he bathed, put on special garments, washed his hands, face, and feet at the laver and came in carrying a basin of blood from the brazen altar and a censer of incense from the golden altar. But, like Joshua in the vision, even after we believer-priests have done everything that the Word requires to be cleansed, when we stand before the ineffable presence of our holy God we realize that compared to Him we are still defiled and polluted.

It is noteworthy, though, that this high priest was not condemned for wearing defiled garments, the angel of the Lord, an Old Testament manifestation of Jesus, said:

Take away the filthy garments from him. And unto him he said, Behold, I have caused thine iniquity to pass from thee, and I will clothe thee with change of raiment (Zechariah 3:4).

This priest was not condemned; he was changed! That which was unholy was removed and replaced with one of Christ's garments of righteousness. Then the Lord said, "Let them set a fair mitre upon his head" (Zechariah 3:5). The mitre, a ceremonial hat that the high priest wore in the holy place, had an inscription on it that read, HOLINESS UNTO THE LORD. Although the priest had done everything he could do ceremonially to be holy, it did not measure up to the holiness of God, so God merely shared His holiness with the priest. So He does with believer-priests today. It is His pleasure to share His nature with those who will come into His presence with as much purity as their faith can appropriate.

God has always been and will always be incomparable in His holiness. His holiness cannot be fashioned in anything that man can see, but whenever God's holiness is made available to man, whether in ritual or reality, cleanness is an integral part, for the removal of unholiness is a prerequisite to the reception of His holiness.

Inasmuch as holiness brings us back into a right relationship with God, it also brings us back into a joyful relationship with life which is the fountainhead of praise and worship, but while both have their source in holiness, each flows in a different stream down the mountain.

16

Praise and Worship

Some ten years ago, when I wrote the book, *Let Us Praise*, I consistently interchanged the words "praise" and "worship" for, at that level of my walk with God, I accepted them as synonymous terms. During the intervening years I have observed that the Scriptures do not interchange these words, but rather teach that praise prepares us for worship, or that praise is a prelude to worship. Psalm 95 is a good example of this principle. It begins:

O come, let us sing unto the Lord: let us make a joyful noise to the rock of our salvation. Let us come before His presence with thanksgiving, and make a joyful noise unto Him with psalms. (verses 1, 2)

That this is praise none would dispute. It is joyful, melodious, demonstrated, and declared praise directed to God. But it is only *after* this praise has been fully expressed unto God that the Psalmist invites us:

O come, let us worship and bow down: let us kneel before the Lord our maker (verse 6).

The order is praise first, worship second. The same pattern is found in Psalm 96 where we are reminded:

For the Lord is great, and greatly to be praised: He is to be feared above all gods. Give unto the Lord, O ye kindreds of the people, give unto the Lord ... the glory due unto His name: bring an offering, and come into His courts (verses 4, 7, 8).

It is only after clearly orchestrating the form of praise that was to be offered unto God that the inspired writer added: "O worship the Lord in the beauty of holiness: fear before Him, all the earth" (verse 9). So while worship may be dependent upon praise, praise is not a substitute for worship; it is, however, a blessed supplement to it.

We Christians use a triunity of terms to describe our responses to God: prayer, praise, and worship, and we often place one word for the other as though they were merely different expressions for the same action. Prayer is usually understood as being concerned with our *needs*, praise is concerned with our blessings, while worship is concerned with *God Himself*. This is not to say that prayer cannot be an avenue of expressing worship or that praise will not be concerned with God, but, generally speaking, this is the pattern that they take.

While I am aware that there are at least eight forms or levels of prayer, the most common prayer Christians of this generation pray is the prayer of petition. This is both scriptural and practical, but petition is not worship. Some persons who think that they are worshipping have merely joined the worshippers as petitioners.

In seeking to differentiate between praise and worship, I see at least six areas of contrast that extend from the stimulus behind them to the mode of their utterance. Praise and worship will differ somewhat in their motivation, in their thrust, in their source of inspiration, in their depth of dedication, in their proximity to God, and even in their method of expression.

Since God is more interested in *why* we do than in *what* we do, our motivations are vital. Generally we praise out of a motivation to be blessed of God. We come, not as a petitioner with a need, but as a praiser with a desire for an emotional lift. In praying prayers of entreaty, we request something from God in acknowledgment of our deep need and utter dependence upon Him; in praise we approach God joyfully and enthusiastically to savour to the fullest the pleasure of His presence; but in worship we present something *to* God as a loving recognition and expression of our deep appreciation of what God is and for all that He has done.

Far too frequently what seems to start out as a motivation to worship God quickly degenerates into a lusting to receive something from Him. But the key to worship is to give, not to get. True worship gives glory to the Lord, it does not seek to get glory from the Lord. A worshipper comes to God not to be blessed but to bless; not to enter God's presence as an asker but as an admirer. Praisers who aspire to be worshippers need to ask themselves if they are praising to give unto God or to get from God. In praising are we ministering unto God or seeking ministry from God?

Beyond this contrast in motivation between praise and worship is the diversity in the thrust of praise and worship. The frontal attack of praise is a positive response Godward, based far more upon His deeds than on His person. Repeatedly the Psalmists urge us to praise the Lord for the *things* He *has done*. Moses wrote the song of praise extolling God's dramatic rescue of Israel through the Red Sea; Hannah sang praises to God for giving Samuel to her after a long period of childlessness; and Psalm 107 three times exhorts us, "Oh that men would praise the Lord for His goodness, and for His wonderful works to the children of men!" (verses 8, 21, 31).

This thrust of praise is prescribed, proper, and very profitable, and it is certainly a step beyond thanksgiving; but it is, admittedly concerned far more with what God has done for us than with who God actually is. Praise tends to be more concerned with God's *presents* than with God's *presence*.

Because praise is act-centered, it often becomes petition in a positive form, or is an attempt to manipulate God to grant us present desires by greatly praising Him for His past gifts to us. It is possible for us to come before the presence of the Lord and to perform proper praise with a motivation to get, not to give, and never go beyond praise into worship.

Actually, at those times, we have stepped backward from praise to prayer instead of forward from praise to worship.

In contrast to praise, worship's main thrust is toward the God who has done these great things. While the injunction to praise is often followed by the word "for," the command to worship points to a Person. "Worship God;" "worship the Lord;" and "worship Jesus" are all scriptural commands. Praise begins by applauding God's power, but it often brings us close enough to God that worship can respond to God's presence. While the energy of praise is toward what God does, the energy of worship is toward who God is. The first is concerned with God's performance, while the second is occupied with God's personage. The thrust of worship, therefore, is higher than the thrust of praise.

Still another disparity between praise and worship can be found in the source of their inspiration. Fundamentally, praise is an exuberance in the human soul/spirit that is expressed to God, while worship flows from God's Spirit who is resident in the spirit of man. Praise is redeemed men calling to God, while worship is God calling to God from within redeemed men. Praise often has its origins in the soul, but true worship will always originate in the spirit, for just as Jesus told the woman at the well, "God is a Spirit: and they that worship Him must worship Him in spirit and in truth" (John 4:24).

All divisions between soul and spirit are of necessity arbitrary and tend to be more theological than practical. Still, we recognize the difference between emotional inspiration and spirit inspiration in our responses to God. Praise is more apt to be an act of emotion while worship is

an act of devotion. Praise springs from the fountain of our feelings, while worship flows from the spring of our spirit. Praise says, "I feel ..." Worship says, "I love." Praise looks to the hand of God; worship looks to His heart. While praise and worship are very much alike, they flow from separate sources in our being even though each must manifest itself through the same body. The manifestation does not always reveal the source, for both praise and worship can be expressed with the same bodily postures or actions.

A fourth difference between praise and worship may be found in the depth of dedication evidenced in the praiser as contrasted to the worshipper, for while praise is an expression of our life, worship is a life-style. The prophet even speaks of Christ giving us "... the garment of praise for the spirit of heaviness ..." (Isaiah 61:3), but nowhere does the Bible speak of worship as a gift from God or something that can be put on as a garment.

Praise is often an act of our will, and it can be stirred into action by the working of our emotions, but worship involves the entire life. A true worshipper is a worshipper whether he is engaged in an act of worship at the moment or not. Worship is far more than an attitude or an action, it is a way of life that affects the worshipper's behavior outside the presence of God as well as inside that presence. You can tell a true worshipper by his actions on the job, his attitudes in the home, as well as his ardor at church. His time with God changes him in all of his relationships in life.

Rev. Charlotte Baker, founder and pastor emeritus of King's Temple in Seattle, Washington has been a longtime pioneer of the message of worship throughout the world. In a recent conference where we shared together she stated, "*Worship is extreme submission and extravagant love.*" This demands a lifestyle, for submission is a long-term commitment. We do not have a "season" of submission as we so often have a "season" of praise. Praise may be as brief a period as a moment, or it may last for an hour or more, but submission to God is for a lifetime, and if worship is "extreme submission" then the worshipper is called upon to be extremely submitted to God throughout the whole of his life.

If worship is also "extravagant love" then surely it is more than an attitude or a mere act. It will take a lifetime to extravagantly love God. Jesus taught us, "thou shalt love the Lord thy God with all thy heart, and with all thy soul, and with all thy mind, and with all thy strength: this is the first commandment" (Mark 12:30), and obedience to this level of expressed love will become a lifetime occupation that produces a life-style in the worshipper.

Daniel is a classic example of these two forces at work in the life of a worshipper. Although captured as a youth and taken to a foreign land, Daniel accepted this as the will of God for his life. In the midst of the most perverse circumstances we can imagine, he continued to pour out his love unto God. Even when the edict of the king made it life-threatening to do so, Daniel continued his thrice daily worship response to God. His life was so surrendered to God that he simply refused to do things the king's way if it conflicted with God's revealed will. Yet his spirit remained loving toward God in the midst of all the pressure. Whether in training, in service, or in the lion's den, Daniel was a worshipper, for it was a way of life for him. His life was one of extreme submission to God and extravagant love poured out unto God.

Praise may be a style of expressing life, but worship is a lifestyle in itself. In praise we express a deep appreciation to God for the things He has done for us, but in worship "we live unto the Lord" (Romans 14:8).

Still a fifth difference between praise and worship has to do with our proximity to God. Praise, admittedly, is not always concerned with the deeds of God; it sometimes looks beyond what has been done and praises the one who did it, but it is usually a response from a distance. As we will point out in the next chapter, praise is the vehicle of expression that brings us into God's presence, but worship is what we do once we gain an entrance to that presence. Praise can be done from a great distance, but worship, before it can flow, requires being in the presence of God. In the Tabernacle in the wilderness, praise was practiced even before they entered the outer court, but worship was confined to the holy place; it required an intimacy not needed for praise.

Praise and worship make a good marriage in the sense of being lifetime partners. We find them linked together repeatedly in the pages of the Scripture, for while praise prepares the believer for worship, it is worship that fulfills praise by lifting the expression of praise from appreciation to adoration and by directing its focus to a person rather than to His exploits.

It is hopeless to try to divorce praise from worship, for they are an eternal team. They work together like a hand and a glove. For instance, to be a true worshipper, whatever we do must be a response to an interaction between our spirit and God's Spirit, not as an interaction between us and the persons in the pews around us. But when we come to church we do not walk into the presence of God, we walk into the presence of people and our initial action will be influenced by those people. We'll join them in singing and in various rituals of the service, and in the midst of this we will often be inspired to praise. Although the initial praise may primarily be an interchange with the ones around us, it often lifts us to a one-on-one encounter with God which, in turn, opens the door for the needed response between our spirit and God's Spirit which produces worship.

In this case, praise was the bridge between earthly function and heavenly unction. We praised ourselves out of the pews into God's presence so that worship could flow unto God. Praise can flow with people, but worship is totally concerned with God!

A final diversity between praise and worship might be the method of expression they use. Each must be expressed through the channel of our bodies so, quite obviously, there will be many similarities between them, but a trained observer will also see great dissimilarities.

For instance, praise is very vocal while worship is often void of much speaking. Some declare that praise is the vocal end of worship, and while there is some truth in that statement, it bypasses the very real possibility and common reality of praising without ever worshipping. Two lovers on a walk have much to talk about, but when they are locked in an embrace words seem superfluous.

So it is, often, in worship.

Praise is often physically demonstrative with great action, while deep worship is far more likely to be physically submissive than physically active. We might say that praise tends to be emotional while worship is devotional, and that praise is often loudly exuberant while worship is more apt to be quietly exultant.

Would we better understand this contrast if we said that praise puts love into words and action while worship puts love into touch and relationship? Each is important, but worship is higher and the more intimate.

We cannot bypass praise or negate it, for it is the route into worship. The musical channel for the release of praise is perhaps the most gentle route into worship that God has given to us. But we do not desire to remain in praise when God's presence makes worship a distinct possibility.

17

Leading Others into Worship

That the hundredth Psalm is the divine pattern for entering into the presence of God is obvious to even the most casual reader. Too frequently, however, we begin the pattern at verse four instead of at verses one and two. Long before we "enter into His gates with thanksgiving" we are instructed to "make a joyful noise … come before His presence with singing" (verses 1, 2).

The Hebrews would have no difficulty understanding this, for they were accustomed to singing on their journey to Jerusalem for the feast days, and they even ceremonially sang the psalms of ascent, or degrees (Psalms 120 to 134), as they approached the holy city for these festivals. Their singing reviewed the purpose of their visit, stirred their faith in the Lord their God, and united their hearts and minds with those of their fellow pilgrims.

These psalms of degrees start with man's need—"In my distress I cried unto the Lord …" (Psalm 120:1)—and end in God's sanctuary with men blessing God (Psalm 134:2). From man's need to God's presence is quite a walk; perhaps that is why they sang fifteen songs.

It is likely that the concept of a song service comes from this Jewish practice, but it has been degraded in some religious circles. Sometimes the song service is little more than a call to order, while on occasions it is used to fill time as latecomers find seating in the church.

Scripturally, singing is provided as an expression of worship that can lift us out of the pressures of life into the presence of God. But this is not automatic, for while singing can unite our hearts in a bond of faith and a united expression of love, it can also sidetrack an entire service and immobilize the best of worship desires.

Just as there is a great difference between getting a mass of people to walk aimlessly down a street and leading a band in a march, so singing can either get people involved in aimless activity or lead them to a specific goal. The first will afford emotional release and some soulish responses, but the second can lead people into the presence of God and a worship experience.

Almost anyone can lead songs, but it takes someone special to be able to lead *people* as they sing. This person must be a worshipper himself if he is to lead others into worship, and he must know where he is, where he is going, and when he arrives.

Leading people always requires beginning where the people are. The song leader must locate their present spiritual position or he will miss them entirely, for few people will run to catch up once the march has begun. In most church services, locating the level of the people will generally be easy, for people have come to church from the activities of normal life and have a very minimum of God-consciousness. Their minds are concerned with people, places, things, and personal needs. They are very self-conscious.

The song leader might well start with a song or chorus of personal experience or testimony—one of the many "I am" or "I have" musical testimonies. This meets the people where they

144

are and gives them something with which to identify early in the service.

In the typology of the Tabernacle in the wilderness, to which this hundreth Psalm alludes, this would be the encampment immediately outside the fence that surrounded the Tabernacle. It was the home of the priests, who, although encamped close to the Tabernacle, could not worship until they had entered the Tabernacle itself. And neither can we. If the song leader will bear in mind that songs about personal condition or experience are songs to be sung when the people are outside the Tabernacle enclosure, he can make excellent use of them to gently get the attention of the singers.

Since the Scripturally-declared purpose of gathering together is to worship, the goal of every song service should be to bring people into a worship experience. That would occur in the holy place, where the illumination of the Holy Spirit (the candlestick) makes fellowship with God (the table of shewbread) and worship of God (the altar of incense) possible, pleasurable, and profitable. We want to bring the singers into the holy place where they are conscious of this; but as it is more than one step from outside the court to inside the holy place, songs of experience should not be immediately followed by songs of God's greatness.

"Enter into His gates with thanksgiving ..." (Psalm 100:4), the Psalmist instructs. Don't leave the people in the priestly encampment all the time; take gentle, progressive steps to move them closer to God's presence. This psalm lists three or four such steps, and *thanks*giving is the first. Let the congregation enjoy singing songs of testimony until they are sufficiently united to begin moving closer to God. Use such songs to move the people through the gate that will separate them from the profane into the sacred, and then introduce songs and choruses of thanksgiving.

It is a matter of bringing them from a consciousness of what has been done in and for them (testimony) to Who did it in and for them (thanksgiving). The procession through the eastern gate into the outer court should be a joyful march, for thanks should never be expressed mournfully or negatively. While the people are singing choruses of thanksgiving, they will be thinking both of themselves and of their God, but by putting the emphasis upon the giving of thanks, the majority of the thought patterns should be on their God. Singing at this level will often invoke a beginning level of praise, but it will not produce worship, for the singers are not yet close enough to God's presence to express a worship response.

Step number two is "enter into His courts with praise" (Psalm 100:4). Once the heart has been lifted in thanksgiving, it is natural for it to take the progressive steps into praise. To thank God for what He has done evokes praise for Who He is, so move the songs from thanksgiving for past favors to praises for His present mercy. The outer court is a fairly large place, so it may require more time singing choruses and songs of praise to move the people toward the holy place than it required to get them through the gates with music of thanksgiving.

Progressing from one step to another may require a few words of transition, but the leader whose goal is to bring people into the worship of God will weigh his words carefully. Many a praise service has been talked to death by an anxious song leader, since a long "commercial" breaks the thought patterns of the singers. A well prepared leader can say what needs to be said in a paragraph or less.

The closer we get to the presence of God in the Holy of Holies, the more the songs will be concerned with God Himself. "Be thankful unto Him, and bless His name," the Psalmist says (Psalm 100:4). Whereas we started singing about ourselves outside the walls, we will end up singing about God inside the holy place, for nothing in there speaks of man; it is in its every aspect a revelation of God. Here is where some of the majestic hymns give expression of higher concepts of God than do some of the simple choruses, but if it is a chorus-oriented congregation, let the choruses be those which direct all of the attention to God, Jesus, or the Holy Spirit.

If the leader has been successful in bringing the people step by step into the outer court and on through it into the holy place, there will be a rise in the spiritual response of the people. Instead of mere soulish, emotional responses, there will be responses from the human spirit that have depth and devotion in them. The emotional clapping will likely be replaced with devotional responses of upturned faces, raised hands, tears, and even a subtle change in the timbre of the voices. When there is an awareness that we have come into the presence of God, we step out of lightness into sobriety.

It is at this point that too many leaders make a serious mistake by jerking the people back into the outer court with an emotional chorus of thanksgiving. Worship takes time; don't rush the people. Let them sing; let them repeat any chorus or verse of a hymn that seems to give honest expression to what they are feeling and doing at the moment. The mind can jump from one concept to another far faster than the spirit can. Allow the spirit to savor the sense of the presence of the Lord. A change of chorus can destroy the entire worship attitude.

Just worship. Cleverness is inappropriate. Talk is unnecessary. Directions for response are superfluous. Let the people worship. Silence may be threatening to the leader, but it is golden to the worshipper. A gentle, sustained chord on the organ and a song of the Spirit on the lips of the leader should be more than sufficient to carry a worship response of the entire congregation for a protracted period of time.

"But that isn't singing," you say.

Of course not. It is the purpose of singing. The saints are worshipping; that's why we lead the singing. Don't let the tool of singing hinder the worship response. Everything we have done has been for this, so stop doing, and let the worship flow throughout the congregation. When the majority seem to have finished their worship, the whole congregation can either be invited to sit down "in His presence," or you may choose one more chorus to lead them back to the outer court for the preaching of the Word or whatever other ministry has been prepared.

Singing should not be considered an end in itself. It should be a release of the Holy Spirit unto God in a worship expression. But people have to be led from the natural to the spiritual and from expression of self-needs to an expression of spirit-worship. This is the task of the song leader. If he succeeds, he will be a leader of worshippers more than a leader of songs.

Of course, singing should not be considered as an end in itself, for our purpose in assembling together is to worship the Lord in the beauty of holiness. Worship is the end; all other activities, ceremonies, or ordinances merely serve as a means to that end. But while worship is the end for all of our means, it, of itself, is a means for transforming our individual lives, for a worshipper cannot help being changed in the midst of his worshipping.

18

Transformation and Worship

M an is uniquely a religious creature. His intellectual superiority over all other animals is undisputed, and he is very aware that he is the zenith of all creation. Surely his supremacy is not because he evolved to a higher level than anything else, but it is because he was created in a different manner than anything else.

The Genesis account declares that God created the earth and all of its inhabitants with His word: "... God said, Let there be ..." (Genesis 1:3). But of the creation of man we read, "And God said, Let us make man in Our image, after Our likeness ..." (Genesis 1:26). Man was created by the hand of God, not merely the word of God. Furthermore, God created man from His own image, formed him into God's own likeness, and "breathed into his nostrils the breath of life; and man became a living soul" (Genesis 2:7). Man, far more than any other living thing, is a specific and special creation of God.

In addition to this, man was created for a very special purpose. Paul succinctly stated it in saying, "... we should be to the praise of His glory" (Ephesians 1:12). Man was unquestionably created a religious creature, for there is in the very nature of man something which causes him to recognize and worship a superior being. Whether this "something" is an inner instinct or the effect of tradition, descending from the first worshippers, through all the tribes of the human family, man is indeed a religious being.

Never in all the explorations men have made throughout the earth has a tribe of men been discovered who did not recognize the existence of a superior being and worship it in one way or another. Man worships something which he believes to be endowed with the attributes of a superior being. It has often been said that man has a God-shaped vacuum within his spirit which produces a universal reaching out to worship a superior being.

But while man is a worshipping being, he needs guidance in the choice of the object of his worship. For man, by worshipping, becomes assimilated into the moral character of the object which he worships as the standard of perfection. Accordingly, then, he condemns everything in himself which is unlike, and approves of everything in himself which is like, that character. This causes him to abandon everything in the course of his life which is condemned by the character and precepts of his god, and to conform himself to that standard which is approved by his god. Obviously the worshipper wants the favor of the object he worships, and he reasons that it can only be obtained by conformity to the will and character of that object. To become conformed to the image of the object worshipped must be the end desire of the worshipper. These very aspirations cause his character to become more and more like his god.

The history of idolatry gives ample proof of this. Consistently the character of every nation and tribe throughout the history of civilization has been molded and shaped by the character attributed to their gods. Indeed, man becomes like the object of his worship.

The early Egyptians illustrate this. These patrons of the arts and sciences were brute-worshippers, having their sacred bull, ram, heifer and goat. Historians report that bestiality, the lowest vice to which human nature can descend, was common at that time. The Egyptian sculpture and paintings reveal that the minds of the worshippers were filled with debased, vile and unnatural desires.

Another example of the power of idolatry to change men into the character of the gods they worshipped is that of the Scythians, who finally overthrew Rome. Their chief deities were ideas of hero-kings, bloodthirsty and cruel. Therefore, the worshippers possessed a horrid delight in reveling in slaughter, mayhem and blood. Since they believed that one of their hero-gods, after massacring much of the human race, destroyed himself, it was considered ignoble to die a natural death. Those who were not killed in battle frequently committed suicide, fearing that a serene death might exclude them from favor in Valhalla. Like god, like people.

Better known to most of us is the example of the goddess Venus, called Aphrodite by the Greeks. Although referred to in literature as the goddess of love, as worshipped by the nations of antiquity she was actually a personification of lust. Acts of worship done in her honor would be "X-rated" in today's society. In Paul's day in the beautiful city of Corinth, whose temple to Venus was world-renowned, the persons who were considered to be the most sacred in the city were prostitutes, consecrated to the worship of Venus. This was the major source of revenue for the temple. Consequently, the inhabitants of Corinth became proverbial for dissoluteness and debauchery.

From the beginning of civilization to the present day, men have clothed depraved or bestial deities with almighty power. They became cruel, or corrupt—bestial in their affections—by the reaction of the character worshipped upon the character of the worshipper. In the words of an anonymous writer, "They clothed beasts and depraved beings with the attributes of almightiness, and in effect they worshipped almighty beasts and devils."

This premise is not only recognized by Christians looking at idolatry from the outside, but was admitted by some of the most brilliant minds in the midst of the corruption. Plato speaks of the pernicious influence of the conduct attributed to the gods and suggests that such histories should not be rehearsed in public, lest they should influence the youth to commit the same evil. Aristotle advised that statues and paintings of the gods should exclude all indecent scenes, except in the sacred temples, which presided over sensuality.

H. Oakley, Esq., a magistrate in Bengal, India, some years ago, was quoted as saying, concerning the worship of Kali, one of India's most popular idols, "The murderer, the robber, and the prostitute, all aim to propitiate a being whose worship is obscenity and without imploring whose aid, no act of wickedness is committed. The worship of Kali must harden the hearts of her followers; and to them scenes of blood and crime must become familiar."

Writing of the latter years of Rome and Greece, the moral Seneca exclaimed: "How great now is the madness of men! They lisp the most abominable prayers, and if a man is found listening they are silent. What a man ought not to hear, they do not blush to relate to the gods." He goes on to say, "If any one considers what things they do, and to what things they subject themselves, instead of decency he will find indencency; instead of the honorable, the unworthy; instead of the rational, the insane."

Such was heathenism and its influence, in its most enlightened ages, according to the testimony of the best men of those times. These men, as men of today, were indeed religious creatures who became conformed to the moral character of the object they worshipped.

But does the Scripture support this thesis? The Psalmist declares, in the picture language of Hebrew: "Their idols are silver and gold, the work of men's hands. They have mouths, but they speak not: they have ears, but they hear not: noses have they, but they smell not: feet have they, but they walk not: neither speak they through their throat. They that make them are like unto them; so is every one that trusteth in them" (Psalm 115:4-8).

The Hebrews to whom this was written recognized that far more than the construction of idols was being discussed. Not only did man fashion the visible representation of their god, but they formed the concepts that were projected to that deity. Their god was a god of their craftsmanship, of their concepts, and of their imagination. And having formed their gods, they became like them.

The first chapter of Romans bears further testimony to this: "And changed the glory of the incorruptible God into an image made like to corruptible man, and to birds, and four-footed beasts, and creeping things. Wherefore God also gave them up to uncleanness through the lusts of their own hearts, to dishonour their own bodies ..." (Romans 1:23, 24).

Whenever man projects the attributes of deity to his own creation and then worships it, whether it be a visible idol, a myth, or a mental concept, he risks becoming exactly like his creation: first, because the worshipper has formed something of his own image; second, because the worship is soon assimilated into the moral character of the object of his worship; and third, because "... God gave them up unto vile affections" (Romans 1:26).

But as dismal as this principle is when applied to idolatry, it becomes an exciting provision when seen from the Christian perspective.

Paul exhorted the saints at Colossi: "If ye then be risen with Christ, seek those things which are above ... Set your affections on things above ..." (Colossians 3:1, 2). For since the worshipper takes on the character of the worshipped he need but worship the true and living God to partake of His character.

"Look up and be changed," Paul was saying.

The New Testament consistently teaches that change in the life of a believer is needful, desirable, and available. It speaks of men having been "darkness" who have now become "light in the Lord" (Ephesians 5:8). It declares, "... Such were some of you: but now ye are washed ... sanctified ... justified ... by the Spirit of our God" (1 Corinthians 6:11). Furthermore, it contrasts the natural works of the flesh with the spiritual fruit of the Spirit (Galatians 5:17-23) and even declares: "[Ye] have put on the new man, which is renewed in knowledge after the image of Him that created Him ..." (Colossians 3:10).

Even more pointedly, Paul told the Corinthian church, "But we all, with open face beholding as in a glass the glory of the Lord, are changed into the same image from glory to glory, even as by the Spirit of the Lord" (2 Corinthians 3:18). "Beholding ... [we] are changed!"

These changes that worship will produce in the worshipper are, then, progressive ("from glory to glory"), imputed ("by the Spirit of the Lord"), and very consistent with what occupies the attention of the worshipper ("are changed into the same image").

But what seems to be overlooked, frequently, is that he is changed only while "beholding the glory of the Lord."

In the setting of the Old Testament Tabernacle we could say that we are not changed appreciably in the outer court where the ministry of the brazen altar and the laver are attended to, it is in the holy place where God's glory is seen as a Shekinah that character changes are effected. It is in the awe of worship that we are altered in our ways.

This is not a crisis experience but a continuing one, "from glory to glory." It is while we are beholding that we are becoming like Him. The adorer is adjusted to whatever level of glory he can see, and this level becomes the platform from which increasingly greater levels of glory may be viewed. Little by little, from faith to faith (2 Corinthians 10:15) and from strength to strength (Psalm 138:3) the Holy Spirit changes us from our depraved character to God's divine character "even as by the Spirit of the Lord." It is not instantaneous nor are there any shortcuts, but there also are no failures, only dropouts.

The rate of change is controlled by the worshipper. The more he worships, the more he is changed. Daily sessions in the divine presence will produce daily assimilation into God's character, while mere sporadic seasons of worship will produce only erratic changes. It is not the capriciousness of God's will but the constancy of man's worship that determines the rate of spiritual maturtion.

Since the object of our love determines the character of our life, and the intensity and regularity of the expression of that love will determine the rate at which we are changed, we can understand why Christ declared that the greatest commandment of God's Word is, "Thou shalt love the Lord thy God with all thy heart, and with all thy soul, and with all thy mind, and with all thy strength" (Mark 12:30), for the character of the worshipper will always be assimilated into the character of the object of his worship.

God's special creation may have been marred and scarred by sin, but it can be regenerated and animated by bringing it into the presence of its Creator as surely as the dried seed can be brought to life by placing it back into the earth from which it came. Man, the religious creature, can be restored to God's image only when he is in God's presence, and worship is the prescribed avenue for entrance into that transforming presence. "Beholding ... we are changed."

If the need for change is so apparent, and if the channel for that change is worshipping God on a consistent basis, would we not expect God, who alone can effect these needed changes, to bring back to this world a revival of worship?

19

Revival and Worship

I was raised with the concept of revival. My heritage had its beginnings in such an outpouring of the Holy Spirit as to raise up a people whose hearts hungered after God. One of the methods they used to promote church growth was the conducting of "revival services," which usually consisted of a guest speaker, special music, and services every night for two to six weeks. As the years passed by, the church grew, and as the world seemed to turn upside down, these revival services often became more "rival services" where one church tried to outdo a sister church across town. Other times the announcement of a "revival" conjured up visions of survival as the people remembered how this evangelist forcefully preached on "hellfire and brimstone." It was not always easy to get a commitment from the members of the congregation to support such a revival and, through the years, these revivals gave way to other emphases.

For some years in my early ministry I carried a negative attitude toward "revival." I saw it as an Old Testament word, and pointed out that we never need to revive that which is alive and functioning, so the church should never need to be revived.

Furthermore, I was convinced that the closer we would get to the end of time, the greater would be the falling away of the saints. I had a devil who was too large, a God who was too small, and a church that was too weak. About the only hope I could hold out to the saints was a secret rapture at some moment when the devil was preoccupied.

What confidence God has in His Church to let individuals of such limited and perverted vision take leadership. Fortunately, God is going to do what He has purposed to do in spite of what His preachers do or say. No amount of preaching about apostasy and falling away is going to keep God from renewing His work in the Church of the last days. We may talk survival, but God is purposing revival. We may expect failure in the Church of the twentieth century, but God intends to expedite success beyond our wildest imagination. The Psalmist was a better visionary than many of us, for he cried, "Wilt Thou not revive us again: that thy people may rejoice in Thee?" (Psalm 85:6).

All students of church history are aware that there have been great revivals in days past, but "wilt thou not revive us again?" We have just come through a twenty-year cycle of the renewing of the work of the Holy Spirit in the churches of America and in the true Church of the Living God, but "wilt Thou not revive us again?" Is Jehovah a God of the past or is He a God of eternity? Did He not reveal Himself as the I AM and then proclaim "Jesus Christ the same yesterday, and to day and for ever" (Hebrews 13:8)? What God has done, He is doing, and whatever He is doing, He shall still do, for there is a continuum in God that cannot be violated.

All through the Old Testament, whatever God set out to accomplish was done with finality. He led His people into the Promised Land almost against their will—certainly in spite of their repeated murmurings—and gave them every piece of territory that they would occupy. No change in the economy and no change in leadership kept God from making His people glorious and holy in His sight. God said that He would take them in, and He did.

Why, then, do we worry about recession, cartels, changes in world leadership, and ungodliness? Can they stop God from presenting to this world a Church which is glorious, spotless, and full of the power of God? America's philosophy of humanism and the rights of the individual has not hindered God's express plan for revealing His Son through the Church; if all the power of Rome could not prevent the birth, and hinder the revelation, of Jesus, certainly there is no political or ideological power on earth today with sufficient strength to even slow down God's program of purifying unto Himself a people who can be presented to His Son as a bride and to this earth as the very Body of Christ. Paul was "confident of this very thing, that he which hath begun a good work in you will perform it until the day of Jesus Christ …" (Philippians 1:6). God never starts something that He cannot complete; He started reviving His church, so we have a right to expect Him to continue reviving her until she is ready for presentation to Christ and to the world.

That the early Church was pure, powerful, and productive is revealed in the Book of Acts, but through the years that followed, religious men, for various reasons and using varied methods, defiled the purity of the Church, depleted her power, and decimated her productivity. That which had been birthed as a living organism was reduced to a lethargic organization. The rule of the Holy Spirit was supplanted by human spirits in the persons of the clergy. The divinely prescribed approach to God was replaced with an elaborate manmade labyrinth so complex that even the priests could not find the presence of God. The marvelous approach to God as revealed in the tabernacle in the wilderness seemed lost to the Church forever.

The early Church brought the light of revelation to the world, but the enchained Church contributed to the Dark Ages.

As in Samuel's days, the light of the Lord was just about extinguished. Although the system was corrupt, some of the men in that system were concerned and genuinely hungry for God. Among them was Martin Luther, whose heart cry reached out to God until God revealed to him the truth that "... the just shall live by his faith" (Habakkuk 2:4). This was echoed by the Apostle Paul, "The just shall live by faith" (Romans 1:17).

Justified by faith, not by fiat! It was revolutionary in Luther's day. His teaching of the Pauline doctrine that it is not by works of righteousness but by God's grace alone that men stand justified before God caused him to be viewed as a radical and a heretic. But God was restoring the brazen altar to the Church through a fresh emphasis on the cross of Christ Jesus. Martin Luther's teaching of justification by grace on God's part and by faith on man's part returned to the Church the realization that we have been completely pardoned from the penalty of sin. God chose to place all the punishment for sin upon His Son at Calvary. As Paul put it, "Christ was without sin, but for our sake God made him share our sin in order that we, in union with him, might share the righteousness of God" (2 Corinthians 5:21, TEV). This double imputation, whereby God imputed our sins to Christ on the cross and also imputed His righteousness to us in return, formed the backbone of the revelation given to Martin Luther. Once again men could begin their approach to God, for the issue of the guilt of sin was adequately handled by God and needed only to be faithfully embraced by men.

Just as Israel's approach to God began with the substitutionary sacrifice of an innocent animal at the brazen altar that stood in the outer court just inside the eastern gate, so our approach to God must begin at God's brazen altar, the cross, where the innocent victim died as a substitute for the sinful person. Until sin's penalty is completely satisfied we dare not approach God, the righteous Judge of all the earth (see

Genesis 18:25; Hebrews 12:23). Because of the cross we are now both guiltless and blameless; therefore, we can "draw near with a true heart in full assurance of faith, having our hearts sprinkled from an evil conscience ..." (Hebrews 10:22). This is the message of justification. This was the ministry Martin Luther shared, and thousands of people joined him until, ultimately, the great Lutheran denomination was founded to continue to promulgate the great truth that the cross has never lost its power.

For 250 years this was *the* game in town; it was the revolutionary message of the dynamic Church. Then, in the mid-eighteenth century God began to move dramatically in the lives of two brothers by the names of John and Charles Wesley, inspiring them to see the truth of sanctification throughout the Scriptures. They had long embraced justification, but they were unsatisfied with the continued presence of sin in their lives even after they had experienced God's forgiveness. Charles Wesley preached that there was a place in God where not only was sin's penalty revoked, but sin's pollution was removed. He was not content to be assured of escape from the flames of an eternal hell; he wanted present deliverance from the fire of sin's inner habitation. He embraced the injunctions of Scripture to "likewise reckon ye also yourselves to be dead indeed unto sin ... Let not sin therefore reign in your mortal body, that ye should obey it in the lusts thereof. Neither yield ye your members as instruments of unrighteousness unto sin ... for sin shall not have dominion over you" (Romans 6:11-14).

Whether he was completely aware of it or not, Wesley was used of the Holy Spirit to return the laver to the service of the Church. The laver, the second piece of furniture in the outer court, was made of the mirrors of the women and was kept filled with water. It was used by the priests for the cleaning of their hands, faces, and feet before going into the holy place to minister unto the Lord, for the Lord had threatened death to any priest who dared to enter the holy place defiled. The laver offered a place of both self-inspection and self-purification, for the same basin that revealed defilement afforded the mans to remove that contamination. This is the image behind Paul's testimony of Christ's love for the Church when he wrote, "that He might sanctify and cleanse it with the washing of water by the Word"(Ephesians 5:26). Those who would minister exclusively to people may get by with little more than justification, but those who aspire to minister unto the Lord must also submit themselves to the sanctifying power of the Word of God.

With the return of the truth of sanctification, the Church had a twofold message: pardon from the penalty of sin (justification) and purification from the pollution of sin (sanctification). These messages that brought men into the outer court of God's presence were without significant addition for the next 150 years. Wesleyanism produced the great Methodist movement and became a denomination with world-wide influence.

It wasn't until the early twentieth century that another major revelation of God was shared with the Church on earth. It began with a world-wide outpouring of the Holy Spirit that was misunderstood, maligned, and misinterpreted by the mainline denominations. Those who got involved in this new thing were often disciplined out of their churches, and through their need for fellowship a new religious organization came on the scene. This early Pentecostal outpouring brought the believers beyond the outer court relationship with God into the holy place. They went beyond the hanging of "Jesus the Way" and dared to enter the doorway marked "Jesus the Truth." God used them to focus the attention of the Church upon Christ the Golden Candlestick. These early Pentecostals had an amazing perception of the Redeemer from sin. God imparted great illumination and revelation to them, and although their experience was the infilling of the Holy Spirit, their message was *Jesus*. So notably did they preach Jesus that many of the fundamental denominations labeled them heretics because they rarely used the name of God—everything was "Jesus." In light of this fresh illumination of Christ they were very evangelistic in nature and missionary-oriented in ministry. They founded churches everywhere, and they sent missionaries to the four corners of the world. They did not emphasize the mere work of Christ; they had caught a glimpse of the Redeemer and they wanted everyone else to see Him "as He is."

The faith, enthusiasm, and inspiration of these who had gone into the holy place became infectious, and before long these Pentecostals were growing faster than any other church body. Their Christ-centered singing, testifying, and preaching reached over the wall to affect even those who had originally rigidly rejected them. With the aid of better transportation and rapid communication, they were able to reach the world with their message in a mere fraction of the time it took to promulgate the truths of justification and sanctification. In contrast to the 250 years between Luther and Wesley and the 150 years between Wesley and the early Pentecostal outpouring, this re-establishment of the lampstand was the "new message" for only 50 years before the next major revival swept the world.

With the ministry of the brazen altar (the cross), the laver (the Word), and the golden candlestick (the person of Christ) well established in the true Church, it was time for the Church to come into fellowship with itself. For too long different segments of the Church had fearfully and suspiciously stood aloof from one another. But a divided body is a defenseless body. So in another outpouring of His Holy Spirit, God brought into being the Charismatics, whose main contribution to the Church has been partnership with the redeemed. Their conventions were billed as "Holy Spirit conventions," but the main ministry was feasting together in spiritual fellowship. This move brought the Church to the golden table of shewbread around which the Old Testament priests met weekly for feasting and fellowship.

In the Charismatic revival, God caused His people to step beyond their doctrinal boundaries and to be united partakers of the spiritual life and strength that is in Christ Jesus. While this revival did not bring new doctrine to the Body, it brought a renewal of the ministry of the cross and the Word with a fresh appreciation of Christ and His many brothers and sisters in this great Body, the Church. Perhaps its greatest contribution was in making the believers aware of the many similarities that exist among us in spite of the differences that have separated us for so long. We have found that as long as we are feasting upon the shewbread (also called "the bread of His presence") we have a common basis for fellowship with one another. It has taught us "how good and how pleasant it is for brethren to dwell together in unity" (Psalm 133 :1).

Some have pronounced the Charismatic renewal as the final revival God has promised before the return of Jesus, but I have grave reservations about this. First of all, there is still one piece of tabernacle furniture that has not yet been returned to the Church: we are missing the golden altar of incense where continual worship was offered up to God. Every time a priest entered the holy place he was commanded to take a handful of incense and to scatter it over the hot coals on this golden altar. This cloud of incense smoke permeated the atmosphere of both the holy place of the priests and the most holy place, which was God's habitation among men. Furthermore, it saturated the skin, hair, and clothing of the priests, causing them to bear the fragrance of the knowledge of God with them to the needy people in the outer court.

By the grace of God the Church has come back to pardon from the penalty of sin, purification from the pollution of sin, a fresh perception of the Redeemer from sin, and into a partnership with the redeemed from sin, but she has not yet experienced much participation with God Himself. Although each revival has brought a renewal of praise, there is a true dearth of pure worship in the Body of Christ today. We can praise our way into His presence, but generally we do not know what to do once we gain admittance to Him.

None who know the ways of God could be comfortable with the statement that "this is the final revival." Certainly God would not return only four pieces of furniture to the Church when it required five stations (five is the number of grace) to allow the Levitical priests entrance to God. God, who has begun a good work, will complete it. If the new wine that Christ produced for the wedding at Cana of Galilee was better than the old wine, should we not expect that the final provision will greatly exceed the first provision? The glory of the Church's inception will be greatly exceeded in the Church's final hours. The power, victory, growth, influence, ministry, and worship of the Church seen in the Book of Acts will be signally surpassed in the coming revival that will bring the Church back to such an intimate relationship with the Father that she will instinctively know how to worship and will distinctively want to worship.

The best is yet to come! I believe that I can prove this from the Word. I know that God has spoken it to my heart, and I can bring the testimony of many, many people who declare that God has equally quickened to them that there is a move of God in the wings just awaiting its cue before coming to center stage. God has told me that it would begin in America and Australia almost simultaneously and would work together and spread across the world in very rapid fashion.

He told me that the nature of the move would be a fresh revelation of God the Father. In the Pentecostal revival there was an unusual revelation of Jesus, and in the Charismatic revival we experienced a supplementary revelation of the Holy Spirit, but our generation has not had a wholesome unveiling of the Fatherhood of God. As a natural outgrowth of this unique presentation of God the Father, worship will spring forth, for throughout the Scriptures, every person who came into an awareness of God immediately worshipped Him.

Since, as we have learned, worship is a response to a *person*, it will require such a revelation of God the Father in order to produce world-wide worship in the Church; but God has promised it, history requires it, and our experiences long for it.

When will it happen? I don't know. Between Luther and Wesley was a span of 250 years. Between Methodism and Pentecostalism was 150 years, but only 50 years separated the Pentecostal revival from the Charismatic renewal. At that ratio, we might expect the next revival "yesterday," for the Charismatic renewal is already 25 years old!

We do not have the dates revealed, but we do know something of the times and seasons. Revival is closer than we may think. Worship will be the theme of that revival, and already some segments of God's Church have entered into this glorious experience. Fortunately none of us need await the forthcoming revival to enter into worship, for that is available to us right here and now.

Other Books by Dr. Judson Cornwall

The Best of Judson Cornwall

Elements of Worship

Heaven

Let Us Abide

Let Us Be Holy

Let Us Draw Near

Let Us Enjoy Forgiveness

Let Us See Jesus

Lord, It's Me Again

Profiles of a Leader

Order today through your local Christian bookstore!

LET US Praise

LET US Praise

by
JUDSON CORNWALL

Bridge-Logos
Orlando, Florida 32822

Bridge-Logos

Orlando, Florida 32822 USA

Let Us Praise / Let Us Worship
by Judson Cornwall

Printed in the United States of America.

Library of Congress Catalog Card Number: 2005936843
International Standard Book Number 0-88270-134-7

Unless otherwise identified. Scriptures quotations are from the *King James Version* of the Bible.

Scripture quotations identified AMPLIFIED are from the Amplified Bible. Copyright© The Lockman Foundation 1954-58, and are used by permission.

Scripture quotations identified NEB are from the New English Bible. Copyright © The Delegates of the Oxford University Press and Syndics of the Cambridge University Press 1961, 1970. Reprinted by permission.

Scripture quotations identified PHILLIPS are from the New Testament in Modern English Revised edition, J.B. Phillips, translator. Copyright © J.B.Phillips 1958, 1960, 1972. Used by permission of Macmillan Publishing Company Inc.

Scripture quotations identified RSV are from the Revised Standard Version of the Bible. Copyright © Division of Christian Education of the National Council of the Churches of Christ in the United States of America 1946, 1952 ® 1971 and 1973.

Scripture quotations identified TEV are from the Good News Bible - Old Testament: Copyright © American Bible Society 1976; New Testament: Copyright © American Bible Society 1966, 1971, 1976.

Verses marked TLB are taken from the Living Bible, Copyright ® 1971 by Tyndale House Publishers, Wheaton, Ill. Used by permission.

G1.316x.N.m604.35220

CONTENTS

Let Us Praise

To Eleanor Louise

wife of my youth and middle age, and the three daughters

she gave me: Dorothy—Jeannie—Justine.

The longsuffering of these women in sharing me with others

has made my ministry so much easier.

Preface

I n recent years, several excellent books on *Praise* have been published by Logos. Why another?

In ministering to pastors and people with the historic church backgrounds, I find that the nuts and bolts of the subject of praise, as a public function, is often quite foreign to them. As they have opened themselves to a fuller flow of the Holy Spirit, there is a strong inner desire to express love and adoration, but an outer rigidity that prohibits their bursting forth into praise. Although they thrill to the testimonies of others who have moved into this dimension, they feel they cannot set aside past training just because of someone else's experience, however glorious it may be.

In conferences and seminars, I have been asked repeatedly, "What is the scriptural basis for praise?" This book is an attempt to answer that question. There are over 350 scriptural quotations or references in the book. I've tried to establish that praise is not Davidic but divine, that we are not emulating man's pattern but God's.

I was ministering in Africa when Logos finally convinced me to write such a book. It has been written in airports, motel rooms, guest rooms, and on conference grounds, for it was not possible to cancel a pre-committed schedule to sit down and write. During the writing, I traveled over 80,000 miles and

ministered in seven countries. May the ministry of praise that *Let Us Praise* teaches find an expression in the Body of Christ that is even broader and more far-reaching than my journeys.

Praise God, from whom all blessings flow!

Praise Him, all creatures here below!

Praise Him above, ye heavenly host!

Praise Father, Son, and Holy Ghost!

1

Presented with Praise

The singer had just finished his second set of gospel songs and had laid his guitar on the chair behind the pulpit. Our musical guest of the evening was apparently going to talk for a while, to give his singing voice a rest and us a change of pace.

"I want to congratulate Pastor Cornwall and the congregation on the wonderful job they've done in converting this old barn into a church …"

Barn? I guess that's accurate enough. It does look more like a place for hay storage than for a congregation.

"Although you're a small congregation," he continued, "you've got a beautiful atmosphere here."

Did he use the word atmosphere as a euphemism for empty parking lot? What was I doing here in this nearly deserted barn? This was a home-missions work, a place for a young, eager pioneer. This was the type of anvil on which the beginning ministries of Bible school graduates were forged and tempered. But I was no beginner—I'd been preaching more than twenty-five years, fifteen of them as a pastor. Before pastoring, I'd put

1

in an apprenticeship under my father in two different churches and then invested another year as assistant pastor in a large church in Southern California.

"I'm impressed with the caliber of your pastor," he continued.

Freely translated, that meant he was shocked to see an experienced man in such a small church. He couldn't possibly be more shocked than I was. By denominational standards, I had been successful. An honor student in Bible college, and one of the youngest ministers ever to receive credentials in my denomination, I had stayed less than a year in my first church, dividing the next fourteen years between two others. I had not climbed to larger churches; I had produced them, conducting successful building programs without incurring large indebtedness. I had taken small, weak works and had left them large and strong. Why was I here?

"I first met your pastor when he was ministering in Yakima, Washington, some years ago ..."

I had left that church only a few months ago. Not only had we re-located the congregation and revamped their program and ministry, but I had spent three of those years teaching in a local Bible school in the mornings, and I had a radio ministry to boot. Part of that time I served as president of two ministerial groups, director of youth camps for my denomination, and organist for the adult camps. In fact, I was on so many committees and the platforms of so many denominational functions that some of my fellow ministers were openly jealous of me.

Not surprisingly, my church had one complaint against me: too much outside ministry. Yet I thoroughly enjoyed being called upon to minister outside the walls of my church, and took pride in my reputation within the denomination as a real workhorse.

"I had heard that Brother Cornwall had not only resigned his church but had turned in his papers to the denomination, stating that he would never pastor another church ..."

The dear old denominational grapevine, transmitting such news faster than the telegraph. Well, I guessed there came a time in every preacher's ministry when the frustrations his ministry produced in his own life exceeded the fruit it produced in his congregation. A time when the challenge of his call was countered by an awareness of his inability to produce. Some said this was evidence of maturity, but, for many, it was merely the beginning of the end.

I had just faced such a confrontation with reality in Yakima. More and more I had questioned the standard by which we were measuring success, until I began to have doubts that the church could ever meet the true call of Christ in ministry. It seemed I was enmeshed in a web of near-fruitless activity, and the harder I drove myself, the less satisfaction I had. I began to doubt that the ideals of my youth could ever be accomplished. It finally got to the point where I felt that if I had been in any business other than religion, such an expenditure of energy, manpower, and finance with so little rate of return would have produced bankruptcy. And so, I had turned in my resignation.

I didn't want to give up the ministry; that had been a call of God on my life since boyhood. I simply wanted out of an area of ministry that was completely void of lasting, vital, spiritual life, even though it was being called successful.

My three years of teaching in a small Bible school had convinced me that the most effective means of producing change in the church was to reach future ministers while they were still in training. I had determined to dedicate the remaining years of my ministry to Bible school teaching. My denomination had offered me a teaching spot in their Washington school if I would get my Master's degree, so I had sent a transcript of my Bible

college credits to several West Coast colleges and universities asking for information on a transfer of credits. The University of Oregon offered me the best transfer, and without hesitation, I moved my family to Eugene.

But as I went to enroll, I made a shocking discovery: to establish residency in the state, in order to avoid the double fees charged non-residents, would take six months! I took a job as a roofer. My wife and I were able to find some work for the Lord in the large downtown church of our denomination as the church pianist and organist. And, all in all, our family enjoyed the relaxed pace this change of life forced on us.

"I'm glad to see that what I heard was not true and that Brother Cornwall is, indeed, pastoring ..."

I wished he would stop talking and start singing again.

Oh, it was true enough that I had turned in my papers and refused to pastor again. But during the six months I was establishing residency, the officials of my former district nonetheless sent several delegations from various churches in Washington to invite me to present myself as a ministerial candidate to their congregations. Although these churches were all larger than the congregation I had just left, there had been no temptation to accept their offers. I had had it with pastoring.

"... and that he has been willing to step down to such a small congregation. I know God will bless him for it."

Step down? Dragged down was more like it! This small church, deeply in trouble and badly in debt, had suddenly lost its pastor, and I was simply asked to fill the pulpit for two Sundays. In the meantime, so serious was the condition of the church that the district officials had voted to close its doors, rather than try to continue ministry in that section of town.

This, of course, was of no concern to me; I was only a guest speaker on assignment.

Informed of the decision to close the work and lock the building, the congregation called a business meeting after I left the premises on my second Sunday. They decided to reject the district's decision and to continue struggling to produce a work in this growing section of the city. They unanimously—all fourteen of them—elected me to be their pastor and informed me of their action by phone about midnight.

Aroused from sleep, I had lacked the grace to keep from laughing out loud over the phone.

"I refused two *good* churches just this past week. What on earth makes you think I would take one like yours?"

I had never served such a small congregation, not even as a teenage pastor. I could not even remember having taught a Sunday school class that small.

"Well, won't you pray about it before making your final decision?" the spokesman asked.

"There's no need to," I replied. "I will *never* pastor another church as long as I live."

The shocked silence on the other end began to make me feel guilty, and so, since it seemed the only hope of getting back to bed was to agree, I finally said I would pray about it the next day, and then call him in the evening and tell him no.

Late in the afternoon of the following day, I was reminded of my promise. Since I was working alone on a shake roof, I just paused for a moment and prayed aloud: "Lord, You know I promised to pray about taking the pastorate of that little church, but I know this isn't Your will for my life. Please do provide the guidance for them that they need. And I thank You for delivering me from pastoring."

I had picked up my hatchet and returned to my roofing when the Lord spoke to me by an inner voice that I knew was

His. I had heard it before. *My son, I won't make you take it, but it would please Me if you did. If you will become their pastor, I will show you a safe way into My realm and My presence.*

"Oh, God, no! You can't do this to me! If I have to pastor, at least let it be something large enough to support my family. I'll not only have to work, I'll probably have to pay off their indebtedness. Besides, it would be a breach of courtesy to pastor a little church in this town now that I've been associated with the large downtown work. And what about the district officials? They voted to close that church!"

Little roofing was done in the ensuing hour, as I wrestled with God. I used every gambit, exhausted every argument. I reasoned. I pleaded, I threatened, I cajoled. He remained immovable.

Finally, I threw my shingling hatchet at the roof with such force that it cut all the way through the shakes and fell into the house as I cried, "All right! If You'll teach me new ways into Your presence, I'll take that wretched little church!"

The disciples could not have experienced greater peace when Jesus calmed the storm on Galilee than I knew in the moments that followed.

My wife and daughters were amazed at my decision, although greatly relieved, for they sensed that my withdrawal from pastoring had heightened rather than calmed my frustrations.

Although I had the promise of God that He would show me a new way into His presence and kingdom, by habit patterns long ingrained, I immediately implemented all the old ways I had learned and used in past ministry. God graciously gave us some people so hungry and needy that they were willing to be led almost anywhere.

We tried the evangelistic center approach, but it did not bring us into the divine Presence.

We entered into demon exorcising long before it became popular in the Body of Christ, but after a while, this seemed to magnify the power of the devil rather than the presence of God.

We emphasized divine healing, then being filled with the Spirit. When each special emphasis failed to bring us into the realized presence of God, we would confess our error, back up, and start over in another direction.

During all this time, we kept a very heavy emphasis upon prayer. People were being saved, healed, filled with the Spirit, and delivered from bondage; homes were being re-united, and we were experiencing such growth that we had to build a new building. But we were not enjoying what I had once tasted in earlier ministry and had been promised in this one: the realized presence of the Lord.

During one week-night service, I vaguely recognized a visitor entering the auditorium during the song service. Although it was unusual for me to do so, I felt strongly led to walk down from the platform and introduce myself. He turned out to be someone I had known back in Bible college days. He had been on the missionary field in South America, and our paths had not crossed for many years.

I invited him to speak to us that evening, but he declined, pleading weariness of body. He had just arrived in town, having driven out from Chicago. He did, however, accept an invitation to testify briefly. His testimony electrified all of us. This man knew God! He was on intimate terms with Him. What excitement he created in my inner spirit! I pled with him to give us a series of services, and, in the will of the Lord, he agreed to stay for a week.

I wanted him to preach on knowing God, on talking to God, on coming into God's presence, but he insisted on teaching on praise, and not just teaching—he taught *us* to praise.

What a task he had! We wanted the power and the presence of God, but were fearful and very doubtful about praise. Although I was a member of a group long ago "born in the fire" and could still remember extended, ardent, praise sessions as a boy, I, too, had departed from this and did not know that anyone in the world was deeply involved in vocal, united, congregational praise. Our own congregational praise was generally limited to a stilted, "Praise the Lord, Hallelujah," and his concept of praising in the Spirit and lengthy congregational responses was as disturbing to me as to anyone else.

Perhaps it was undue pride in our lovely new auditorium, so much more elegant than the "old barn" in which we had started, but this man seemed to lack the refinement and decorum to which we had grown accustomed. When we would introduce him as the speaker, instead of coming to the pulpit, he would put a chair alongside it, strap on his accordion, and begin to sing Scriptures set to music. Once we learned a verse, he would repeat it again and again. We were not used to this and grew very impatient with it.

Little by little, however, we began to learn that singing from the intellect is not the same as singing in the Spirit. He was teaching us how to move from a body function to a Spirit response. He would emphasize the truth of the words and then have us sing them again, until there was something within us reaching out in our song.

Another thing struck me: he never seemed to be in a hurry. I feared he had been in the southern hemisphere so long he had forgotten that Americans keep rather regular hours. After he felt we had initiated some response from within to the song we were singing, he took off his accordion, and we expected

him to begin preaching. But he didn't. He insisted that all of us leave our padded pews and stand close together at the front of the auditorium.

Then he exhorted us to raise our hands and vocally express our love, praise, and adoration to the Lord. Few of us knew how. I could express myself emotionally on the organ, but not vocally. He often read a psalm and emphasized that praise is a vocal expression. Then he urged us to try it again.

The patience and great faith of this man did eventually overcome our timidity, and suddenly we found ourselves, however weakly, expressing worship and praise! What's more, we looked around at one another, and if we felt more than a bit foolish, at least we were all in the same boat.

Morning and night, this brother exhorted, exemplified, and encouraged us in praise. He urged us to raise our hands unto the Lord. Now that was going a bit far! I've never seen such an instant plague of arthritis. Not only did our hands feel like they were lead weights, our arm muscles ached after only a few seconds. I think we could have done twenty push-ups easier than we could raise our hands unto the Lord for thirty seconds. What bondage had to be broken in our lives! Each of us felt that the entire congregation was gazing only at us. If we happened to touch another while raising our hands, we felt we had to apologize and start over. How God must have shook His head at us!

Finally, in one last do-or-die effort to break our fears and acute self-awareness, this dear man of God urged us to march around the building one night. And after that, he suggested *dancing* before the Lord! How glad I was that it was so late that no passersby might chance to look in on us. This was positively unreal! And, yet, unmistakedly, all of these were clear commands in the Bible, and I had to admit that every time we obeyed them, it seemed to bring us a little nearer the presence of God.

Nearer the presence of God ... And then I remembered what He had promised that day on the roof. So this was how He was going to do it! I think from that moment all of my deepest resistance was broken, but it would be some time before I could embrace these new ways with anything approaching his enthusiasm. Toward the end of his stay, he brought a tape recording he had made in a church that knew how to relax in praising the Lord. He intended to play it for the evening service and was kind enough to give me a preview of it in private. Just listening to it proved embarrassing to me. How could they worship so uninhibitedly, so naturally, so honestly?

I couldn't give him any reason why I didn't want that tape played in our evening service, but he recognized and respected my fears. He did say that if I continued to lead my people in vocal worship, the day would come when we, too, would enter into just such unrestrained, open praise. I only smiled, for I no more believed that than Martha believed Lazarus would come out of his tomb.

As the week ended, we all had mixed emotions. Relief and regret. The pressure had been heavy, but we had come a long way in seven days. Most of us somehow regretted having the ministry end, for we had experienced something of God hitherto unknown to us—the warm glow that His presence produces, a flow of love that exceeded our former experiences, an operation of spiritual gifts that brought us communication from God. We certainly felt we had been "in heavenly places in Christ Jesus" (Eph. 2:6).

And when our visitor left, we were glad that he had promised to return, although that schedule was many weeks in the future.

2

The Purpose of Praise

"We worship and adore Thee ..." sang the sanctuary choir as an invitation to worship. The opening words were lost amidst muffled whispers from the congregation. The impact of the new choir robes was sensational, and I smiled at the "coincidence" of their arrival, the very Sunday after the second visit of the man of God. It was so much greater than the one two months before. We had gotten over the shock of having to praise vocally, and actually, it hadn't seemed too hard to praise last week. In fact, I rather enjoyed standing with my congregation in front of the pulpit and praising in whatever manner the visitor suggested. At times, it seemed he went too far, but I guess all teaching requires an over-emphasis of the subject to enforce the learning process.

"Bowing down before Thee ..."

I shifted my weight gently, to turn inconspicuously toward the soprano section and get a good look at the robes. Yes, gold was the right color. It blended perfectly with the new carpet and the birch pews.

Slowly turning back to face the congregation, I could see that the pianist, organist, and the choir director were also resplendent in new robes. Now everything was in balance. I had nearly driven the men of the congregation crazy with my obsession for having this auditorium balanced. They had to re-do the steps to the platform twice because I had found them of slightly different heights.

"Songs of praises ringing ... " the choir continued.

The congregation was listening now, not just looking. I wondered just how much I should emphasize praise this morning. It would be different now that *he* had gone.

We had come a long way from the day when I had thrown my hatchet through the roof, and I didn't want to rock the boat too severely—especially right now. Having finished the building, we were starting mortgage payments now, and this was no time to create dissension.

"Hallelujahs ringing ... "

I didn't want to give them too much praise. But how much was too much? Life was full of praise. Manufacturers praised their product. Parents praised their children and were outdone only by the grandparents. Men praised their automobiles or their favorite football teams; women praised their hairdressers, their culinary prowess, or their wardrobes. Children praised, sportsmen praised, pastors praised, and even politicians liked to "point with pride."

Praise was certainly not foreign to our way of life; it was an integral part of it! It seemed to be ingrained in our basic human nature to spontaneously praise whatever we valued. Could we view a great masterpiece of art without giving an exclamation of praise? Could we listen to a symphony skillfully performed without loudly praising the conductor and the orchestra by clapping our hands? We even sent compliments to the chef after enjoying an unusually delicious meal. It was not so much that

these things were "deserving" or "worthy," but that in order to fully savor our enjoyment, we had to give expression to our feelings. It completed us. It enhanced our delight. It seemed to seal the feeling of pleasure within us.

The choir director asked the congregation to stand and join the choir in a repeat of the chorus, "We worship and adore Thee ... "

"Adore Thee ..." Of course! If God was among the things we valued, it was normal to release our inner being in praise to Him and about Him. It was not so much that He needed to hear it as that we needed to say it and to hear ourselves saying it. The conductor of the symphony didn't "need" to hear our applause (although, obviously, he enjoyed and rightly deserved it) as much as we needed to release our inner feelings in an acceptable way.

Yesterday's crowd at the football stadium would have gone crazy if they hadn't been allowed to express themselves at our first win of the season. The team didn't need the praise in order to make the touchdown; they made it before the crowd began praising. It was the spectators who benefited from the clapping, yelling, and waving of hands, hats, and banners.

"You may be seated. Let's turn in our songbooks this morning to page ... "

Songbooks! We didn't use them at all last week. He had us sing from the New Testament. It was an interesting experience to sing directly from God's Word. The very singing became praise, and we never stumbled searching for words. It was going to take a while to develop a praise vocabulary.

In his book *Reflections on the Psalms,* C.S. Lewis wrote, "I had not noticed how the humblest, and at the same time most balanced and capacious minds, praised most, while the cranks, misfits and malcontents, praised least. The good critics found something to praise in many imperfect works; the bad ones

continually narrowed the list of books we might be allowed to read. The healthy and unaffected man, even if luxuriously brought up and widely experienced in good cookery, could praise a very modest meal; the dyspeptic and the snob found fault with all. Except where intolerably adverse circumstances interfere, *praise almost seems to be inner health made audible.*"[1]

"Inner health made audible ... " Spiritual health made audible. Those who had spiritual health found praise to be quite natural to their inner nature, although, with many of us, it had been repressed by religious training. But praise was there! It was an expression of inner strength to praise, and it was an exercising of that strength when praise was expressed. I remembered, as a boy, attending camp meetings where Dr. Charles Price was the speaker. Praise was often the keynote in his services. I had seen congregations rise to their feet during his sermon and spontaneously praise for up to an hour while he joined us in worship, then concluded his sermon when we were seated again. It was as though they could not help themselves, something within so cried out to be expressed.

And there was an invitation to it, a spontaneous appeal for others to join in. And after all, that's what "Hallelujah" really meant: "Praise *ye* the Lord." It was much like asking, "Wasn't that delicious? Isn't that beautiful?" We want to share our enjoyment, for life unshared is life half-lived.

Yet it wasn't simply inner health that caused us to praise at a concert or ball game. Without that health, we might be unable to praise, but the motivation was an outer stimulus. It seemed that the emotional response was in direct proportion to the emotional stimuli. The greater the excitement, the greater the shouting. I wondered if we'd ever get so excited over Jesus, and what He had done for us, that we'd just have to release the pressure of excitement in shouts of praise. This was why our guest spent so much time talking about Jesus and what He had

provided for us: it stimulated us to excitement and anticipation, and we somewhat spontaneously rejoiced!

The more he had talked about the Lord, the warmer my heart had felt toward Jesus. My love had grown greatly this past week. And, come to think of it, this, too, had motivated me to praise.

Just as one of the keys to successful courtship was communication, and the act of communicating love not only expressed it but completed it, so one of the keys to a more intimate relationship with the Lord Jesus Christ was love communicated. It amplified the love within us, it enhanced our enjoyment of Him, it enlarged our capacity for Him and made our existence more meaningful. The Scottish catechism said that man's chief end was "to glorify God and enjoy Him forever." Fully to enjoy was to glorify. In commanding us to glorify Him, God was inviting us to enjoy Him. And in enjoying Him, we would, because of our very nature, invite others to enjoy Him with us.

"Let's stand together and sing this chorus once more before pastor Cornwall comes to lead us in praise and worship."

I wondered if I could do it. It seemed so easy the way he did it. But I must keep it balanced. But balanced to what? To their inner spiritual health that demands expression? To the stimulus of God's presence? Balanced with their love responses to God? To God's commands to praise? Yet we've been spiritually healthy without praise. We've been greatly stimulated by God and His Word. We have shown our love for God by many selfless deeds without praising. Why didn't we praise then? And why did we have the beginning desire to praise now?

C.S. Lewis said, "I had never noticed that all enjoyment spontaneously overflows into praise, unless (sometimes even if) shyness or the fear of boring others is deliberately brought in to check it."[2]

Shyness, fear...checking it? Of course, that was the trouble: our reluctance to overcome this "shyness"—a polite term for self-centeredness.

At the close of the song, I said a fast prayer, stepped into the pulpit, and said, "Let's lift our hands unto the Lord and praise His name."

I realized that I was on display. I was not standing with my people, I was facing them. A few people began to lift their hands, and some braver souls were already gently expressing vocal praise, but I was paralyzed. My arms didn't want to move. I felt a flash of terror, knowing that the congregation in front of me and the choir behind me were all watching to see how I would lead them in praise. All sense of spirituality had drained out of me, leaving me with a familiar back problem: a broad yellow stripe which extended from the base of my skull to where my spine met my pelvis. Jesus, help me! By sheer force of will, I got my hands lifted to the pulpit level and managed to express a few praise-the-Lords. Nervous coughs and shuffling revealed that I was not alone in my self-consciousness. We wanted to praise, but it was hardly "flowing like a river."

This was the crucial moment. Under the faith and guidance of another, we had entered into some enjoyment of praise. Could we maintain it and grow in it on our own? If I couldn't break through my self-consciousness today, right now, no matter what it might cost me, I was convinced we would plunge back to where we had started from, worse off, because we had had a taste and knew the promise.

"Look," I said, "let's all gather together at the front of the auditorium. Choir, come off the platform and join the congregation. God's Word declares in Psalm 100, verse 4, 'Enter into His gates with thanksgiving, and into His courts with praise.' " As they came forward, I went on to explain, "In the tabernacle in the wilderness, God's place of habitation was the Holy of Holies. It sat in a courtyard surrounded by a linen

fence which had only one gate. Anyone approaching God came through that gate and walked through the courtyard to get to the tabernacle in which God dwelt. The gate is called "thanksgiving" and the court is called "praise." That is why Psalm 22:3 declares that God inhabits the praises of His people. The place of His dwelling is in the midst of the courtyard of praise. If we desire to approach God, we must come through praise. If we would enter petitions before God, we must also come through thanksgiving, as Philippians 4:6 tells us: 'With thanksgiving let your requests be made known unto God.'

"All right," I said, looking around at all of us sheepishly gathered up front, "now that we're united physically, let's get united in the activity of praise. So no one will feel he is being looked at, let's all close our eyes and focus our attention on our lovely Lord Jesus. Now, even if it takes all the will-power you've got, lift your hands and faces Godward and tell Him that you love Him."

I strapped on the roving microphone to free me from the pulpit, lifted my hands, and joined my congregation in telling God that I loved Him. Slowly I moved from one end of the platform to the other, praying and praising with more than a little desperation.

Finally, when in my heart I had utterly given up, the log-jam began to move. Almost imperceptibly, the volume of praise began to increase.

A pair of half-raised arms reached to a full stretch. A bowed head became a lifted head. Whispered words became exclamations of praise. Some wept, some shouted, some sang softly, and a few gently clapped their hands. Bit by bit, we seemed to be tuning one another out and tuning God in.

It was obvious, from facial expressions and the changing level and pitch of the vocal praise, that as some broke through to victory, others were coming under the dealings of God. What

had started as a simple praise session had, for some, become a time of direct confrontation.

Our reactions to this manifestation of the presence of God were as varied as our individual personalities. But by this point, our reactions no longer mattered. We felt like Mary, who had sat at the feet of Jesus, or like Lazarus, who had just come forth from the tomb at the call of the Lord.

As the level of praise subsided, I led them in a chorus of praise that sparked them to a renewed outpouring of worship to God. Gently, but very pronouncedly, we became conscious of a sense of the Divine Presence of God greater than we had ever known before. It was as though we had bridged the gap between His world and ours, and we were on the outskirts of His glorious realm.

An overwhelming peace filled the auditorium, and there was an inner experience of alternating love and joy—like ocean waves, one after another, cascading onto the beach. It seemed the light of God's countenance had pierced to the very depth of our souls, not only revealing hidden things, but bringing life and healing to the inner man.

My wife, seated at the piano ready to assist me with any worship chorus I might signal, was allowed to see angels of the Lord walking in our midst.

The crisis was over. We had survived a strong emphasis on praise without the high faith level of our visiting minister. We were on our way to becoming a praising church.

During the year that followed, I preached on praise almost exclusively. Having been shown that the path into the presence of God was praise, I wanted to learn about individual praise, collective praise, praise from our spirit, praise in the Holy Spirit, praise in song, praise with the Word, and so on. And I not only preached praise, I continued to have the people gather at the front to practice it.

Needless to say, all this was not done without some repercussions. Some of our people decided it was time to change churches, and they did. Others felt it was time to change pastors. But I remained convinced it was time, instead, to hold fast to our new approach to God.

It was not long until our new form of worship was known throughout the community and then in our denominational circles. We received little encouragement and lots of criticism, but we really didn't care: we were finding a freedom and fellowship with God we had not experienced before, and we had no desire to return to our former arid and sterile ways.

We were excited—and a little awed—with what God was doing. Our praise was producing the realized presence of God, moving us beyond the rituals of worship into a vital, personal confrontation with Him. It was lifting us out of a self- and need-centeredness, to a Christ-centeredness. And now that we seemed to have the handles, we were not about to let go.

There were other unexpected benefits of praise. It brought a new honesty into our midst. It helped us enlarge our concepts of God. In teaching us how to release our emotions of love and joy, it began to have a noticeable effect in our church's marriages and inter-personal relationships. It moved us from negative to positive attitudes. It changed our services from identification to participation. It began to mold our congregation into a family unit, for once we learned to flow love to God, we began to learn how to love one another.

Again and again, in the weeks that followed, God told us, through a prophetic word, that our praising delighted Him, that He enjoyed it, that it brought us into a warm relationship with Him that was very satisfying to Him. One particularly forceful word of prophecy was given in which the Lord declared that our worship and praise had brought great pleasure to Him.

Pleasure to God? That was a new thought. Somehow I had thought only of God bringing pleasure to us. Yet one of the last five praise psalms declares, "For the Lord taketh pleasure in his people." (Ps. 149:4). And the Psalmist cries, "Bless the Lord, O my soul" (Ps. 104:1), *not* "Bless my soul, O Lord." We, the lesser, are invited (commanded) to bless, honor, magnify, extol, give pleasure to the greater.

Two New Testament books seem to reflect this truth. In Revelation 4:11 we read, "Thou art worthy, O Lord, to receive glory and honour and power: for thou hast created all things, and *for thy pleasure* they are and were created."

Ephesians 1:12 states, "that we should be to the praise of his glory." The Twentieth Century New Testament translates it, "that we should enhance His glory." As surely as God made woman to enhance the man, God made man to enhance His God. As woman became an extension of the man (Ephesians 5:28 commands "men to love their wives as their own bodies"), so man became somewhat of an extension of God. It was the breath, or Spirit, of God that put life in the first man. That man was said to have been created in "the image of God." God told Adam that to be completed, he must be joined to his wife. The two of them made one. She completed him, and he her.

Just so, man completes God, and God completes man. Not in the sense that God is incomplete as a person without the man, but that His sense of satisfaction is not complete without man. God desires and yearns for a close relationship with man.

When a small daughter crawls up on her father's lap, hugs him, and kisses him, does this make him a complete man? No. Does he have to have this? No. Does he desire and enjoy it? Oh, yes! This completes his enjoyment of fatherhood. Just so, my expressed love and adoration for God completes His enjoyment of being our Father. God loves me as an extension of Himself, and delights and receives genuine pleasure when I respond to that love in expressions of praise and worship.

One morning, as I sent the congregation back to their seats to prepare to worship the Lord in giving, I reflected on the fact that it always seemed to be during the praise time that God had communicated with us. I remembered the 29th Psalm which begins, "Give unto the Lord ... the glory due unto his name; worship the Lord in the beauty of holiness," and then continues, in verses 3-5, 7-9, speaking of "the voice of the Lord." I also remembered Psalm 68:32-33 saying, "Sing unto God ... O sing praises unto the Lord; ... *lo, he doth send out his voice, and that a mighty voice.*" As we enter into His presence in praise, we open a channel of communication that gives God an opportunity to speak to us and to be heard.

I remember when I was taking flying lessons that I was very nervous the first time my instructor had me fly out of a radio-controlled field. I had practiced the procedures repeatedly, but this was "for real." I picked up the microphone, pushed in the button on the side, and said, "Eugene tower, this is 5723W, ready for take-off." Total silence. I repeated my message, but still no answer. After what seemed a very long period of time, I made my call again. This time the instructor noticed that I had not released the mike button. In my fright, I had frozen "on" the switch which made it possible for me to speak, but cut off all reception. As I released the button, I heard the tower saying, "Seven, eight, nine, zero ... how do you read me, 23W?"

They had been speaking all the time! I had just blocked out all reception pressing down on the "talk button" on the microphone.

Too often, prayer causes us to hold the switch on the communications, blocking off reception from God. When we praise, we give Him a chance to speak to us.

Proverbs 27:21 says, "As the fining pot for silver, and the furnace for gold; so is a man to praise."

So often it is during praise time, when we have heated our spirits in worship and have the touch of the presence of God around us, that sublimated thoughts, desires, and attitudes rise to the surface. We may have thought we had dealt with these things, but we had only stuffed them down into our subconscious. As we are broken and heated in His presence, these things are separated from the precious metal of our spirits, and rise to the surface. Only then are we able to get them to His cross, to be cleansed from them by His mighty power, to be freed from them by the action of the Divine Smelter's nail-scarred hand, skimming them from our surface.

When asked how he knew the silver was sufficiently pure to be poured into the molds, an old-time refiner said, "I know it is ready when I am able to see my face mirrored undistorted in the molten metal." Will our Divine Smelter give up on us before He has removed the impurities that distort His image in our lives? Will He not encourage us to heat and reheat our lives again and again until all the inner impurities have been released and submitted to His hand? Praise is the pot and the furnace that gives God a chance to further purify our lives. The greater the heat, the greater the release.

How often, during praise sessions, have I seen individuals go to one another to make things right. Fathers straightened things out with children, wives with husbands, and vice versa. Many were saved just standing during a praise session. More people were filled with the Holy Spirit while we were in praise than when we laid hands on them. And the healings that took place—outstanding is the only word for them!

During the week, tradesmen would remark that they could "feel a presence" even in the empty building. God was, indeed, keeping His pledge to show me a safe way into His Divine Presence!

EndNotes

1 C.S. Lewis, *Reflections on the Psalms* (London: Collins Fontana Books) p. 19.

2 Ibid., p.23.

3

The Pattern of Praise

At the time our congregation began to enter into praise, we already had members from at least twenty denominational backgrounds, worshiping together. Although they were, for the most part, Spirit-filled, they did not classify themselves as Pentecostals nor did they consider themselves members of the denomination whose name was on the church building. In fact, each seemed to retain an inner identification with the denomination in which he had worshiped for so many years. Although we never used the title, I suppose we could have been classified as a community church.

With such diversity of backgrounds, not surprisingly, there was an equal diversity of concepts of praise. Our members from a liturgical background saw praise quite differently from the classic Pentecostals in our midst, and though we all agreed that praise was proper, we found ourselves divided on a proper way of expressing that praise.

Realizing that up to this point we had simply copied the method of praising that had been brought to us, we set ourselves to search the Scriptures to see if God had revealed a pattern of

praise. It seemed far better to go directly to the original pattern than to copy something that has been "adapted" from it.

I remember violating this principle once as a young pastor. We were constructing a new church in Kennewick, Washington, and doing it entirely by volunteer labor. When it was time to raise the rafters, we borrowed a large radial saw to cut them to size and shape. The chief carpenter in our church drew a pattern on the first 2 x 10 piece of timber and cut it to shape. He told me to use this as the pattern for all succeeding cuts. Most of our work was done at night, and I had volunteered to spend my days that week pre-cutting the rafters so that when we had a crew of men, they could raise the rafters into place.

It soon became obvious to me that using the pattern meant the handling of that twenty-four-foot piece of heavy lumber repeatedly, whereas the board I had just cut was already in position to act as a pattern for the new board. All I had to do was draw a line at the end with a pencil and cut it.

I was rather proud of my shortcut and happily showed the large stack of pre-cut rafters to the builder when work-night arrived. He properly congratulated me for my work and began supervising the raising of the rafters.

It was not long, however, before it was obvious that something was wrong. There was an inconsistency in the length of the rafters. Each board was longer than the preceding one by the thickness of a pencil mark because I had not continued to use the original pattern. Such a minute variation had not seemed worth considering at the time—but it was multiplied one hundred times (the number of rafters I had cut).

The rafters were useless. The work-night was lost, the days of labor were wasted, and ninety-nine rafters had to be re-cut (the first one, made from the original pattern, was usable).

Would it not be equally foolish to pattern our praise solely on the behavior pattern of men who learned it from other men

who learned it from others, and so on, back to those who may have originally learned it from the Scripture? Why not seek out the Divine pattern at the beginning?

So, continuing our search for a Divine pattern, we rediscovered two books of the Bible that give us glimpses into the heavens—in the Old Testament, Isaiah, and in the New, Revelation. While other writers of the Bible had visions of the living creatures of heaven (notably Ezekiel), it is Isaiah and John, living hundreds of years apart, from diverse cultures and different physical circumstances (Isaiah, tutor of kings; John, prisoner of kings), speaking separate languages, who see and similarly report the magnificence of heavenly praise.

Isaiah's account is given in chapter six. The first four verses tell us, "In the year that king Uzziah died I saw also the Lord sitting upon a throne, high and lifted up, and his train filled the temple. Above it stood the seraphims: each one had six wings; with twain he covered his face, and with twain he covered his feet, and with twain he did fly. And one cried unto another, and said, Holy, holy, holy, is the Lord of hosts: the whole earth is full of his glory. And the posts of the door moved at the voice of him that cried, and the house was filled with smoke."

The seraphim described here are very high-ranking beings of the angelic order. Many feel they are the highest of God's angelic hosts, while others feel the cherubim described by Ezekiel are the first rank of God's heavenly order (Ezek. 1). Isaiah records that at the time of his visit to the temple, these great creatures of God's service were exchanging praises unto the Lord upon the throne in a sort of antiphonal chant or cry. So great was the volume of their praise that the "posts of the door" moved (v. 4).

We also read that the house filled with the smoke or incense of worship. Little wonder, then, that the Psalmist often speaks of a loud shout being germane to praise, or that the New

Testament writers tell us that the Lord's return will be "with a shout" (1 Thess. 4:16).

From the shout of Israel at Jericho (Josh. 6:20), to the shouts at the laying of the foundation of the Temple (Ezra 3:11-13), through the exhortations of the Psalmists and prophets, shouting, as part of worship, is mentioned often in the Bible. Very rarely (Hab. 2:20) are we told to "keep silence before him," while many times we are enjoined to shout: "Clap your hands, all ye people; *shout* unto God with the voice of triumph" (Ps. 47:1); "Let all those that put their trust in thee rejoice: let them ever *shout* for joy" (Ps. 5:11).

It is not that God desires the volume or puts a premium on noise, but that man needs the release of his pent-up joyful emotions that shouting can bring him.

Think of our earlier analogy. Just let your favorite football team unexpectedly intercept a pass and run it all the way back for a touchdown, and the stimulated emotions rise to such a high peak that they are released in a loud shout, often accompanied with emphatic physical gestures. The same emotional rise occurs when saints actually see the Lord *seated* on His throne; the work is accomplished, the victory is won, nothing remains to be done. It is not amiss or improper to express those infused emotions in an electrifying shout of praise, when this is an honest expression of inner feelings.

True, not everyone shouts at football games and not everyone shouts in a worship service, but I have sometimes wondered if the non-shouters really understood what was going on down on the field. Can we see Christ as the complete conqueror of all our enemies and not at least "feel" a shout rising within us? It is obvious, from Isaiah's vision, that the angelic hosts cannot! Just the sight of the Conqueror at rest evoked loud praises unto His name!

When we turned to the book of Revelation, we saw varied forms of worship transpiring. The four living creatures (RSV) cry, "Holy, holy, holy, Lord God Almighty, which was, and is, and is to come" (4:8). They are giving *"glory* and *honor* and *thanks"* to the Lord (4:9). The twenty-four elders prostrate themselves "and worship him that liveth for ever and ever, and cast *their crowns* before the throne, saying, Thou art worthy, O Lord, to receive glory and honour and power: for thou hast created all things, and for thy pleasure they are and were created" (4:10).

All, except the casting of the crowns and prostrate bowing, is vocal, audible expression from living, rational beings unto the Lord. In chapter five, a great multitude of angels joins the living creatures (RSV) and elders of chapter four. John tries to describe their number by saying, "The number of them was ten thousand times ten thousand, and thousands of thousands" (Rev. 5:11) which, if we dared to take it literally, would be in excess of one hundred million angels, all praising with a *"loud voice"* (Rev. 5:12).

In verse thirteen we read, "And every creature which is in heaven, and on the earth, and under the earth, and such as are in the sea, and all that are in them, heard I saying, Blessing, and honour, and glory, and power, be unto him that sitteth upon the throne, and unto the Lamb for ever and ever." This is in complete harmony with Psalm 148 which also calls upon all the creation and created beings to unite in praising God. The day is coming when *everyone* shall praise the Lord vocally and unitedly.

In Revelation 7:9-10, we read, "After this I beheld, and, lo, a great multitude, which no man could number, of all nations, and kindreds, and people, and tongues, stood before the throne, and before the Lamb, clothed with white robes, and palms in their hands; And cried with a loud voice, saying, Salvation to our God which sitteth upon the throne, and unto the Lamb."

In the next two verses, all the angels, and elders, and living creatures (RSV) in heaven join in this vociferous expression of praise, saying, "Amen: Blessing, and glory, and wisdom, and thanksgiving, and honour, and power, and might, be unto our God for ever and ever. Amen" (Rev. 7:12).

In January of 1973, while I was ministering on this theme in the downtown Presbyterian Church in Bogota, Colombia, the pastor told me that my sermon had given him increased motivation to want to go to heaven: he wanted to see twenty-four elders who would consistently fall down before the presence of the Lord and worship. Every mention of the Elders in Revelation shows them worshiping.

A group in heaven express their praise in song: "And they sing the song of Moses the servant of God, and the song of the Lamb, saying, Great and marvellous are thy works, Lord God Almighty; just and true are thy ways, thou King of saints. Who shall not fear thee, O Lord, and glorify thy name? for thou only art holy: for all nations shall come and worship before thee; for thy judgments are made manifest" (Rev. 15:3-4).

Both the Song of Moses and the Song of the Lamb are songs of deliverance. Both declare that the work is already done. They are not songs of faith looking forward to deliverance, but songs of fact, looking back at deliverance. This group is motivated to praise by remembering Christ's finished work.

In chapter nineteen, we again see mass worship and praise with shoutings, adulations, prostration, and declarations of the greatness of God. So *overwhelming* was the laudation, that John seemed to be at a loss for descriptive terms. He writes, "And I heard as it were the voice of a great multitude, and as the voice of many waters, and as the voice of mighty thunderings, saying, Alleluia: for the Lord God omnipotent reigneth (Rev. 19:6). A colosseum of shouting people—a cascading waterfall of praises—a thundering of praise!

From these visions into the heavenlies, then, we got a beginning pattern of the nature and performance of praise. It is vocal, often voluminous. It is sometimes antiphonal, sometimes united, sometimes singular. Often it is sung, even more often it is shouted. Not infrequently it is accompanied by standing, raising the hands, bowing, prostrating, casting of crowns before Him, etc.

We did not see these things as demands of the Scriptures, nor as exhortations similar to those in the Psalms, but what holy men of old actually witnessed taking place in heaven— not merely what should be done, *what was being done.* This is the Divine pattern, the exemplar, the protocol of praise! Anything less than this may be fine, but must accept the tag, "Made according to man's pattern."

During our search for a pattern of praise, we also noted the many instances where angels were commissioned to communicate with man. Their communication usually included praise to God. The best-known example is the appearance of the angelic host to the shepherds on Bethlehem's hillsides to announce the birth of Jesus: "And suddenly there was with the angel a multitude of the heavenly host praising God, and saying, Glory to God in the highest, and on earth peace, good will toward men. ... And the shepherds returned, glorifying and praising God for all the things that they had heard and seen, as it was told unto them" (Luke ?:13-14, 20).

Because there are so many different terms used in Scripture for adulation and praise unto God, we sometimes miss seeing the full role it plays in the Word. These glimpses into heavenly praising helped our congregation see that all praise is worship. We sometimes called it the "vocal end" of worship. It is even one aspect of prayer, a portion of thanksgiving, a releasing of joy, the "lesser" blessing the "greater."

We soon assembled twenty or more similes or analogies for praise. Some refer to various ways of expressing praise vocally. Some point to the use of the hands in praise, while others direct attention to the posture of the body in praise. (The serious student of praise will find a listing of methods of praise in the appendix.)

During the year that I preached almost exclusively on praise, I decided to see how widely praise is taught throughout the Bible. In re-reading the Bible that year, I kept an orange felt pen handy and underscored verses that mentioned praise. I was continually astonished at the frequency of mention, although this was exactly what I was searching for.

It became excitingly clear to us that praise was hardly confined to the book of the Psalms and that praise did not originate with man; it began with God. Well-meaning religious men have not commanded us to praise, God has!

If praise had had its origins in man, we would have had both the right and the responsibility to criticize it, revise it, to question it, or even completely disregard it as not being germane for the twentieth century.

But since praise had its origins in God's heaven, we felt we had to accept and participate in it. We observed, that there had developed such a discrepancy between the original pattern of praise and worship and the present product called "worship" as to challenge the credulity of the most naive among us. We had been using each latest cut as our pattern for the next rafter. Now we felt it was time to get back to the original, Divine pattern, and "do our first works over."

4

The Paradigms of Praise

In the early 1950s at the church I was pastoring in Kennewick, Washington, we were bursting at the seams and had to build. But how and what? We had as many ideas as we had people. It seemed everyone wanted to build a church just like the one back home. In a denominational paper I saw a picture of a church that interested me. I wrote to the pastor on the East Coast, and asked if I could borrow a set of plans to study. The sketches and elevation drawings that he sent completely satisfied both me and my board that this was the type of structure we needed. It would nicely fit our property, it was so simple to construct that the men of the congregation could do most of the work, yet it was of an architectural style that blended well with the homes in the area.

We posted the architect's drawings on the bulletin board, expecting the congregation's *instant* approval. Instead, we found them confused, unable to visualize the proposed structure from the drawings. They could not transform a drawing into three-dimensional thought. Although we had

what we thought was the perfect pattern for our building, people only became bewildered.

After two weeks of increasing confusion, I decided to do something about it. I would make a scale model. It involved many hours of work, but when it was accurate in every detail, including lighting, I put the model on display in the front of the church in place of the sketches. The reaction was most gratifying. When they could see a model of what the architect had in mind, members of the congregation were thrilled. That week, at a business meeting, they voted unanimously to build "according to the model." We broke ground within a week.

In the same way, God's patterns are often difficult for us to translate into action because of our inability to properly visualize or comprehend spiritual things. Since we are so dependent upon our senses, and our acquisition of knowledge demands a proceeding from the known to the unknown, God has often given us paradigms—models—on earth that represent the reality of the heavens.

The Old Testament abounds with models, types, symbols, or paradigms of the reality that was to be revealed later. Who has not thrilled at the abundant (over 100) types of Christ to be seen in the life of Joseph; or at the pattern of faith seen in Abraham; or the pattern of redemption seen in the paschal lamb? These gave us a foretaste, a prefiguring, a perception of that which was yet to come. They presented us with keys of understanding that we might recognize the real when it arrived, as surely as my sending a photograph of myself to a pastor before arrival in his city makes it easy for him to identify me as I step off the airplane.

While there are, unquestionably, many more paradigms of praise than I have yet discovered in the Bible, there are three major models that richly illustrate praise.

Judah, a Paradigm of Praise

The very first use of the word "praise" in the Scriptures is in Genesis 29:35 in connection with the birth of Judah whose name means "praise."

There was a serious conflict between Leah and Rachel, the two wives of Jacob. Leah, who was forced upon Jacob in a most deceitful switch at the wedding (Jacob had labored seven years for Rachel), had, as her only claim to her husband's affections, borne him three sons: Reuben, Simeon, and Levi. It was at the birth of the third son that she felt that she and Jacob were really "joined" (Gen. 29:34). Up to this time, there had been a legal and physical joining, but now, she felt, there would be a joining in the spiritual union of the marriage. Following this "joining," this coming into a true, spiritual relationship one with the other, she conceived again and bore a son. It is in this circumstance that Scripture declares, "Now will I praise the Lord: therefore she called his name Judah [Praise] " (Gen. 29:35).

How fitting an introduction to the ministry of praise, for it is not being "legally" related to the Lord that brings forth praise but the "spiritual" union that brings us into a relationship—spirit, soul, and body—with Him.

The son that was the outgrowth of a complete union was himself to be the father of a family, a tribe, and a nation—all bearing his name of *Praise*. From this man was to come the great King David, and the greater than David, the Lord Jesus Christ Himself! Keep in mind that Judah *always* means praise, no matter where you find it in the Bible.

Let's look at a few key references to Judah in the four major divisions of the Old Testament.

Judah in the Pentateuch

In the Pentateuch, the first five books of the Bible, the name Judah appears more than forty times.

The historical portions of these books of the law do not reveal Judah as being perfect nor his ways totally pleasing unto God. Yet when the dying Jacob called his sons to his death-bed and spoke prophetically to each of them, his words to Judah were, "Judah is a lion's whelp: from the prey, my son, thou art gone up: he stooped down, he couched as a lion, and as an old lion; who shall rouse him up? The sceptre shall not depart from Judah, nor a lawgiver from between his feet, until Shiloh come; and unto him shall the gathering of the people be" (Gen. 49:9-10).

I am not aware of any disagreement among scholars as to the basic meaning of this prophecy, a clear prognostication of the coming of the Lord Jesus Christ. In his complete concordance to the Bible, James Strong says of the word *Shiloh,* that it is "an epithet of the Messiah." Of Jesus it is said, "The Lion of the tribe of Judah, the Root of David, hath prevailed to open the book, and to loose the seven seals thereof" (Rev. 5:5).

Whether he was Lion or Lawgiver, the promise was that Shiloh, the Messiah, the Christ, would come out of Judah, *Praise*. Does not our deliverance, our defense, our directive consistently come out of praise? Non-praisers often live in terror of the adversary who "as a roaring lion, walketh about, seeking whom he may devour" (I Pet. 5:8) while the true praisers live in trust that the Lion of the tribe of Judah shall prevail over every onslaught of the devil. Psalm 81 teaches us that if we will praise God, "There shall no strange god be in thee" (81:9). Praise is our greatest defense against the eruption of demonic activity in our generation.

Another graphic illustration of praise is the order in which God had Israel set up camp in the wilderness. According to

Numbers 2:2-3, the camp of Judah was placed on the east side, facing both the rising sun and the only entrance into the tabernacle enclosure.

It is always the praiser who gets the first glimpse of the rising of the "Sun of Righteousness" (Mal. 3:2) over the horizon, because the man who praises has set his face expecting the rising sun to pierce the darkness. Others will see the light later. He will see the advanced rays of the sunrise!

It was the standard of Judah, bearing the symbol of the lion, which was pitched directly east of the tabernacle. Only the priesthood itself had readier access to the place of worship than the tribe of Judah. While everyone in the camp had access to the tabernacle and its outer court of worship, many of them had quite a journey to get there. The praisers, Judah, dwelt next-door to the gate! I do not doubt that there are non-praisers who gain access to the presence of the Lord, but their route is often long, arduous, and wearisome, and when they finally arrive, they find they must enter in through praise, for that is the name of the court.

Deuteronomy 33:7 records a fourfold blessing of "praise" (Judah). Moses was prophetically blessing each of the twelve tribes of Israel, and to Judah he said, "Hear, Lord, the voice of Judah, and bring him unto his people: let his hands be sufficient for him; and be thou an help to him from his enemies." This, too, is a *working* model of praise. Note first that Moses asked God to hear the voice of Judah, *Praise*. Praise will pierce through any hindering force and gain an audience with God.

Secondly, Moses pled that "praise" should unite the family ("bring him unto his people"). How moving it is to see how God is using praise to bring His body of believers together in this day and age. Praise is a magnet that draws believers of differing concepts and backgrounds together, uniting them in worship, fellowship, and family.

Observe, also, that praise was to have strength equal to the task ("Let his hands be sufficient for him"). How appropriate that the Psalmist couples praises to the Lord with strength, "shewing to the generation to come the praises of the Lord, and his strength" (Ps. 78:4). The secret of strength for the Christian is a praising heart! Well does the Word declare, "The joy of the Lord is your strength" (Neh. 8:10).

The fourth promise in this blessing of Judah is contained in, "Be thou an help to him from his enemies." Never lose sight of the truth that the praiser has access to Divine protection that the non-praising Christian does not have. The pledge of help was given to Judah, Praise.

Judah in the Historical Books

In the books of the law, we saw Judah prophetically. In the books of history, we see Judah performing. In Joshua fourteen we read of Caleb, the man chosen from the tribe of Judah to be one of the twelve spies sent to reconnoiter the land beyond Jordan. He, with Joshua, brought back a report of faith, and although the report was rejected, Caleb was allowed of God to live through the forty years of wandering during which the unbelieving Israelites died and were buried in the sands of the desert. In chapter fourteen, Caleb is reminding Joshua how the two of them had stood against the other ten spies in delivering the minority report. He declares, "I wholly followed the Lord my God" (Josh. 14:8); "the Lord hath kept me alive" (v. 10); "As yet I am as strong this day as I was in the day that Moses sent me" (v. 11); and "Now therefore give me this mountain" (v. 12).

A man who was of the tribe of *Praise* was preserved from disobedience, destruction, dissipation, and disinheritance. He took, as his inheritance, the very land that had been the possession of the giants that so terrified the children of Israel.

Thank God for this small model of praise which reveals some of what praising can do for the practitioner.

The four areas of success reported by this man of *Praise* are often the main objectives of our Christian endeavors. Success in these areas comes to the man of the tribe of *Praise*.

In Judges 1:1-2 we read, "Now after the death of Joshua it came to pass, that the children of Israel asked the Lord, saying, Who shall go up for us against the Canaanites first, to fight against them? And the Lord said, Judah shall go up: behold, I have delivered the land into his hand." *Praise* shall enter the battle first! And God has already delivered the territory into the hand of *Praise*.

How literally this was proved in the case of Jehoshaphat, king of Judah, when he was secretly invaded by Moab and Ammon (2 Chron. 20). God's instructions to him, given through a prophet, were to "stand ... still, and see the salvation of the Lord" (v. 17). Jehosphaphat worshiped the Lord, and then sent singers ahead of the army singing praises to the Lord (v. 21). Imagine sending the choir and orchestra ahead of the warriors! Yet it worked, for God moved in the camp and set the enemy against Himself in an act of self-destruction. The army of Judah never drew a sword, but did spend three days collecting the spoil and loot from the dead bodies.

Saints who would learn to do battle for the Lord should first learn how to praise, for God sends praise as the shock troops to drive the enemy back before the rest of the army is allowed to join the battle.

In the beginning stages of our building program in Eugene, Oregon, I had a chance to personally try this use of praise. Stage one of the program required removal of the roof on the existing church, raising the walls to match the height of the joining structure. No sooner had we completed tearing off the old roof, than the sheriff served us with a cease-and-desist

order which carried a penalty of $400 per day for continued construction. We had a legal building permit and had met all county requirements, as far as we knew. I immediately phoned the building department of our county government and was informed that our new building violated setback requirements of the zoning ordinance. I admitted knowledge of this but told them that the planning commission had granted us a waiver of this provision well over a year previously. The official with whom I was speaking was unaware of this variance grant and could not find it in his files. I offered him my copy but he would not accept it. He said his secretary was on vacation and we would have to wait her return to find the official copy in his files.

Anyone who has lived in Oregon knows it is apt to rain at any time of the year. Our entire church was exposed to rain damage. We had all materials on hand and had scheduled sufficient work parties to have the new roof completed within a week. Delay meant almost certain damage amounting to hundreds of dollars. Continued construction would open us to fines and penalties.

I reported the impasse to my work crew and asked them to join me in prayer. Then I instructed the men to continue working while I went to the prayer room. There I laid the official document on the bench and asked the Lord to read it. Then I began to praise Him for breaking through this hindrance. I paced back and forth in that room with my hands raised, doing nothing but praising God for stopping this hindrance to our building program.

In about an hour, the phone rang. It was the head of the county planning commission phoning to apologize for the inconvenience. The document in question had been found, and the mistake was obviously theirs. I asked to have permission to resume construction given in written form as protection against the legal paper that had been served. In less than an hour the

sheriff drove up with the written apology. What could have been a month-long hassle with county officials was cleared up in less than two hours simply by praising the Lord. "Judah [Praise] shall go up [first] ."

In 2 Samuel 2 we read that following the death of Saul in battle, it was the men of *Praise,* who "anointed David king over the house of Judah (v. 4). It is usually the men of praise who first enthrone Christ as Lord of all! Verses 8-9 tell us that Abner choose Ish-bosheth and anointed him king "over all Israel." Yet Judah recognized that the Lord had anointed David to be king, and they stood by God's choice. "The house of Judah followed David" (v. 10). It was seven and one half years before David was received as king by anyone else. During those years, Judah had the joy of the divinely appointed leader and ingratiated themselves with him. Praisers are usually among the "firsts."

Praise produces proclaimers. We see this beautifully illustrated in I Kings 13:1: "And, behold, there came a man of God out of Judah by the word of the Lord unto Bethel." There are many workers for God and many ministers of the Gospel, but usually the worker, or minister, who is called out specifically to be a "man of God" comes out of Judah, *Praise.* God seems to choose worshipers, praisers, men who understand the Divine Presence and are comfortable in it. What a shame that so few of our seminaries and Bible colleges offer courses in praise.

First Chronicles 12:23-40 lists the men who came to David to help him in his battle against the kingdom of Saul. The first group listed are "the children of Judah that bare shield and spear." These praisers knew how to use the shield of faith as well as the two-edged sword. They were men of combat. Of the groups listed, only Judahites and Naphtalites are said to be bearers of shield and spear. The praiser is as apt in defense as in offense! He can push the enemy back without exposing himself to the "fiery darts."

Judah in the Poetic Books

While the poetic books deal with praise very directly, the Psalms speak also of Judah as a paradigm of praise. "Let the daughters of Judah be glad" (48:11). "The daughters of Judah rejoiced" (97:8). The praisers and their children know joy and gladness, for they are dealing with the God of promises even more than with the promises of God. The Psalms say, "For God ... will build the cities of Judah: that they may dwell there, and have it in possession" (69:35), and "Judah was his sanctuary" (114:2). People who praise will have a place of habitation and thereby will give God a sanctuary in which to dwell: "But thou art holy, O thou that inhabitest the praises" (Ps. 22:3).

Judah in the Prophetic Books

Judah is mentioned more than 290 times in the prophetic books! Hosea 10:11 says, "Judah shall plow." How foolish to plant seed in unprepared soil that has become rock hard either from idleness or the many trampling feet of life's behavior patterns. The prophet suggests that praise can well plow the soil prior to the planting of the seed. As a pastor of a praising congregation for some years now, I can certainly attest to this truth. After we began to praise unitedly in our worship services, we had a great increase in the harvest results. Praise turned and softened hearts and prepared them for the richness of God's Word.

Hosea 11:12 informs us, "Judah yet ruleth with God, and is faithful with the saints." In this day when many are so caught up on authority, rulership, titles, and positions in the Body of Christ, it is refreshing to read that it is *Praise* that yet ruleth with God. We may not all come into an apostleship, but we can all come into praise and therein rule with God.

Joel 3:18 promises, "And it shall come to pass in that day, that ... all the rivers of Judah shall flow with waters, and a

fountain shall come forth of the house of the Lord, and shall water the valley of Shittim." How true this is in today's move of the Spirit! Out from the midst of the people of praise there is flowing a fresh stream of the Holy Spirit that is irrigating the dry valleys of religion. Praise is not only the overflow of the Spirit, it is the source, the fountainhead of the Spirit's flow! Praise can cause a springing up of the waters of the Spirit after a parching day at the office, or in the home. Verse 20 adds, "But Judah shall dwell [Hebrew *abide*] for ever and Jerusalem from generation to generation." Praise is not a novelty to the present charismatic move, any more than it was developed by the classic Pentecostals some seventy years ago. Praise always has been and always will be.

Malachi brings the Old Testament to a close, affirming, "Then shall the offering of Judah be pleasant unto the Lord, as in the days of old, and as in former years" (3:4). The first three verses of the third chapter speak of the dealings of the Lord in the lives of His people, and verse four gives the reason—that praise might be pleasant unto the Lord once again.

What a model, or paradigm, of praise is Judah! Imperfect, at times rebellious, sometimes hasty, sometimes slow, but intended to be a pleasant offering of praise unto the Lord.

Rituals of Worship, a Paradigm of Praise

God would not command His people to worship without giving them a pattern for worship. Inasmuch as praise is an integral part of worship, one would expect to find a pattern for praise woven into the required ritual, and it is there. Some people seem to feel that Old Testament worship was a dull routine of confession, slaughter of innocent animals, and fasting. This is not so at all. Far more of the worship was marked with rejoicing, thanksgiving, and feasting than with solemn fastings.

Take, for instance, the provision for the feasts. Three of these were compulsory, and each Hebrew male was required to return to Jerusalem for them. They were: (1) Feast of Passover (also called Feast of Unleavened Bread); (2) Feast of Pentecost (also called Feast of Weeks, Harvest, or First-Fruits); and (3) Feast of Tabernacles. In addition to these three compulsory feasts, two optional feasts were offered: (4) Feast of Trumpets, which formed the "New Year" of their civil year; and (5) The Feast of Atonement.

All these feasts were joyous occasions, regular family reunions. The sacrifices offered gave only a token part of the animal to the priest, and the rest was returned to the sacrificer for his part of the feast. It was somewhat like the old-fashioned "basket social" or the more recent pot-luck supper many of us have enjoyed. Then as now, eating, drinking, fellowshipping, and rejoicing were the keynotes of the day.

During the rebuilding of Jerusalem, its Temple, and its worship, Nehemiah and Ezra gathered the people into the street by the water gate and read God's law to them. Nehemiah 8:8-10, 12 records the reactions: "So they read in the book of the law of God distinctly, and gave the sense, and caused them to understand the reading. And Nehemiah ... and Ezra the priest the scribe, and the Levites that taught the people, said unto all the people, This day is holy unto the Lord your God; mourn not, nor weep. For all the people wept, when they heard the words of the law. Then he said unto them, Go your way, eat the fat, and drink the sweet, and send portions unto them for whom nothing is prepared: for this day is holy unto our Lord: neither be ye sorry; for the joy of the Lord is your strength. ... And all the people went their way to eat, and to drink, and to send portions, and to make great mirth, because they had understood the words that were declared unto them."

Such was the original way of celebrating the feasts of the Lord. While there is certainly a place for solemnity, there is

equally a place for hilarity. There is a time for fasting but also a time for feasting; a time for judging and a time for joy. Once the Israelite had met God's requirements for sin, he was urged to rejoice in His saving God.

God's ordinances of worship began with a feast (Passover) and will end with a feast (Marriage Supper). The first was just before the Exodus, the second will be just after the entrance! In between the beginning and the end, there was a constancy of feasting before the Lord, for the feasts had three aspects to them: (1) Past (a memorial), (2) Present (an experiential involvement for the individual), and (3) Future (prophetic of greater things to come).

And so there are three aspects of praise to the praiser. We praise as a memorial for His past doings, we praise because of a present involvement in His doings, and we praise because of a prophetic vision and hope. Whether looking backward, outward, or forward, we are motivated to praise the Lord, and feast before His presence with rejoicing and singing.

Take the provision made for a drink offering. This was not, as some have supposed, an offering of wine for the priest's consumption, for although our King James translation has named it a "drink offering," it was actually a "libation offering." The Hebrew word used here literally means "to pour out." It was an offering that was poured out before the Lord. It was not intended for man; it was presented to God.

This illustrates what happens in a man's spirit when he begins to praise. Something from deep within his spirit is "poured out" before the Lord. There is a flowing from him to God. Love, appreciation, adoration, and worship flow from his spirit, through the Holy Spirit, into the presence of God. It is not intended for man, nor is it presented to man. It is an offering from man's spirit to God.

A second offering worthy of note when considering praise was called the "heave offering." The Hebrew word signifies "a present or a gift." It is also translated, in the King James version, as a "freewill offering." All the gifts given for the construction of the tabernacle were called "heave offerings." These offerings were not required; they were totally "freewill" gifts unto God.

What a fitting symbol for what happens to a man's soul when he begins to praise! His emotions begin to open to God, his will responds to the urgings of his spirit, and he finds himself of his own free will giving praise, adulation, magnification, and exaltation to God with delight and pleasure. There is no pressure, no constraint, no coercion, for his soul "delights in the Lord his God." He finds himself joining David in crying, "Bless the Lord, O my soul: and all that is within me, bless his holy name" (Ps. 103:1).

Finally, a third offering worth remembering in this connection is called the "wave offering." In this offering, the priest took of the sacrifices of bread, cakes of meal, and shoulder of the ram and waved them before the Lord. The Hebrew word signifies, "shaking, waving, beckoning, or rocking to and fro." Exodus 29:24-25 tells us that after these offerings were waved before the Lord, they were to be burnt upon the altar "for a sweet savour before the Lord." But first, man's body was to get involved in waving it, shaking it, rocking it to and fro before the Lord.

I remember as a young boy seeing great congregations in camp meetings waving their hands before the Lord in praise and worship. Often they would take out their handkerchiefs, or lift a song book, and wave it before the Lord. I did not understand that they were simply entering into the "wave offering" that becomes a "sweet savour before the Lord" if offered in the fire of the Holy Spirit. It is difficult to get deeply involved in praise without having a physical participation in that praise. God not only expects, but anticipates and invites

bodily participation. He views it as a "wave offering" before Him that will soon be consumed in the fire of His Spirit.

The "drink offering" illustrates the flowing out of man's *spirit*. The "heave offering" pictures the free will responding of man's *soul*, while the "wave offering" involves the man's *body*.

Praise is not confined to the heavens; it has been consigned to earth. Although we see the Divine pattern of praise in the heavens, we also see the Divine model of praise on the earth. In God's choice of Judah to exemplify and expound praise, we have paradigms of praise applied to the life of the individual believer. In God's rituals of worship, both as to feasts and offerings, we see the extent of man's involvement in praise—spirit, soul, and body.

5

Persons in Praise

Standing behind the pulpit with my hands raised in praise one morning, I opened my eyes and was suddenly struck with the great diversity of manifestations. Some persons had their hands raised, others clasped their hands together. Some stood with bowed heads, while others had upturned faces. A few were kneeling, and there was a scattering of people seated, reading their Bibles. And it came to me: the church does not praise, individuals praise. Although united in a concept of adoration, our performances were very individualistic and personal.

My first impulse was to lead in a chorus to unite us in doing the same thing together. Then I realized how needless this would be, how typically this was me reacting in the flesh. We were united in praise, our thoughts were united on Jesus, it was only in our method of expression that each was "doing his own thing." The variety actually made it less ritualistic and more vital.

The comprehensive purpose for everything we had seen thus far was to involve people in praising the Lord. People

praising—What of a few of the individuals in Scripture who represented a special group or class of people, who were worshipers and praisers?

Adam

The first man was Adam. The Bible tells us very little of what he said; however, we do know he had intimate, personal fellowship and communication with the Lord, for the Lord came down into Eden in the cool of the day to walk and talk with Adam (Gen. 3:8). Certainly this is the ultimate end of praise, to bring us into the Divine Presence.

Enoch

Of Enoch, Genesis 5:24 says, "Enoch walked with God: and he was not; for God took him." Again, praise's ultimate!

Noah

Noah also was brought into intimate communication and communion with God. After the flood, one of his first acts was to build an altar for worship (Gen. 8:20).

Abraham

The next emphasis of Scripture upon specific men is with the great patriarchs of old—Abraham, Isaac, and Jacob. Abraham was a man of the altar, a man of feasts, a man of prayer, a man of sacrifices, one who humbled himself before God. He was a man of faith, called in the Bible, "a friend of God" and "a righteous man." Jesus said of him, in John 8:56, "Abraham rejoiced to see my day."

Isaac

In sharp contrast with his father, Isaac seemed to be a quiet, peace-loving man. The Scriptures tell us that God appeared to him, reaffirmed the Abrahamic covenant to him, blessed him, and that, under the blessing of God, Isaac blessed his two sons (Gen. 21-27). He was also known for re-digging his father's wells after the enemy had filled them (Gen. 26:15-18), much as the Spirit reopens the wells of our spirits after religion has filled them up. Praise needs the water of the Spirit and is willing to dig for it.

Jacob

Jacob was a true "character." Yet he was under the Abrahamic covenant, and God was faithful to him. Can we ever forget his great vision of the ladder stretched from earth to heaven with the Angels of God ascending and descending on it? (Gen. 28:12). Jacob responded, upon awakening, by anointing a rock, the pillow upon which he had been sleeping (v. 18). It was Jacob, who upon returning to his own land, wrestled all night with an angel of God (Gen. 32:24-26). We see him before his altar and demanding purity of worship in his whole household. His relating to God finally changed his nature as well as his name (32:27-28). This is another purpose of praise, that we might be changed into His image.

Joseph

It was Jacob who, under the guidance of God, took the chosen family into Egypt where his long-lost son, Joseph, was a co-regent to the throne (Gen. 46). Who can fail to see that Joseph was a true worshiper of God, offering unto Him the praise of his life as well as his lips. In the midst of idol worship, he maintained true worship unto God, and even when standing

before Pharaoh, who was himself looked upon as a God, Joseph proclaimed the name of Elohim!

Little of the speech of these brethren of old is recorded, but the fruit of their worship and praise is easily seen.

Moses

Four hundred years passed with virtually no history recorded in Scripture. Then God raised up a deliverer and lawgiver named Moses. Although God had to deal sorely and lengthily with him, no other man had such face-to-face communication with God, or was ever led so consistently by the supernatural hand of God. After the victorious crossing through the Red Sea, and the subsequent destruction of the enemy forces, Moses lifted his voice and began to sing a song of triumph that was both a proclamation and a prophecy.

Exodus 15 records the song. The first two verses declare, "Then sang Moses and the children of Israel this song unto the Lord, and spake, saying, I will sing unto the Lord, for he hath triumphed gloriously: the horse and his rider hath he thrown into the sea. The Lord is my strength and song, and he is become my salvation: he is my God, and I will prepare him an habitation: my father's God, and I will exalt him."

Moses' pledge to prepare God "an habitation" reveals his unusual understanding of praise, for as we have already seen, God inhabits the praises of Israel (Ps. 22:3). Revelation 15:3 tells us that after our victory is complete, and heaven is gained, we will join the great multitude on the sea of glass and sing the song of Moses! So great was the prophecy of Moses' praise, that it will suffice as a song of deliverance for us!

Melchizedek

One of the first provisions of the law, given through Moses, was for a priesthood. God had already revealed his acceptance of a priesthood long before Abraham's first son was born. Genesis 14:18-20 tells us, "And Melchizedek king of Salem brought forth bread and wine: and he was the priest of the most high God....And he...said, "Blessed be. . .the most high God, which hath delivered thine enemies into thy hand.""

Aaron

When God began to reveal his design for a priesthood, he chose Aaron as the first high priest. He was to become a man of the altar, a man of the censer, the man who entered, annually, into the Divine Presence of the Holy of Holies. He it was who offered the wave offerings before the Lord and poured out the libation offerings as an act of worship. Little wonder, then, that Psalm 115:9 implored, "O house of Aaron, trust in the Lord." Years later the Psalmist pleaded with the progeny of Aaron to continue in blessing and praising the Lord: "Bless the Lord, O house of Aaron" (Ps. 135:19).

Deborah

For many years, the guidance for God's people came through the priesthood. The Book of Judges, however, records times of spiritual decline which encouraged Israel's enemies to rise up against them. Repeatedly, God raised up deliverers who became rulers under the title of "Judges." Many of these offered praise to God during times of victories, but the most outstanding praise comes from the lips of Deborah, who, with Barak, gained a rousing victory over the Canaanites. The song is recorded in Judges 5. Verses 2 and 9 highlight the song: "Praise ye the Lord for the avenging of Israel, when the people willingly

offered themselves. ... My heart is toward the governors of Israel, that offered themselves willingly among the people. Bless ye the Lord."

Samuel

Following the rule of the judges was another period of rule by priests which ended with the godless rule of the household of Eli. Then Samuel took the reigns of leadership, functioning both as prophet and priest, living a life above reproach in its godliness and worship. Toward the end of his rule, the people demanded a king, and the rest of Israel's history is connected with kingly rulership.

David

As touching praise and worship, David was undoubtedly the most outstanding of all the kings of Judah and Israel. His Psalms have given rise to praise for many generations. We can hear David saying, "I will bless the Lord at all times: his praise shall continually be in my mouth. My soul shall make her boast in the Lord: the humble shall hear thereof, and be glad. O magnify the Lord with me, and let us exalt his name together" (Ps. 34:1-3).

David was not only a praiser himself, but he continually exhorted others to join him in praising the Lord. He taught singers to praise the Lord, he trained choirs and orchestras and appointed them to the service of praising the Lord twenty-four hours a day. He seldom lost sight of the fact that until the Lord came on the scene he was just a despised shepherd boy. He continually gave the glory to the Lord.

Isaiah

Concurrent with the reign of the kings was the reign of the prophets. They often played a pivotal role in the political as well as the spiritual affairs of the nation. They frequently were spiritual advisers to the throne, and in the case of Isaiah, a prophet was tutor to the king. The messages they received from God often became the guidelines for a generation.

Isaiah's writings are filled with praise. It was Isaiah who first saw into the heavens and witnessed Divine praise. Little wonder, then, that he executed the commission that was born in praise, with much expression of praise. The entire twelfth chapter is a chapter of praise: "And in that day thou shalt say, O Lord, I will praise thee ... Therefore with joy shall ye draw water out of the wells of salvation ... Praise the Lord ... make mention that his name is exalted. Sing unto the Lord ... Cry out and shout, thou inhabitant of Zion: for great is the Holy One of Israel in the midst of thee." Isaiah 25:1 cries, "O Lord, thou art my God: I will exalt thee, I will praise thy name; for thou hast done wonderful things; thy counsels of old are faithfulness and truth." In 35:10, he promises, "And the ransomed of the Lord shall return, and come to Zion with songs and everlasting joy upon their heads: they shall obtain joy and gladness, and sorrow and sighing shall flee away." Isaiah 42:10 implores, "Sing unto the Lord a new song, and his praise from the end of the earth," while 43:21 declares, "This people have I formed for myself; they shall shew forth my praise."

Habakkuk

All of the minor prophets (minor meaning "briefer," not "less important") contain some message of praise. Note-worthy among them is Habakkuk. He begins his book with criticism of the ways of God and questions of "how long" (1:2), "why" (1:3), and "wherefore" (1:13). He seems to be at the end of his

wavering faith, and goes to his prayer tower to seek a visitation from God. He ends the second chapter with, "But the Lord is in His holy temple: let all the earth keep silence before him" (2:20). The third chapter is a vocal embodiment of praise. It begins with, "His glory covered the heavens, and the earth was full of His praise" (3:3) and ends with, "Yet I will rejoice in the Lord, I will joy in the God of my salvation. The Lord God is my strength, and he will make my feet like hinds' feet, and he will make me to walk upon mine high places. To the chief singer on my stringed instruments (double harp)" (3:18-19).

This preferrer of charges against God becomes a proclaimer of praises unto God after a season in God's presence.

Jesus

In the New Testament, who can see Jesus without seeing praise? As soon as Mary was assured of her pregnancy, she burst forth into magnificent praise. The angels announced His birth with peals of praise. The shepherds observed the Christ-child with praise and wonderment. Men and women from all walks of life praised Him while He walked among them. He, Himself, publicly gave thanks to the Father. Hebrews 2:12 quotes Him as saying, "I will declare thy name unto my brethren, in the midst of the church will I sing praise unto thee." Everything about Jesus spoke of praise; everything in His earthly life; from birth to death and resurrection and ascension was attended and surrounded with praise!

Paul

Every New Testament book Paul authored, except Titus, which deals almost exclusively with church government, contains expressions of praise. He called for singing praise, rejoicing praise, praise of thanksgiving, sacrifice of praise, and

the lifting up of hands in praise. Unquestionably, his heavy emphasis was, "Rejoice in the Lord." He exemplified his philosophy of praise in the Philippian jail when he and Silas began to sing praises unto God in the midst of the pain and persecution (Acts 16:25). He not only lectured on praise, he lived it as well!

John

That John the Beloved understood praise is more evident in his writing as the revelator than as the historian. His book of Revelation is filled with multitudes praising the Lord. Who can read this book of "endings" without being caught up in the great wealth of praise and adoration that the ransomed pour out upon God and His Christ!

Such a fast walk through the Bible cannot hope to give a complete picture of the praisers of God whose names are recorded in Holy Writ, and is intended only to show how many more praisers there were than David and his Psalms. Every era of God's dealing with men has produced its praisers, and thank God that through His present dealings by His Spirit, the church is being reawakened to praise.

6

The Pact of Praise

"**N**ow if you will just sign here ... and here ... and here, it's all yours."

The widespread use of installment credit today makes us more aware of the power of a contract than ever before. When the first party has fulfilled certain stated obligations, the second party is bound, by this written covenant, to perform stated services. Once the parties have entered into the pact, it is enforceable by law. Society demands that the obligations be fulfilled, and this is the security of the covenant.

The Scriptures declare that in the life of the believer, praise is beautiful, necessary, and pleasing to God. But we sometimes fail to realize that praise is a pact, a covenant—not a covenant man makes with God, but a covenant that God has made with man. In Psalm 81, we have a recital of this pact of praise that God offers to His children.

Throughout the Old Testament, we distinguish God's covenants with Adam, Abraham, Jacob, Moses, David, and through the prophets, with His chosen people. In the New

Testament, we find that both salvation and the infilling of the Holy Spirit are covenant promises. Whenever God makes a covenant, He binds Himself by the oath of His Word to fulfill His part; indeed, most of the basic benefits we derive from God are the result of a covenant that God has made with His people. The entire Old Testament is a covenant. "Testament" means "covenant" in modern English. The Old Testament is still called the "Old Covenant" in some translations of the Bible. It is the "old pact" God made with His people. At the Eucharist, Jesus said, "This cup is the new testament (covenant, pact) in my blood" (1 Cor. 11:25).

The Old Covenant is not something Abraham made with God, but something God made with Abraham and many others; neither is the New Covenant something you make with God. The covenant is not in your submission to it, the covenant, He said, "is in My blood." It is true that if you would become a participant in the pact, there are certain things you must do, but your doing them does not produce the covenant—it only makes the covenant valid for you because you have met the pre-existing conditions of the pact.

Psalm 81 gives us the concept of God making a pact or entering into a covenant with His people. "Hear, O my people, and I will *testify unto thee:* O Israel, *if thou* wilt hearken unto me ...

" (v. 8). In this Psalm, God is stating previous promises made and is making a record of them or reiterating them as a legal witness for all to see. The strong implication is the making of a "testament" or entering into a pact or covenant in the matter of praise. "Hear (and heed) my people, and I will make a testament, covenant, pact with thee."

Covenants are generally conditional: "If you'll do this, I'll do that." When we buy a car or a house, and need financing, we sign a contract or pact wherein we agree to make regular payments of a specified amount, and the other party agrees to

let us have possession of the property and later, upon completion of our payment schedule, full title to it. It is an "I will if you will" pact or contract. This is so with God's covenants. He says, "If My people will—I will ... "

The pact presented in Psalm 81 suggests, first, the conditions that must be met in order to enter into the covenant, and then lists God's promises or pledges to the person who will meet the conditions. The final three verses give some covenant benefits, or five things that accrue to the person of the pact.

Our side of this pact is given in the first seven verses. Five methods of praise and five motivations for praise are spelled out, and unless we fulfill the basic condition—praising God—we will be cheated out of the benefits of this covenant of praise. (See chapter seven, "The Performance of Praise," for a discussion of methods of praise.)

In the New Testament, we find an interesting verse which is not usually quoted in its entirety. In 1 Peter 2:9, we read, "But ye are a chosen generation, a royal priesthood, an holy nation, a peculiar people." This is where we usually stop, but it is not where the verse stops. What it says after the semicolon is: "That ye should show forth the praises of him who hath called you out of darkness into his marvellous light." For this He has called us. For this He has made priests of us. For this we are peculiar and different. That we might get together to show forth His praise.

The covenant condition, therefore, is obviously praise. As we praise Him, He moves toward us. But, you may ask, what is a proper motivation for praise? Is it proper to praise just so I can get something from God? What should a Christian's motivation be for praising the Lord? In Psalm 81:4-7, the Holy Spirit gives us six strong reasons for praise, reasons we can understand and relate to, reasons that combine the dealings of God with the deliverance of man.

The first reason for praise is given in verse four: "For this was a statute … and a law of the God of Jacob." This alone should be sufficient. God's Word commands it! Note that it is not listed as an option, for those who want a deeper experience with God; it is given as a repeated command.

"Praise ye the Lord" means, "*All* ye people praise the Lord." Psalm 47:1 declares, "O clap your hands *all ye people*," while Psalm 40:16 says, "Let *all* that seek thee rejoice and be glad in thee." This is the word of the King of kings and Lord of lords. Refusal to praise is rebellion against God's Word.

The second reason for praise is that praising people are God's testimony. "This He ordained in Joseph for a testimony" (Ps. 81:5). The cornerstones of many of our massive cathedrals dedicate the building, "To the Glory of God," and much of the greatest music ever written has been inscribed, "To the Glory of God." Yet the Bible teaches that "*We* should be to the praise of his glory, who first trusted in Christ" (Eph. 1:12). Jesus said, "Ye shall *be* my witnesses."

Contrary to a prevalent belief among many new charismatic Christians, it is not the demonstration of power that God has chosen as a testimony unto Himself, but a declaration of Praise! Praise is a testimony unto God understood both in the heavens and on the earth. As a matter of fact, it is dangerous to get very involved in a display of divine power until you are well entrenched in praise. I've seen what the misuse of spiritual gifts can do to destroy an individual or a church by bringing them into high pride levels. Praise, on the other hand, is conducive to humility, for the only direction praise can go is upward. Until we have learned to worship and praise, we do well to shy away from the power. Where there are people who will praise, there is testimony of Christ; the expressed attitudes have been to Him. He is center and paramount. Then out of this atmosphere of praise, we can safely release the Divine power to minister to

the needs of people. Let's have the adoration of Jesus first, then the authority of Jesus can safely follow. Praise, then power!

A further reason for praise is our deliverance from slavery. "I removed his shoulder from the burden: his hands were delivered from the pots. Thou calledst in trouble, and I delivered thee" (Ps. 81:6-7). How this thought should produce praise! God freed and delivered His people. And He is in the same business today. Slaves are still being transformed into free men. Hallelujah!

In Egypt, the people were the servile vassals of their captors. Their tasks included carrying all the burdens—they were treated much the same as beasts of burden. Their hands were constantly "in the pots," both in cooking and cleaning.

Then the Lord delivered them, and just listen to Miriam with her tambourine leading the women in response to the song of Moses in Exodus 15.

Are you losing your own desire to praise? Bring to remembrance exactly where and what you were before knowing the deliverance and security found in Jesus Christ. Take another look at some of the scenes you were a part of when you were a servant of sin. Are you glad to be free? Tell Him so.

Not only has God delivered His people from the slavery of sin, He is also delivering them from servitude to "religion." I use the word in a negative sense, as Moffatt translates it, having a form but no force ["Though they keep up a form of religion, they will have nothing to do with it as a force" (2 Tim. 3:5)].

Other than Satan himself, there is probably no sterner taskmaster than organized religion. It often forces us to carry burdens that are not our own—to stir pots for other people. If God has delivered you from bearing the burden of "need orientation," praise Him for it. If the Lord, in His grace, has delivered you from ceaseless toil in the pot of "the

denomination," freeing you to be involved in the things of God, praise Him for it. If you have found relationship with Christ instead of dead ritual, praise Him for it. We do well to remember our deliverances, mark them upon our foreheads, recite them unto our children, use them as reason for praise day and night. We were bondsmen, we were slaves, and He has delivered us! (Rest assured that I am speaking of a lifeless "religion" that substitutes itself for a relationship with God. I am not against organization or churches, nor dare I be, for God and His Word are for them.)

A fourth reason for praising the Lord is, "I answered thee" (v. 7). Not only were the people delivered from slavery, but they barely got across the Red Sea before God started answering their prayers. There was the request for sweet water and manna. He provided for their every need when they called upon Him. They should never have lost the awe they felt as God performed miracle after miracle in their behalf.

What about us today? Do we still feel a sense of awe as we think about the God of all the universe listening to our prayers and answering them? Who am I that the King of kings should pause and listen, much less pay attention and answer me. Here am I, one infinitesimal segment of society. I cry, "Oh, God, for Jesus' sake, will You do this for me?" And He answers. If that cannot evoke a sense of wonder and response of praise, then somewhere along the line I have forgotten my relationship and think I deserve this response.

There is a prayer that often comes from my lips: "Thank You, God, that I do not get what I deserve." I do not ever want what I deserve. I am grateful that God has offered me grace, not justice. God listens when I pray. And consistent with His will, He answers. Let that thought evoke praise within you! Praise Him for answered prayer whether the answer was, "Yes," "No," "Later," or "I will if you will."

We often fail to praise the Lord for His provings, testings, trials, and temptations, yet the fifth reason given for praise is, "I proved thee" (Ps. 81:7). We fail to realize that God never tests our weak points, only our strong ones. "I will test my man to reveal what I have put in him." Satan likes to present the situation to us as a temptation, and we often refer to the same situation as a trial. But God says, "Call it a temptation or call it a trial, I initiated it as a test."

Now why does God test us? For the same reason that a manufacturer tests a new product before a new product is put on the market. After many and varied testings, the laboratory writes a certified report to the manufacturer saying, "You can easily guarantee that this product will take seventy years of normal usage. We have abused it far beyond that point." So the advertisement declares, "Lifetime Guarantee." How dare they do this? They have put it to the test and discovered its strength. God does that with you. He wants you to discover how great is His strength within your life.

Have you ever tripped and fallen flat on your face on what you thought was one of your "strong points"? This seems to be where I fall. When I think I am strong, then I am weak. Then the grace of God comes, and God begins doing a work in me. He cleanses me and stands me up in His faith again. But from that time on, I am very apprehensive about a repeat situation. One day I may be brought right into the presence of the same "trial" or "temptation," and there seems to be no escape. My heart cries, "Oh, God, not again!" All the while, the devil is whispering in my ear, "This is the end. You've had it!"

Suddenly I find myself moving right on out of the situation, as if it were not even there. As I look back in amazement, I say, "I did *not* fail. In fact, it did not even bother me. Oh, Lord, thank You." The Lord replies, "The reason for the test is to let you know that I have been building strength

in you, that My grace is sufficient and you need not live in fear. I have proved you."

Can you identify with the Psalmist as he cries, "The Lord is my strength ... The Lord is my rock ... The Lord is my shield ... The Lord is my reward ... The Lord is my buckler ... The Lord is my high tower"? You *are* strong in the Lord! How did you find out? Because He tested you, because the devil tempted you, because you were terribly tried and came forth as pure gold. He wants you to praise Him for that. You would never know the strengths within you if He didn't test you once in a while.

Our part of the pact, then, is simply to praise the Lord! Verse eight of this 81st Psalm ends, "If thou wilt hearken unto me." What has He been talking about? Praise! You dare not apply this statement to the law, ordinances, commandments, or statutes, for that would take the verse completely out of context.

What God has been asking for is praise; He has been talking about praise. He simply says, "If you will, I will." If you will praise, I will ... and in verses 9-10 He lists four things He will do. These are the promises of this pact or covenant.

"There shall no strange god be in thee." Through the Old Testament, "strange gods" is merely a euphemism for "demons." Behind all idolatry is demonic power. Men think they are bowing to stone or silver images, but demons accept it as direct worship to themselves. Little wonder that God is so opposed to idolatry of any kind.

Moreover, we are living today in the midst of an occult explosion. Since there has also been a restoration of the ministry of exorcism to the church, many believing Christians have become unduly demon conscious and live in the mistaken fear of becoming inhabited by alien forces themselves. How

reassuring that the first provision of this pact made by God is that He will be our protection from all Satanic attack!

Deuteronomy 32:9-18 reveals why some Christians have trouble with the Satanic and others do not. To me, this passage coincides beautifully with this first promise of the pact of praise. Verse nine informs us, "For the Lord's portion is his people." Without us, He has no inheritance. The tenth verse tells us that God found them, led them, instructed them, and protected them as He would the "apple (pupil TAB) of his eye." Verse 12 says, "So the Lord *alone* did lead them, and there was no strange god with him." As long as we stay in a praising relationship, we have the assurance of this covenant that God will secure total protection from the Satanic for the children of His inheritance.

Deuteronomy 32:13-14 shows how God's provision for His people is more than ample, it is luxurious. "It is your Father's good pleasure to give you the kingdom" (Luke 12:32). Verse 15, however, says that after these people were totally satisfied and had actually gotten "fat" on God's provision, they began a four-step, downward progression that moved them from the realms of the Divine to the demonic.

First, they "forsook God" (Deut. 32:15). This was one of God's complaints throughout the Old Testament. As long as He blessed His people with abundance, they tended to forsake Him. When He sold them into bondage, they called on His name. How God yearns to give us the best of everything, but He fears it will cause us to rise in self-will and self-love instead of praise ... to forsake rather than to follow ... to become self-oriented instead of God-centered. Is it not easy to become gift-oriented, or power-centered or structure-conscious the moment God begins to share His Divine provisions with us? While none of these things are necessarily evil in themselves, if they replace the affection we once had for God, if they occupy our attention,

we are "forsaking God" just as much as the man who seeks to return to "the pleasures of this world."

After forsaking God, the second step (Deut. 32:16) was, "They provoked him to jealousy with strange gods." I've seen this pattern repeated often in my years of ministry. People come through redemption, into praise, then on to provision until they start getting fat on the provision of the Lord. Then they start looking around for something new, a new "kick," and faster than you might realize it, they're playing the "demonology game." They, like the disciples of old, are excited because "even the devils are subject unto us." [I wonder if the sharp rebuke that Christ gave His disciples for that prideful report wouldn't do our generation of "demon-chasers" some good: "Rejoice not, that the spirits are subject unto you; but rather rejoice, because your names are written in heaven" (Luke 10:20)].

God warned His people, in His very first visitation at Sinai, that He was a "jealous God;" that He would tolerate no other gods before Himself. Happy is the saint who learns, early in his walk, not to try to mix the Divine and the demonic—the light and the darkness; not to share his attention and affections with both.

The next step downward is, "They sacrificed unto devils, not to God (Deut. 32:17). Sadly does 2 Kings 17:33 report, "They feared the Lord, and served their own gods." We may never lose our reverential respect for God, we may still maintain a love for Him, but where are we investing our lives? It is a short step from "playing" with strange gods to "sacrificing" unto them; from curiously reading about the occult to actively experimenting in it.

Nor is the use of idolatry limited to the strict literal sense: are we also serving Mammon, the god of affluence? What investment do we have in the gods of success, recognition, possessive love? What gods are we allowing to insinuate themselves between us and our God?

The final step is, "Thou ... hast forgotten God that formed thee" (Deut. 32:18). By four restoring steps, God had brought them to a place where "there was no strange god with him." By four rebellious steps they had taken themselves away from God into the demonic realms. It is an easy, age-old progression: we tend to forsake God when we do not feel that we need Him. Very few people seek God because they *want* Him—they seek Him because they *need* Him. That is why He created need levels in us.

Amazingly, when we become interested in strange things, we begin to make sacrifices to follow this interest. They soon become part of us, and we fall into a total forgetting of God. The greatest protection anyone has from the Satanic is to keep your mind on God: "Thou wilt keep him in perfect peace, whose mind is stayed on thee" (Isa. 26:3).

The second promise of this pact of praise is concerned with purity of worship. Psalm 81:9 pledges, "Neither shalt thou worship any strange god." Not only is Divine protection offered to the praiser, but purity in his worship is equally assured. We will never be able to develop purity in worship because we are pure, but because He is going to take care of the purification. He and He alone can cleanse the impure motives from our lives, and keep our worship Christ-centered rather than church-, self- or program-centered.

Isaiah 43:12 states, "I have declared, and have saved, and I have shewed, *when* there was no strange god among you: therefore ye are my witnesses, saith the Lord, that I am God." When God has a Divine monopoly in our midst, He will declare, deliver, and demonstrate. But when we bring in a second "god," be it of self or of Satan, God withdraws from the scene and no longer speaks, saves, or shows. As R.A. Torrey used to say, "God will be Lord of all or not at all."

But how will we maintain such a realm of purity? We all have our selfish motivations, our self-love, our self-will. The answer is simply to praise God, and He will keep us pure. If there is to be any purity in our worship, it is going to be because we have given ourselves to the covenant of praise— we have accepted God's pact and are not trying to formulate one ourselves.

With real sorrow, I remember a dealing of God in my life some time ago while I was pastoring a church in Eugene, Oregon. In searching for greater reality than the denominational approach had brought to us, we found ourselves involved in casting out demons. We were very successful in it, although this was years ahead of the present emphasis that is becoming so popular. We soon discovered, however, that if you stir the demonic pot during the week, you can expect the services to be really boiling with demonic powers on Sunday. Week after week my associate pastor would struggle with a song service, finally signaling me for help. I would walk to the pulpit, ask for all heads to be bowed, eyes closed, and I would command the demon forces to leave the building. Almost immediately, there was a release in the midst, and the service could proceed unhindered. However, we usually had to repeat the performance for the evening service and the midweek sessions.

One morning, as I was in prayer, the Lord spoke to me and said, "My son, I would be first in your church." I quickly responded, "But, Lord, You always have top billing. You are Number One in this church. You are the center of our song and sermon. No one is above You in our affections or worship."

But the Lord said, "You do not lead your people to worship Me until you have led them in the worship of demons."

"Not so, Lord," I cried. "Far be it from me to bow my knee to a demon, much less lead a congregation in such worship.

He continued, "Each service you stand before your people and request that they bow their heads before the demons who are present, close their eyes in respect to them, and then you begin to talk to the demon forces. Their world accepts this as worship. Demon forces from far and near attend your services, for they have heard they will be worshiped if they come."

You can well imagine how this broke my heart. I was appalled to think that I had led the saints in the worship of demons. After much weeping and repenting, I asked the Lord what I should do.

He said, "Just ignore the presence of the demonic. Praise and worship Me. You are My people; this house has been dedicated unto the worship of Me. Center your people in praising Me, and I will deal with the demonic."

The following Sunday morning, I had hoped there would be a great liberty of worship. I had prayed much and pled with God to take care of the bondage. The service, however, was even more bound than usual. The song leader asked me to intervene. The moment I stepped into the pulpit, every head bowed and eyes closed, for this was the way I had trained them. This time, I asked them to look at me, and when I had finally gained their full attention, I said, "Isn't it wonderful that Jesus is here in such a glorious way?" They looked at one another as though I had gone crazy. I repeated it, but got no positive response.

I said, "Let us praise the Lord." They tried, but could not. Then I called them to the front of the church and told them that we would not deal with the demonic interference anymore; we were going to "major in God" and let Him take care of any opposition. It took quite a time, but finally the congregation broke through in praise, and when they did, real liberation came. From that day to the day I resigned as pastor of the assembly, we never publicly acknowledged the presence of demonic

forces. We began every service with praise, and the Lord Jesus broke whatever bondage there may have been. Once the evil spirit forces were convinced that their days of being worshiped were over, once they knew that they could no longer hold our attention, they left. And they did not return. The answer to purity in worship is the same now as it was in Moses' day:

"If you will praise me, thou shalt not worship any strange God." Jesus still cleanses the temple when He comes in, and I'll tell you something: I can't prove it, but I suspect that the sweet aroma of heavenward praise is as acrid in the nostrils of Satan and his hordes as sulphur and brimstone are in ours. I'll just bet they can't stand it!

The third promise of this pact of praise is personal relationship. Psalm 81:10 says, "I am the Lord *thy* God." How does one come into this relationship? As you begin to praise God, something wonderful happens to your confidence in your relationship with God. You become aware that He is, in fact, what you are declaring—your Lord. There is a drawing of your spirit and His Spirit together. This strengthens your faith, your worship, your whole being, to know that God is intimately related to you. "I am thy God."

How desperately this is needed today. Only when we are secure in our own relationship to Jesus are we able to offer Jesus to anyone else. We may seek security in relationships in our families, our church, our friends. We may feel secure knowing they are interceding for us. But it is only as we come into the realization of His desire to be our sufficiency, that we can find complete freedom in our relationship with Him. This security is not dependent upon the people we are with, or the culture, or the circumstances. As we praise Him, we come into this glorious closeness and comfort.

And there's something else that happens in our relationship with Him when we start to praise. If there has been a hardness

of heart on our part, a root of bitterness that has effectively blocked whatever He might have wanted to do on our behalf, there is nothing like praise to change one's heart attitude, soften one generally, and set into motion all that Divine machinery which is just poised and waiting. Some of the hardest times to praise—when praise began through gritted teeth in blind obedience to the commands of Scripture—have ended in the greatest victory.

We must never forget that we did not choose Him. He chose us, ordained us, set us as a testimony, and revealed His grace through us to a sinful world. He has put His name on us, His nature within us, His Word in our heart, and His praise in our mouth. The whole spectrum of our intimate relationship with Him is what He *has* done. It is completed. He simply asks us to *praise Him* and thereby enter into the fullness of this personal relationship. He is not just the Redeemer, Creator, Lord of the universe; He is your Savior, your Lord, your Bridegroom, your soon-coming King. Hallelujah!

The fourth promise is certainly a manifestation of Divine grace. "Open thy mouth wide, and I will fill it" (Ps. 81:10). With what will He fill our mouth? What has He been talking about in the whole Psalm? Praise! So, not only does He set praise as the condition we must meet to gain the benefits of this pact, He Himself then supplies that praise. It is one of the promises of the covenant.

This reminds me of my situation as a father. When my daughters were small, they occasionally needed money to buy me a gift. They would approach me and, in their child-like way, get across the message that they needed some money. I was not supposed to know that they were going to buy me a gift. So I gave them the money, and their need was met. The point is, they could not give "unto," until they had received "from." There was no other source of supply for them. Their joy in bringing me their gift was not lessened because they had to

come to me as their source of supply. In fact, it tied us more closely together. This is what God wants. He yearns for a praising people. He is willing to meet our needs by giving us the praise so that our needs are again met as we give that praise to Him.

This provision is consistent with an equation found throughout the Scriptures: if you cannot come to God *with* what He requires, come to Him *for* what He requires. Before forgiveness, we are told to bring repentance to God. Sometimes we do not have a genuine repentance. Yet the New Testament tells us that repentance itself is a gift of God: "In meekness instructing those that oppose themselves; if God peradventure *will give them repentance* to the acknowledging of the truth" (2 Tim. 2:25).

We are told that without faith it is impossible to please God, but who among us can produce faith? Praise God, none of us needs to, for faith also is spoken of as a gift of God: "*God hath dealt* to every man the measure of faith" (Rom. 12:3); "Faith *cometh* by hearing, and hearing by the word of God" (Rom. 10:17); and "To them that have *obtained* like precious faith with us through the righteousness of God and our Saviour Jesus Christ" (2 Pet. 1:1). So if you cannot come to God *with* praise, come to God *for* praise, but come with a mouth wide open! He will fill it for you.

It is unfortunate that the next three verses of this Psalm had to be written. It would be glorious if the Psalmist could tell us that God's people did, in fact, become praising people and enjoyed all the benefits of this glorious covenant. But historically, each succeeding group of "called out ones" have embraced the covenant of praise for only brief periods of their early history and then turned to their own ways, methods, ideas, and programs. Psalm 81:11 sadly reports, "But my people [1] would not hearken to my voice; and [2] Israel would none of me." The voice of God ignored, the presence of God rejected!

"So [1] I gave them up unto their own hearts' lust: and [2] they walked in their own counsels" (Ps. 81:12). God's punishment was simply to let them have their own way—and have it, and have it. If we won't walk after God's heart, He lets us walk after our own heart's desires. If we won't hearken to His voice, He lets us walk according to our own voice, and what desperate consequences accrue. The moment we feel that we can "do it," God stops doing. If we're going to be our own defense, God will get out of the way.

Like little children who do not want to do as they are told but want to do what the parents are doing, we seek to usurp God's authority and expressed responsibility and to do His work for Him. We feel that the part He has asked us to play is "beneath our dignity," below our maturity level, or demeaning to our station in life.

As we look at the closing verses of this Psalm, we cannot help but sense the pathos as God says, "Oh that my people had hearkened...and...walked in my ways! I had purposed good things for them." Then are listed five covenant benefits that could have been theirs.

"I should soon have subdued their enemies" (Ps. 81:14). It was God's desire to bring them into rest, to deliver them from their struggles. But we cannot enter into that rest until we have ceased from our own labors. As long as *we* are going to do it, God will not do it. But if we are going to let God do it, we do not have to do it.

Speaking to religious people of His day, Jesus said, "Come unto me, all ye that labour and are heavy laden, and I will give you rest. Take my yoke upon you, and learn of me; for I am meek and lowly in heart: and ye shall find rest unto your souls" (Matt. 11:28-29).

For years I could not understand this. When I am worn out, the last thing I want to do is stick my neck in a yoke. What

did Jesus mean? Meditating on a yoke of oxen, I found that when you get your neck in His yoke, you will begin to learn. You will learn that if you try to go before He goes, all you are going to get is sore shoulders. You will learn that if you refuse to go when He goes, you are going to have sore ears. You will find that when He turns left and you do not want to turn in that direction, you will get a real crick in the side of your neck. You will learn to eat when He eats, because that is the only time the neck yoke goes down. You will find one of the most glorious lessons to be learned—that your job is simply to hold up your end of the yoke. He will do the pulling. If you are yoked with Him, you will realize that you are just going along for the walk—you are there to learn, not to work. There is a rest. We do become a participant, but it is *His* work, *His* way, *His* will, *His* time, *and His* place. You will learn that a result of praise will be a contentment in moving with God because you are beginning to really know Him.

The second provision of covenant blessing would have been Divine battling. "I should soon have ... turned my head against their adversaries" (Ps. 81:14). It is a marvelous thing when God undertakes against our adversaries, and we do have them, in the flesh and in the spiritual realm. Do not pick up the closest tool at hand and go to battle. Praise the Lord, and He will turn *His* hand against them.

Some years ago when I first began ministering on foreign soil, the Lord gave a beautiful vision to a brother in my congregation. He saw God lowering a dome-shaped canopy of glass over me as hordes of demon powers came against me, and they just hit the glass and bounced off. Later, I went to an area of ministry and faced a great demonic force in the community. To my rejoicing, the vision was fulfilled. I was gloriously protected, untouchable because of His "hand" that was for me and against them.

There is a beautiful truth in Psalm 8:2: "Out of the mouth of babes and sucklings hast thou ordained strength because of thine enemies, that thou mightest still the enemy and the avenger." Jesus quotes this in Matthew 21:16, but He changes two words. Instead of "Thou hast *ordained strength,*" He says, "Thou hast *perfected praise.* " Using the "Jesus translation," look at the verse again. "Out of the mouth of babes and sucklings hast thou *perfected praise* because of thine enemies, that thou mightest still the enemy and the avenger." Could anything be presented more clearly? God has perfected the pattern of praise as a powerful weapon against the enemy. As we praise, God's hand moves against them.

The third benefit of this pact is the pledge that our victories would be perpetuated. "The haters of the Lord should have submitted themselves unto Him: but their time (the Berkeley translation adds 'of retribution') should have endured forever" (Ps. 81:15). I cannot perpetuate spiritual victories. I may win one, but I will have to fight it again and again. In desperation I cry out, "My God, what can I do?" He replies, "Let Me perpetuate the victory." This, too, is part of this covenant of praise: what He provides, He perpetuates!

The fourth provision is given as, "He should have fed them also with the finest of the wheat" (Ps. 81:16). God chooses to give the very best to His children, yet we spend so much of our time struggling and grasping to provide for ourselves. As we fulfill our part of the covenant, we find Him amply filling His part, providing for our every need—spirit, soul, and body— with the very finest possible joys and blessings.

The final provision is also in verse 16: "And with honey out of the rock should I have satisfied thee." Satisfaction! How we search and strive for it. And all of the time God is waiting to give us complete satisfaction in every area of life. Picture after picture is painted in the Old Testament of the struggles of the Israelites to find satisfaction. They turned to strange gods

for religious satisfaction; they turned to foreign practices and people for answers to their physical needs. Yet all the time God was reaching out toward them with His hands full of the good things which were their rightful inheritance as His children. But instead of just praising God as He had commanded, and partaking of his bountiful supply, they sought after broken cisterns that could not possibly hold water. They spent time and money for things which could not fully satisfy—exchanging the lasting things of God for temporary pleasures.

Full satisfaction is to be found in being like Jesus. Although we have not yet attained the fullness of Christ, the Holy Spirit is at work in us at the present, seeking to produce the Divine image in us. 2 Corinthians 3:18 reminds us, "But we all, with open face beholding as in a glass the glory of the Lord, are changed into the same image from glory to glory, even as by the Spirit of the Lord." Is there any time in our Christian discipline when we behold the face of the Lord more than during praise? Is that not one of the prerequisites of praise, that we look away from ourself and see Him? It is in this seeing that we are changed into His image. "Beloved, now are we the sons of God, and it doth not yet appear what we shall be: but we know that, when he shall appear, we shall be like him; for we shall see him as he is" (1 John 3:2).

Read again the 81st Psalm in its entirety. Read it as a pact or covenant that God is presenting to you. He has signed it for eternity in the blood of His son, Jesus Christ. Will you sign your name as party of the second part?

7

The Performance of Praise

Probably the most important instruction in praise given in the entire Bible is given in the first four words of Psalm 149. "Praise ye the Lord." This is, of course, a translation of the Hebrew words *Haw-lai jah* (our "hallelujah"), but we need to realize that the injunction of the Word is more than simply to praise the Lord; it is for *you* to praise the Lord.

So often, as I have ministered in camp meetings, conferences, retreats, and conventions, people have told me that if they could have been a member of my congregation on the West Coast, they, too, would be praisers. I have regularly told them that long before the Lord requires congregational praise, He calls for personal, individual praise. Whether your church praises the Lord or not, "Praise ye the Lord." Whether your prayer group or house meeting gives time for vocal expression of praise or not, "Praise ye the Lord."

Praise is not a mass function, it is the response of an individual to His God. When a group of individuals choose to unite in praising, their individual praises may blend into a group response, but every expression of the praise comes from a

separate individual. My response to God need not be affected by another's response or their lack of response. Since my salvation, my free moral agency has been returned to me; I am an individual in my own right, and if I choose to exercise my will, I can praise the Lord, regardless of the pattern of behavior of those around me.

Don't blame the pastor for lack of praise, don't blame the denomination for praise-lessness, "Praise ye the Lord." You don't have to be led in praise, you don't even need emotional stimuli, just raise your hands and "Praise ye the Lord." Some of Scripture's greatest praisers praised in spite of circumstances and as a solo performance. Once we have learned to praise as individuals, we'll have little difficulty participating in group praise. So say it, sing it, share it, show it, shout it, or strum it— but *start it*! Determine that you *will* praise the Lord!

Often we have difficulty voicing our praise for lack of vocabulary. "Okay, I'm willing to praise the Lord. I really want to, but how do I begin? What do I say?"

God has provided for that contingency. Those of us who have never uttered one word of praise before can begin to praise by using the praises of the great praisers. When you read, "Bless the Lord, O my soul, and forget not all His benefits," you can say, "That's the way I feel about it, too." As you read the words of John, "Worthy is the Lamb," you can add, "Amen, that's what I'm trying to say!"

At times when I was more confused than filled with joy, I have taken the Psalms and read them aloud unto God. As my spirit began to respond to the Words of God's Spirit, there was a lifting that brought rejoicing and victory. Using God's own Words is a marvelous route to high-level praise.

The second instruction about praise, as listed in Psalm 149, is, "Sing unto the Lord a new song" (v. 1). Not many of our major modes of worship and praise are mentioned as often in

the Bible as singing. There are more than three hundred injunctions scattered throughout the Scriptures that tell us to sing. Singing played an important part in the Hebrew worship. When David returned the ark to Jerusalem, he appointed singers and provided that singing should be done before the ark day and night. "And these are they whom David set over the service of song in the house of the Lord, after that the ark had rest. And they ministered...with singing" (1 Chron. 6:31-32). First Chronicles 9:33 adds, "They were employed in that work day and night."

Almost every great general in history knew the tremendous power of song. When the pressure was greatest and fear was rampant, Jehoshaphat caused his troops to begin to sing (2 Chron. 20). How many times has a seemingly beaten body of men been rallied and given new heart by the singing of a beloved marching song or battle hymn? And not just rallied, but transformed? General Booth, the founder of the Salvation Army, once said, "Who said the devil had all the good music?" and countless sidewalk bands in red and blue have known the power of stirring gospel music.

Singing has traditionally been one of the Christian's secret weapons. The martyrs in the arena, faced with being torn apart by wild animals, came out singing. Corrie Ten Boom, in solitary confinement, began each day by singing "Stand Up, Stand Up for Jesus."

I myself have seen congregations gripped with fear and unbelief begin to sing. Soon they sing themselves into reception of faith and then into a release of that faith. They sing themselves from darkness to light, from defeat to victory.

Every revival the world has known has been accompanied with singing. True, in many churches the singing is by remote identification: the choir sings and the people say amen. But

where there is a fresh moving of God, people sing because they want to express something within toward God.

Praising in song performs at least three valuable things for the praiser. First, it affords him a ready-made praise vocabulary. When we begin to sing songs of praise, we have before us words that have been meaningful to others and with which we can easily relate. Some songs have been born in the midst of great experiences with God, and the very singing of them allows us to identify with a high level of praise expression.

Singing praise also contributes to a unity in our response. David was always urging others to join him in praising the Lord. The greater the awareness of God and His glory, the greater the desire to join others or have them join us in lauding that glorious Lord. In song, there is a quick uniting of hearts in praise. We are singing the same words, at the same tempo, to the same tune at the same time, and the cumulative effect is often dynamic! Even if we are singing alone, there is still the sense of uniting with the author and with many others who have, in times past, sung the same song.

A third value of praising in singing is that it helps release the inner emotions that have often been locked up behind the veneer of our culture. For instance, men are taught that it is unmanly for them to weep or show tenderness. In learning to repress weeping, they usually repress all expression of tenderness as well. They find expression in "manly" ways that are acceptable to our culture. Yet boisterous behavior, kidding, physical aggressiveness, and so on, are not conducive to praise. When men and women begin to sing with understanding and anointing, they often find a release for the emotions that is acceptable both to themselves and to their peers, and to God.

Eight separate Hebrew words in the Old Testament are translated "sing" in the King James version of the Bible. According to James Strong's Hebrew dictionary, (appended

to his complete concordance to the Bible), the definitions of these words indicate that singing in Old Testament times was more than the sweet, melodious choral and congregational singing of our churches. One of these words means "to shout or sing aloud for joy." Another, "a shrill sound, or a shout of gladness and rejoicing." Yet another, "joyful voice singing and triumphing," while still another suggests the idea of a strolling minstrel.

Obviously, then, there was a releasing of joyful, triumphant, shouting emotions when the people were singing unto Jehovah. I believe that singing praise will always have some of these factors in it. Congregations have sung together for years and never gotten involved in praise, but when they do get involved, their singing seems not only to come alive, but to explode with emotion.

"Sing unto God. Sing praises to his name" (Ps. 68:4). Don't sing songs; sing praises—with your mind *on* the meaning of the words, and your heart *in* them. Don't sing to people; sing to the Lord. Don't concentrate on musical perfection; concentrate on releasing your inner self in the song. For singing to be praise, the praiser must consciously be singing the song about the Lord or unto the Lord. Not all songs lend themselves to praiseful singing. They should have a Christ-centeredness, either as to His nature and person or as to what He has done. Even songs that are testimony-oriented can be songs of praise if we are less conscious of what we have become and more conscious of all that He has done for and in us.

Just as it helps to create a mental image when talking to someone on the phone, lest you become impersonal in your communication, so it is necessary to have some mental image of the person to whom you are speaking when singing praises. Don't just sing into the air; mentally place yourself in direct communication with God and sing unto Him.

In Hebrews 2:12 Christ is quoted as saying, "I will declare thy name unto my brethren, in the midst of the church will I *sing* praise unto thee." The Greek word used for "sings" is *humneo,* from which we derive our word hymn. It means to sing a religious ode or to celebrate God in song. If this is the type of singing Jesus uses for praising, we would do well to emulate Him.

As valuable as it is for us to use the songs of others, while learning a praise vocabulary, the Spirit within us would like to release the singing of a "new song"—that which is particularly expressive of you and your experience. Don't hesitate in releasing new songs during your praise time. God delights in hearing the "new song." For instance, in the present move of God there is a good deal of emphasis on singing Scriptures.

Singing the Scriptures can become double-praising. There is the melodious release of the inner feelings plus the anointed words of the Bible. What melody? Well, there are many traditional tunes, but if you don't happen to know any, just lean out on the Holy Spirit. Start, and see what happens. You may be very happily surprised! When I begin singing the 150th Psalm, I start to feel what the author felt and to sense and see what he was experiencing, and soon I respond as the writer was responding to God's goodness. In times of pressure, instead of turning on your television or going to the refrigerator, take the Word, read aloud one of the Psalms and declare it to be the expression of your own heart to God. It will bring you into liberty and victory.

When Paul the apostle spoke of singing, he declared, "I will sing with the spirit, and I will sing with the understanding also" (1 Cor. 14:15). "Singing with the Spirit" refers not only to singing a song inspired by the Spirit but singing in the language of the Spirit. This language of the Spirit has not come as a prayer language only, but also as a praise language. Don't be afraid to release that language melodiously. How I used to thrill hearing

our congregation sing in the Spirit, using a variety of languages and rising and falling in pitch as though all knew the song ahead of time. The conscious mind seemed to be bypassed, and the spirit within was unhampered in releasing praise unto the Lord.

It is not unusual for a person given to praise to awaken in the middle of the night aware that the Spirit within him is praising the Lord in song. If our conscious mind did not establish such a rigorous censorship, I would not be surprised if this would occur frequently during the waking hours too.

A third way to perform praise is listed at the end of verse 1 of this 149th Psalm: "And his praise in the congregation of saints." Here it is suggested that spoken, shouted, joyful praise can also be part of our public worship and testimony when we come together. One sometimes cannot help but wonder if much of our assembling is not self-centered or duty motivated. If we came together to "behold Him," would we not involve ourselves in praise far more than we do? If we had a common vision, would there not be more of a common expression?

You will recall how awkward it was to bring our whole congregation into praise. Individuals had learned to praise, our prayer groups did fairly well, but it seemed so strange to do it in the main auditorium. We had found it helpful to take a portion of the service time and invite everyone to leave the pews and gather at the front of the church and down the center isle. When we were packed together, shoulder to shoulder, I would lead them in vocal, united expressions of praise. There was something about breaking the pattern of sitting in the pew, plus the closeness and even physical contact, that seemed to break down inhibitions and made it easier for the people to be released in praise.

Eventually, we made the transition from having to come to the front for praise to being able to praise standing in the pew rows, and what heavenly music it was to hear such variety in

expression, but all praising. We had more than twenty different denominations represented in our congregation, and the differences in heritage and custom made for great variety. I was reminded that the incense used in the Holy of Holies of the tabernacle was compounded from several different fragrances to produce what God desired. How fragrant will be the praises of His people as we stand in His presence in heaven from every tribe, nation, language, culture, and religious heritage and sing and shout His praises in the eternities! Second Chronicles 29:28 gives us a beautiful picture of a praising people: "And all the congregation worshipped, and the singers sang, and the trumpeters sounded: and all this continued until the burnt offering was finished."

Do you have any concept of how long it might have taken to totally consume a bullock on the grates of the altar, reduce it to ashes, cool the ashes enough that men could take them out with shovels, put them in basins, and carry them outside the camp for burial? I have a suspicion that it took from early morning until late evening, and during this whole time, the congregation praised the Lord!

[For additional Scriptures on congregational praise, see the appendix.]

In verse 2 of the 149th Psalm, a fourth method of praising the Lord is given. "Let Israel *rejoice* in him that made him." The Hebrew word translated "rejoice," means, literally, "to brighten up." In Psalm 68:3, the word "rejoice" comes from the Hebrew word "to be bright, cheerful, make mirth." To rejoice in the Lord, then, is more than reciting words of praise and adoration; it is a total change of attitude, countenance, and expression.

The Old Testament priest never came into the Divine presence until he had stopped by the laver for a fresh look, a cleansing, and a refreshing. We need to learn how to use

the "laver of the Word" for "brightening up" on preparation for worship.

We do this regularly in the secular world. Have you ever stepped into a store just in time to overhear the manager angrily disciplining one of his employees, and before you could slip out, you were seen? To your amazement, the manager instantly changed his manner, the tone and inflection of his voice. His face softened, and he even smiled a little as he approached you with a cheery, "May I help you?" For the sake of potential profits, he rapidly exerted his will to brighten up, to become cheerful. To have done otherwise might very well have cost him a customer. He recognized that he had no right to inflict his personal feelings of anger and resentment upon the public.

This matter of "rejoicing in the Lord," is one of learning to be controlled by your *will* levels instead of your *emotional* levels. It is learning not to inflict upon the Lord all your angers, bitternesses, and resentments that the frustrations of life have produced in your emotional nature.

Oh, how often our public worship services are ruined because we've never learned to rule our emotions instead of being ruled by them. Our worship is affected by the weather, stock market, physical condition, or home relationships. This should never be allowed. We do not praise as a release of natural emotions; we praise as a release of emotions stirred by seeing that Jesus is Lord in everything. We learn that all things "come to pass" – nothing comes to stay! We learn to respond to God the Father who has accepted the responsibility for our lives whether they are in a good cycle or a bad one.

What does your life, as you are living it now, have to do with the excellence and greatness of God, of His gifts, graces, and benefits? Paul and Silas, in the midst of the dungeon at Philippi, chose to rejoice in the Lord in praise. Happy is the saint who has learned not to base his praise upon his feelings.

Discipline yourself to praise the Lord no matter what your circumstances in life may be. God sees this discipline as a form of praise in its own right, and His Word calls it, "a brightening up."

Blessed is the Christian, who, when asked "How are you," does not give an "organ recital" but instead expresses the brightness of the Spirit within him. People do not need to hear your problems; they do need to hear your praises.

The last of Psalm 149:2 suggests still a fifth way to praise the Lord. "Let the children of Zion *be joyful* in their King." Being joyful, or joy filled, is one of Christ's goals for His people. He told His disciples, "These things have I spoken unto you, that my joy might remain in you, and that your joy might be full" (John 15:11). Peter wrote, "Whom having not seen, ye love; in whom, though now ye see him not, yet believing, ye rejoice with joy unspeakable and full of glory" (1 Pet. 1:8). Jude reminds us, "Now unto him that is able to keep you from falling, and to present you faultless before the presence of his glory with exceeding joy ... " (Jude 24).

God has purposed joy for His people. Happiness is dependent upon happenings, but joy is dependent upon Jesus. Jesus brought joy to people wherever He went, and He is still doing it! Those who are seeing Him, hearing Him, and believing Him are being filled with "exceeding joy" and "joy unspeakable and full of glory."

However, it is not the possession of the joy that produces the praise, but the release of that joy. "Make a joyful noise unto the God of Jacob" (Ps. 81:1). Have you ever heard the expression, "Well, I can't sing, but I can make a joyful noise?" The Bible makes no reference to any inability to stay on pitch, but emphasizes that we are to speak out our praises unto the Lord.

We need to recognize that until praise is vocalized, it is not completely expressed. There is a difference between thinking and thanking. We see this in our day-to-day relationships. You may be sincerely grateful for something, but until you express your gratitude to the giver, something is missing, incomplete. Similarly, praise is not just a heart attitude, it is the expression of that attitude. Attitudes of praise should produce expressions of praise. Lift up your voice—lift up your hands—let others know of your appreciation and joy.

Just as the uninhibited child who is filled with the emotions of joy will leap and jump and can hardly be made to sit still, so God knows that reception of His Divine joy will produce similar reactions in His joy-filled children.

I am not suggesting that we take our liberty to spin around like a top before the Lord in the downtown cathedral, but wouldn't it be nice to want to? Wouldn't it be proper to give a physical evidence of some kind to the joy God's presence brings to us even if we must restrict it to non-public worship sessions? It is not wrong to let your body demonstrate what your spirit feels, as long as it does not affect the liberty of someone else too adversely.

The sixth method of praise listed in Psalm 149 is, "Let them praise his name in the dance" (v. 3). The *International Standard Bible Encyclopedia* tells us that dancing in Old Testament times was primarily a leaping, often to musical accompaniment. When we read that "David danced before the Lord with all his might" (2 Sam. 6:14), we have a picture of him leaping higher and higher as he ran before the returning ark. His joy was unbounded. He had laid aside his kingly robes and wore the simple linen ephod, as a priest before the Lord, and excelled all the priests in his expression of joy that the symbol of the Lord's presence was returning to Jerusalem.

Psalm 150:4 also calls for us to "Praise him with the ... dance." Literally it says, "Praise Him by leaping before Him." Why? Perhaps this "leaping" has best been explained by David in Psalm 30:11-12: "Thou hast turned for me my mourning into dancing: thou hast put off my sackcloth, and girded me with gladness; To the end that my glory may sing praise to thee, and not be silent. O Lord my God, I will give thanks unto thee for ever." David's leaping and dancing before the Lord was simply a physical demonstration of the great change God had effected in him. It was an expression of the emotion of gladness, and he saw it as a method of giving thanks unto the Lord.

Perhaps the greatest point of resistance in praise is in allowing one's body to become involved in responding to the Lord. Repeatedly I have seen people become angry at even the suggestion that they lift their hands before the Lord, much less dance before Him. I've spent many hours counseling with people who "just couldn't see the sense in raising hands as part of worship," yet without exception when they finally overcame their rebellion and raised their hands, they broke into beautiful beginning praise.

At a conference in Florida recently, a woman reported to me that she had broken into praise the previous day because, for the first time in her life, she had been able to raise her hands in public. When I congratulated her for such an exercise of will, she said it was not due to her will, but because her husband had reached over, taken her hands, and jerked them up into the air. Nonetheless, it brought her the desired release.

There is something about getting the body involved that brings an inner release. I suppose there is something in our pride that does not want to "make a spectacle of ourselves." We have not yet learned to release ourselves fully in the presence of the Lord. We get physically involved in releasing our emotions at sporting events, but feel it is beneath our precious dignity to do so in church. We are urged, nevertheless, to lift our hands

(Ps. 63:4); clap our hands (Ps. 47:1); stand before the Lord (Ps. 135:2); bow down before the Lord and kneel before Him (Ps. 95:6); and dance, or leap, before the Lord (Ps. 149:3).

Finally, this 149th Psalm suggests, in verse 3, "Let them sing praises unto him with the timbrel and harp." Playing instruments in connection with praise and worship is mentioned at least sixteen times in the Old Testament and four times in the New. Although some other species of God's creation can make limited musical intonations, man is the only one of God's creatures that can make a mechanical contrivance and then play music on it. Man is not only creative and artistic, but he has a soul that cries out for expression in various forms of music including instrumentation. Psalm 150 lists every class of musical instrument known in that day and says, "Praise Him with these."

Israel used the trumpet to sound the alarm, to rally her armies, and to call the people to worship. Psalm 81:3 refers to the call throughout the land to return to Jerusalem for one of the three required feast days: "Blow up the trumpet in the new moon, in the time appointed, on our solemn feast day." The keynote of the feasts was joy and praise.

Often we feel that praise must be a private thing, yet as we have seen, the Scripture clearly teaches us that praise should also be a public expression. The purpose for our coming together is worship, and praise is a vital part of that worship.

Let Psalm 149 be your handbook on beginning to praise. First, get involved personally, "Praise ye the Lord." Second, "Sing unto God." Third, unite in congregational praise. Fourth, learn to "brighten up" when coming into His Presence. Fifth, we need to allow ourselves to be "joyful" and to release our emotions Godward. Sixth, we can praise the Lord in the dance. Allow your body some participation in worship. And seventh, play whatever instrument you can as a praise before the Lord.

Recently I was a speaker at a large youth gathering in a major Canadian city. I was startled to see a young man, in his mid-twenties, stand up on the platform with two tiny bells in his hands. As we sang, he played those two tiny bells, and with over 2,000 people singing, several guitars being amplified, and a hugh pipe organ blasting forth, I doubt if he was heard even in the front row. But as I watched his face, I realized he wasn't playing to be heard; he was praising the Lord on those two bells, and he was lost in his praise.

You need not do great things to become a praiser, you need only do something! Praise is neither thought or feeling, it is expression! It should not be governed by emotion, it should be a releasing of the emotion. Praise begins in the spirit of man, is governed by the will of man, and in its expression uses the whole of man.

Praise ye the Lord.

8

Persuasions to Praise

As a teenage preacher, I did not get involved very much in dating girls and was quite sure that I would never marry. But about the second month I was in Bible college, I noticed a young lady who had arrived late in the fall term. Before long, she was assigned as the pianist to the ministry team in which I was the preacher. There was something different about this girl. Just being with her persuaded me to drastically reappraise my stand on dating. Before the school year was over, I had been so persuaded by her company that I proposed marriage to her, and on June 20, 1943, Judson "the woman-hater" became Judson the married man. Oh, the power of persuasion!

Twenty-six times the New Testament uses some form of the word "persuade." Perhaps the two most familiar instances are: "For I know whom I have believed, and *am persuaded* that he is able to keep that which I have committed unto him against that day" (2 Tim. 1:12); and "For I *am persuaded,* that neither death, nor life, nor angels, nor principalities, nor powers, nor things present, nor things to come, Nor height, nor depth, nor any other creature, shall be able to separate us from the love of God, which is in Christ Jesus our Lord" (Rom. 8:38-39). Saul

the persecutor became Paul the persuaded! Something happened that caused him to reverse his viewpoint.

This is the way the Lord brings us into praise. He does not use force, but He does present facts. He is far less commanding in this matter of praise than He is conciliatory. He does not want to make us praise Him, He wants to motivate us into praise. Unless there is an inner desire that is responding to Divine stimuli, our praise would be no more pleasing to God than the "thank you" of a child who had been threatened with punishment if he did not say those words of appreciation. An old song we used to sing included the words, "He would not force them against their will, He just made them willing to go." How illustrative this is of God's methods of bringing us into praise and worship. He persuades us!

In the first seven verses of the 149th Psalm there are at least seven motivations for praise listed, seven persuaders God uses to move us to respond to Him in praise.

The first persuasion is to praise God for who He is! "Praise ye the *Lord*" (v. 1). Until we get a glimpse of who He is, we'll never be good praisers. We must see Him as gracious; we must see Him as merciful; we must see Him as plenteous in love and full of compassion. We must see Him as He is revealed in His Word, not as He is expressed in religion.

When God began to lead our church in Oregon into praise, it didn't take us two years to learn to raise our hands or say "Hallelujah" and "Praise the Lord." But it took us two years to come into a praise that was a real release of what was within us. We found it necessary to re-evaluate the Lord in our concepts before we could fully praise Him. Because of our religious heritage, some of us were bound in legalism. Our concept of God was the concept of an officer of the law, observing us with an eye to our failures, and it's hard to praise that kind of a God.

Others, because of their background, had such a high and lofty concept of God that they considered Him unapproachable. They couldn't imagine His being involved with us personally. Trying to come into His presence with praise was akin to seeking an audience with the President of the United States or with the Queen of England. But slowly the Holy Spirit re-guided us through the Bible to see that the Word makes God very available and deeply related to us. He is revealed as "Father," "Brother," "Husband," "Bridegroom," enabling us to respond to Him on a comfortable level.

When my wife and I were ministering in Indonesia at a minister's institute, we were told not to expect much in the way of emotional response. Because of the extremely crowded living conditions on the island of Java and the depth to which they were rooted in their ancient culture, emotional response had been greatly repressed. In this conference we had about 350 pastors representing some twenty-eight different denominations and foundations, which was quite a cross-section of religion for Indonesia.

All we did was lift up Jesus as we taught the Word. We were not preaching on praise or worship; we taught on the call of God to Moses. But when these brethren began to see what David had seen, they also began to feel what David had felt—and to do what David had done. Without instruction or urging, they began to weep, shout, clap their hands, praise, and on one occasion, even marched around the building rejoicing in the Lord. As their concept of God was lifted to a fresh orientation, their response was spontaneous and free. They praised because they saw the person of God. They got involved with the Divine Presence.

One of the finest and strongest motivations to praise is simply seeing Him as He is presented in the Word. As we lift up Jesus anew and see Him as loving and gentle, as the total provision for our needs in this life as well as King, there will be

a response of praise unto the Lord, because love must find an expression, and praise is a natural response of love. We Praise Him, first of all, for who He is.

Secondly, we praise Him for what He has done. "Let Israel rejoice in him that made him" (Ps. 149:2). Over in Isaiah 43:1 we read, "Now thus saith the Lord that created thee, O Jacob, and he that formed thee, O Israel, Fear not: for I have redeemed thee, I have called thee by thy name; thou art mine." He has created us; He has formed us; He has redeemed us; He has called us, and He has accepted a father's responsibility over us. This should evoke praise responses within us. Some of us have needlessly created problems for ourselves that have hindered praising. A problem that I had for many years, going way back to my boyhood days, was that I did not like my physical build. My father was the runt of his family, being only six feet, one inch, tall. When my brothers came along, they out-distanced dad by several inches. There was a tradition in our home that when one of us boys passed the height of dad, he got a free milkshake, which, in the depth of the Depression, was a great reward. Well, after many years of "struggle," I finally passed the height of my mother and got an ice cream cone. My brothers are tall, well-built, athletic men, but by stretching my frame to its maximum height, I reach barely five feet nine inches.

For years I carried a tremendous sense of inferiority when I was around my brothers. They made the football team; I made cheerleader. They possessed all the qualities considered "manly," while I was interested in music and books.

But one day, as I was reading Isaiah 43:1, the Holy Spirit said, "Judson, I made you short and gentle."

Previously, I had figured that since I was the first child in the family, God had seen His mistake and corrected it on my brothers. But as I meditated on that verse, my inner bitterness and resentment began to fade. *He* had made me exactly as I am.

96

As this truth began to overwhelm me, He spoke further: "My son, I not only made you, I re-made you. I not only formed you in the womb of your mother, I have also formed you in the womb of the Spirit, and I have re-created you so that you are becoming what I chose you to be from the foundations of the earth."

You will never know the new realm of praise this released within me. God made me, and He re-made me. He formed me, and He re-formed me. He created me, and He re-created me. He caused me to be born and to be born again.

I believe that you are what you are because of a pattern God has chosen for your life, as well as the choices you have made in your life. But even though your choices haven't been wise, He is nonetheless able to overrule them and bring them into His wisdom, and this should bring forth praise. Don't condemn yourself because you have a Catholic heritage, or Lutheran, or Presbyterian. I had to stop condemning myself because I had a Pentecostal heritage. It isn't what we were, it's what we are becoming that is of concern to God.

In spite of our background, he is bringing us into His foreground, and by a process of melting, molding, and shaping, He is forming us into His own image, making us accepted in the beloved, and causing us to be seated with Him in the Heavenlies. And that should produce a praise within our hearts that demands an expression through our mouths. (What I was never able to effect within me, He is able to perfect in me through the operation of His Spirit, so I just stand back and rejoice and praise the Lord that He is doing what I could not do.)

A third persuasion to praise is also given in this second verse: "Let the children of Zion *be joyful* in their King." How important it is to learn to direct our emotions, for if we do not direct them, they will direct us, and what a miserable life it is to

be directed from the emotional level. Obviously, we have only one set of emotions, and these must be used by our spirit and our soul, as well as God's Spirit. Unless there is some means of discharging these emotions safely, they will become overloaded and potentially dangerous. There is nothing more prone to danger than a group of people who are emotionally charged. This forms the basis for all sorts of mob actions. Somehow it causes people to lose sensibility. If overcharged emotionally, we tend to respond to further stimulus without rational consideration. Praise is a God-given, scripturally taught channel of release for the emotions. It enables us to release pent-up feelings in a safe, positive fashion that blesses God and builds us up.

It seems unfair, and potentially unsafe, to build high levels of emotional feeling in our worship service through singing, exhortation, and preaching of the Word if we are not going to give worshipers an opportunity to discharge those emotions. Praise is the divinely appointed manner of release. One of the charges assessed against services with an emotional content is that they tend to produce looseness of behavior among the people. The charge is worth looking at seriously. If the worship service tends to charge people emotionally, and we offer no united way of discharging the emotions, we can expect emotional actions and reactions among the people as they meet socially afterwards. Deep stirrings of love are easily transferred from one person to another. The feeling of joy easily finds as its object something other than that which produced the joy.

It is not too uncommon for people to transfer religious feelings to physical feelings, and nothing delights Satan more. As an answer to this danger, some have felt it safest not to arouse emotions in their religious ritual. Yet Oswald Smith wisely observed, "If you take emotion out of religion, you'll have no motion." The answer is not to restrict the emotion but to release it! Let the saints "be joyful in their King." Learn to release

your inner feelings in praise and adoration of God. Let Him benefit from what He has produced within you. If He has stirred you to love, let your love responses be toward Him. If He has stirred you to the deepest love and appreciation you have ever felt, release it back to Him. He desires it and warmly receives it, and in the process of releasing it, you have spent your emotions and leave them clear for stimuli from other sources.

In my earlier days of pastoring, I used to wind myself to a high emotional pitch each Sunday. I would pray late on Saturday night, rise early Sunday morning for prayer, teach a class in Sunday school, and preach twice on Sunday after conducting the preliminaries of the worship services. By Sunday night, I was so keyed up, I couldn't relax enough to go to sleep, so in pre-television days, I would read until two in the morning, when exhaustion overtook the nervous tension. In later years, I did it the easier way by watching TV until exhaustion overwhelmed me. Usually my Sunday would be followed by a "blue Monday," and it would often take all of Tuesday to bring me out of the slump, for all emotional highs will have equally emotional lows, if we allow them to rule us instead of ruling them.

When I began to move into praise, I learned that the thing that had been wrong was simply that I had not learned to discharge my emotions so that I could relax and sleep. So I learned to release this pent-up emotion unto Him in praise—in song, in clapping my hands, in leaping before the Lord, or whatever avenue of worship seemed most appropriate at the moment. Delightfully, I learned that this not only released me emotionally so I could relax, but it was accepted by the Lord as love and praise. Now when I get all keyed up and can't sleep, I just have a praise session and release all the emotions Godward. It is a good thing to express your emotions to God, and praise is the finest expression that the Scripture has given to us.

A fourth motivation to praise God is given in verse 4 of Psalm 149. "For the Lord taketh pleasure *in his people.*" *In his people.* When we read, with our limited understanding, the Scriptures concerning the heavens, we tend to feel God must get great pleasure out of all of that. We read of His angels, His glory, His grandeur, His beauty, His throne, and His dominion and power, and we say, "That must give great pleasure to God." Then we read of His creation and again feel this must give great satisfaction to God. We are ourselves so overwhelmed with the creation of God that we have spent billions of dollars to send a few men to the moon just to pick up some rock samples.

But the Scriptures speak of the creation as simply "God's handiwork" (Ps. 19:1). The Hebrew word used here means "needlework, such as crochet or tatting." The entire stellar system that stirs our deepest imaginations is little more than God's hobby expression—just something He did with His hands in a little spare time.

The Scripture says, however, that He takes pleasure *in His people.* We are the object of the pleasure of God. (We dealt with this in chapter two when considering the God-ward side of the purpose of praise.) God's program is to take pleasure in His people, to be completed in His people, to be satisfied in His people. Man is His glory.

When you genuinely love a person, you are constantly looking for some little way to please them. You listen for every hint or suggestion, because you know a birthday or Christmas is coming. We don't want to ask them outright, nor do we want to miss pleasing them. If we do catch a word, a hint, a suggestion, we hide it in our heart until we can fulfill that expressed desire. God has suggested that praise is the finest gift you can give Him.

Why? When God says, "This gives me pleasure," don't wait until you are mature enough in your relationship to understand

why, for you will never mature in that relationship until you obey Him without having to understand the whys. The fact that He says He likes it should be sufficient motivation for you to do it.

Some years ago, as we were becoming aware of this truth in our church, my sister, under the inspiration of the Spirit, wrote an entire Christmas cantata with praise as its theme. The chorus woven into the cantata repeatedly was, "Sing praise to the Christ of Christmas." It shocked people the first time it was presented, for few had thought of actually praising on Christmas. The second reaction, however, was to take another look at it. We used the cantata repeatedly, for it seemed more appropriate to praise on Christmas than to do anything else. Jesus doesn't need the gold, and frankincense, and the myrrh, but He is obviously pleased with our praise. Psalm 103:21 declares, "Bless ye the Lord...ye ministers of his, that do his pleasure." It is in the blessing of the Lord, in praising Him, that we are giving pleasure unto God.

A fifth motivating persuasion to praise is seen in Psalm 149:4: "The Lord...will beautify the meek with salvation." We are, moved to praise Him when we see what we've become! Please stop saying, "No good thing dwelleth in me," for God dwells within you. He is putting His Spirit within, with all of His glory and beauty. Even the most homely of us have been beautified with the workings of God. As you read the Song of Solomon, you will note that again and again he describes the beauty of the girl. It is a conferred beauty, it is a Divine beauty, it is a glorious beauty—but it has become her beauty!

Some years ago, the Lord spoke to me and said He felt it was time for me to see my inner self as He saw it. I pleaded with Him not to give me such a revelation at that time. I felt it would completely devastate me. I was headed to South America for ministry and was fearful and full of self-doubts already. However, He was most insistent that day, and more against my

will than with the cooperation of that will, the Lord began to describe me.

I will never forget the experience! For more than an hour the Lord spoke of the way the Godhead saw me. He described ministries I have not yet come into. He spoke of inner qualities I know I do not now possess. He described my motivations as He saw them, my mannerisms, my methods, and my ministries. After a lengthy period of hearing, I interrupted the flow of the Spirit by protesting that this certainly was not a description of me. He must have someone else in mind, for the picture He had painted bore very little resemblance to the Judson Cornwall I had lived with for nearly half a century.

His reply to my protest was, "My son, I have been describing you as We see you, for We are looking at the blueprints of your life. As a master architect sees the building completed when he is looking at the drawings, so We see the finished product from the beginning. As you see yourself, you are only an excavated hole in the ground with footings poured and some steel reinforcing in place. Everything around you seems to be in disarray. But We see you as complete in Christ and have described what you shall be in Him." Hallelujah!

When Jesus comes for His church, He is not coming for a worn-out, beaten-down, decrepit, aging bride that He has to sneak out in the dark of the night because of shame. The Scripture says He is going to come for a church that is glorious—without spot, or wrinkle, or blemish, or any such thing. Does that fit your present observation of the church? How, then, can the necessary change be effected? He is cleansing the church, changing the church, and conferring His beauty upon her. He will present the bride unto Himself in the form He desires her to be. As she praises Him, He changes her. What a persuasion to praise! Every look into a mirror should motivate us to further praising of the Lord.

The next major persuasion to praise given in Psalm 149 is that it brings us into God's presence. Verse 1 speaks of praising "in the congregation of saints," while verse 6 speaks of letting "the high praises of God be in their mouth." When Ken Taylor translated Ephesians 3:15 in *The Living Bible,* he wrote, "I ... pray to the Father of all the great family of God—some of them already in heaven and some down here on earth ..."

How short-sighted most of us are in believing that the true church of God is totally here on earth, some of us even believing that it is in the walls of our denomination or even our local church. God's church is far greater than anything on earth right now. It is composed of saints of all the ages, some of whom have already gone on to their reward in the presence of the Lord, and others now living and representing Christ on the earth. Some are worshiping God on earth, the rest are worshiping God in heaven. But all are praising.

In Hebrews 12:22-24 we read that we, the living and earthbound, "*are* come unto" nine "things:" "But ye are come unto mount Sion, and unto the city of the living God, the heavenly Jerusalem, and to an innumerable company of angels, To the general assembly and church of the firstborn, which are written in heaven, and to God the Judge of all, and to the spirits of just men made perfect, and to Jesus the mediator of the new covenant, and to the blood of sprinkling, that speaketh better things than that of Abel." All these things are in the heavenlies.

As we looked at Isaiah 6:1-4 and Revelation 19:1-7, we saw everything praising and worshiping the Lord! Praise seems to be the main occupation on high. Praises on high, or "high praises."

When Psalm 149 calls us to join the "congregation of saints" and to enter with "the high praises of God ... in their mouths," I believe it is saying that there are times when the church on earth rises in her praise levels to join the praise level of the church

in heaven. All our praising is imperfect, but that part of the church that has already entered into the heavenlies has, by now, learned a far more perfect form of praise. They have "seen Him as He is" and are motivated by spiritual vision, not earthly and carnal reasonings. When we can join our praise with their praise, we enter into a much higher realm of praise. We have already mentioned that Psalm 22:3 states that God "inhabitest the praises of Israel." Here, however, we see that not only does God come down to join us in our praising, but there are times when our praising elevates us into the spiritual heavenlies, and as Paul, we find ourselves "caught up to the third heaven" (2 Cor. 12:2).

To transcend time and space and enter into that "other world" that is entirely spiritual is a desire deep in the heart of almost everyone, although often so repressed as to be hidden even from the individual. In fact, it is this repressed craving that gives rise to the occult and witchcraft. Man wants to break the barrier of his small world. God has offered us a "time-space machine" that enables us to enter into His world and presence. He calls it high praises. Shouldn't this persuade you to become a praiser of the Lord?

The seventh persuading motivation to praise in this Psalm is that praise becomes the key weapon in our battle against Satan, verse 7. But since this is at the heart of the next chapter "The Power of Praise," we will not discuss it now beyond saying that rebuking Satan was beyond even the scope of authority given Michael, who was of equal rank with Lucifer in the heavenlies. Praise is our greatest weapon against the Satanic!

Are these motivations sufficient to cause you to magnify the Lord? Lift up your voice and praise the Lord. Praise Him for who He is. Praise Him for what He has done. Praise Him to release your emotions of joy. Praise Him to give Him pleasure. Praise Him for the beauty He is producing in you. Praise Him to enter into His presence. Just praise Him.

9

The Power of Praise

"**W**hy boastest thou thyself in mischief, O mighty man?...God shall likewise destroy thee for ever ... I will praise thee for ever, because thou hast done it" (Psalm 52:1, 5, 9).

The 149th Psalm, that has given us some guidelines in the performance of praise and has gently sought to persuade us to praise, also teaches us that there is tremendous power in praise. God has not left us defenseless, He has given us mighty spiritual weapons, and praise is chief among them.

In Psalm 149:7-9, there are five specific functions of praise that illustrate to us the greatness, the magnitude, the loftiness, and the power of praise, when it is used as a weapon. First, it says we can "execute vengeance upon the heathen" (v. 7). Secondly, it declares that we can execute "punishments upon the people" (v. 7). Third, praise is "to bind their kings with chains" (v. 8), and fourth, "to bind ... their nobles with fetters of iron" (v. 8). The fifth function of praise is "to execute upon them the judgment written" (v. 9).

Praise is immensely powerful! It is eternally effective! It enables us to deal directly in the spirit world. It allows us to come to grips with rebellious men and demonic forces and gain the victory over them. All with praise—high praise!

In seeking to understand this, let's define the enemies listed here, then seek to understand the weapon offered, and finally see if we can comprehend the nature of the conflict. As to the nature of the enemy, there are two classes of men mentioned and two categories in the spirit world. The men are called "heathen" and "the people." The expression "heathen" in the Old Testament consistently refers to those who are without God—those who have no knowledge of God, no acceptance of Him, and no relationship to Him. There is to be an execution of vengeance upon them.

"The people," in contrast to "the heathen" in verse 7, most likely refers to God's covenant people who were often called "the Lord's people" or simply "the people." These are not to know God's vengeance, only punishment from God. God deals with the heathen one way, and with His people another. The Scriptures declare, "For whom the Lord loveth he chasteneth, and scourgeth every son whom he receiveth" (Heb. 12:6). Also, "But when we are judged, we are chastened of the Lord, that we should not be condemned with the world" (1 Cor. 11:32).

The two categories of the spirit world mentioned are "their kings" and "their nobles" (v. 8). The king of the heathen is Satan. He is considered the god of this age. Jesus himself referred to him as "the prince of this world" (John 14:30; 16:11), and Paul called him "the prince of the power of the air" (Eph. 2:2). If their king is Satan, then their nobles would be the lesser powers in the Satanic realm. Ephesians 6:11-12 lists the Satanic kingdom's five levels of authority: "Put on the whole armour of God, that ye may be able to stand against the wiles of [1] the devil. For we wrestle not against flesh and blood, but against [2] principalities, against [3] powers, against [4] the rulers of

the darkness of this world, against [5] spiritual wickedness in high places."

While it is not in the scope of this book to try to fully define each of these levels, we are aware that Satan's kingdom is patterned after God's kingdom and has decreasing levels of power from Satan, through the other fallen angels, to the demons (evil spirits). (See "Demons" in the appendix.)

All are under the control of Satan their king as Revelation 16:13-14 affirms: "And I saw, issuing from the mouth of the dragon [a New Testament name for Satan] ... three foul spirits like frogs; for they are demonic spirits, performing signs, who go abroad to the kings of the whole world" (RSV).

Also, remember that the Jews charged Jesus with casting out demons through Beelzebub the chief of the devils (Luke 11:15). Strong, in his Greek dictionary, (appended to his complete concordance) affirms that "Beelzebub" is a name of Satan. Satan, in Christ's time, was recognized as chief of the devils. The demons are certainly not "free agents;" they issue from Satan's mouth and are under his headship as Beelzebub.

There is a noticeable progression in this listing of the enemies in Ephesians 6:11-12. From the heathen, who are quite non-threatening to most of us; to "the people" to whom we are far more vunerable because of the fellowship of love; to Satan, with whom few of us will ever have a direct confrontation; to the progressively depreciating power of his kingdom, against which we probably struggle more than against all the others put together. Yet, we are taught that praise is a weapon against them all.

We need to look at this weapon called "high praises." There are degrees of praise, just as there are degrees of anointing. We usually start praising in the lower levels of faith and anointing, often getting involved first in the realm of the soulish, the emotions, and then moving into the realm of the mind, the will,

and finally through our spirit, into His Spirit. When we begin to release God's Spirit through using praise, we are reaching a higher realm of praise.

The praise spoken of here as being a weapon against the enemies of the Kingdom of God is called, specifically, "high praises of God." This refers to the praises being offered on high: "Let the saints be joyful in *glory* [in heaven]: let them sing aloud upon their beds [on earth]" (Ps. 149:5).

We are not yet made perfect. We are still greatly limited in our perception of spiritual things. We are not aware of being surrounded by an innumerable company of angels, although the Scripture teaches us that we are. Yet there are times when we begin to soar in the Spirit, and are allowed of God to enter into the praise of the full church of Christ. The segment that we belong to here joins the praise of the segment that is up there. The main activity of the church that has gone on is worship and praise, and they have come into perfection in this because they behold the face of the One they are praising. They have come into an understanding of justice. They've come into an understanding of vengeance. They now comprehend the true Lordship of Christ over the earth. They see into the purposes of God. They can praise better and higher because they can see what we cannot see.

We're performing in faith; they're performing in fact. We're functioning in flesh; they're functioning in spirit. They have been taught by the angels; we have been taught of man. We are very limited; they are unlimited. Were it not for the common bond of the blood of Christ and the love of God, there might very well never be anything analogous between these groups. Yet Hebrews 12:1 speaks of the heavenly group being "a cloud of witnesses," cheering the earthly group on in the race of life.

At times God allows us, in our praises, to rise above our emotional levels, and even above our faith level, and join praises

with the heavenly forces. Often, when this happens, we are not consciously aware that we have joined praises with angels and the spirits of just men made perfect. But just as surely as there was a joining of Jesus with Moses and Elijah on the Mount of Transfiguration, so, I believe, there are times of joining of the Saints on earth with the Saints in glory, in responses of praise that enable us to let the high praises of God be in our mouth. When we get so joined and involved, when the saints are in communion, if you like, our praise is purer, stronger, and more properly directed—even though we may be saying the same words we've always said. And there comes a new direction, a new flow, a new depth of faith, a fresh authority in our praise.

It is interesting that where our translation says these high praises are to be in our "mouth," the literal Hebrew is "in their throats." Just as Jesus did not say it would be out of the brain but out of the belly that rivers of living water should flow (John 7:38), so here it does not say the high praises would be in the mind but in the throat. As surely as tongues go beyond the conscious level (supraconscious), so some praises go beyond the mental level of the conscious mind and are the result of direct inspiration of the Holy Spirit. It is as though the Spirit Himself is doing the praising. It may be in tongues, yet is more likely to be in your own language. But your intellect is not feeding your vocal chords, the Holy Spirit is directing the expression of praise. He is taking the heavenly "high praises" and flowing them into your mouth. When this happens, you are not just dealing with praise as an expression, you're dealing with praise as a weapon, and what a fabulous weapon praise is!

"Let the high praises of God be in their mouth, and a two-edged sword in their hand" (Ps. 149:6). Never reverse God's prescribed order. The praise is to be in the mouth, not the sword. The first chapter of Revelation shows the sword in the mouth of Christ, but nowhere does the Scripture put the sword in the mouth of the saints. It belongs in their *hand.* Ephesians 6:17

calls this, "the sword of the Spirit, which is the word of God." When we try to battle with the sword in our mouth, we only wound, divide, and slay. How the Body of Christ has been hurt by indiscriminate quoting of Scripture one to another as "proof texts" or "Scripture clubs," to force or coerce another to our viewpoint. It's not the quoting of Scripture that is going to bring us into victory, but the release of the high praises of God through our mouth!

Yes, we need the Scriptures, but keep them in the hand. What we really need is the combination of the Spirit and the Word, praises based upon the promises, spoken words flowing from the written Word, responses Godward based upon revelations manward from the Word.

Now that we've seen the enemies, and something of the weapon God has given us to use against these enemies, let's seek to understand the nature of the conflict and how to use our weapon of praise.

The 149th Psalm says our weapon can successfully "execute *vengeance* upon the heathen, and *punishments* upon the people; ... *bind* their kings *with chains,* and their nobles with *fetters of iron;* ... execute upon them the judg*ment written*" *(v. 7-9).*

It is difficult for some to see God as both a God of love and a God of judgment. The concept of using praise to bring vengeance, punishment, binding, and judgment upon others causes some people to cringe. They declare that this is not New Testament at all, that this isn't the God that they know. But it really is the New Testament and the God that you *should* know!

In Revelation 6:10 we hear the voice of the martyrs crying, "How long, O Lord, holy and true, dost thou not judge and avenge our blood on them that dwell on the earth?" and in Revelation 11:17-18 we hear the twenty-four elders worshiping God saying, "We give thee thanks, O Lord God Almighty ...

because thou hast taken to thee thy great power, and hast reigned. And the nations were angry, and thy wrath is come. . .and shouldest destroy them which destroy the earth."

God declares in His Word, "Vengeance is mine; I will repay, saith the Lord" (Rom. 12:19). God doesn't want you to have a vengeful spirit, because He knows it will destroy you. Man is not strong enough to handle vengeance, so Jesus said, "Love your enemies, do good to them which hate you, Bless them that curse you, and pray for them which despitefully use you" (Luke 6:27-28).

God simply says, "I'm strong enough to hold this in remembrance, and if they will not submit to the love that is flowing through you, vengeance is Mine. I'll take care of it for you."

When I read, in the church history books, of the thousands who have been slain by the heathen; or review *Fox's Book of Martyrs* and see the inhumanities of man to man because of his testimony of God; and when I see, in my ministry to pastors throughout the world, what people—Christian people—have done to some of God's servants, something inside me cries out, "Oh, God, don't forget Your promise that vengeance is Yours! Don't forget to repay them!" It is not because I am harsh or hard-hearted; I am, in reality, quite soft-hearted. But I cannot handle seeing people destroyed by other people, and continue to love the destroyers, unless I know that God is a just God as well as a justifier. I must be aware that God ultimately will pour out His vengeance upon those who reject His love. Since I know that vengeance is His, and the punishments are written, I can continue to love—because that is the only hope of yet reaching them for Christ.

Our position is not to plead for vengeance or judgment, we are to let the high praises of God be in our mouth. We can praise God, when normally we would be calling for vengeance,

because we know God is a just God. And we know that He will take care of it His way.

Some years ago, on a Sunday morning in our church, we were moved into a very high level of praise. It flowed like a river, and continued to lift us higher and still higher into realms of praise, greater than we had ever experienced before. We could see no visible results among us, but there was a sense of understanding that God was doing something very extraordinary. That afternoon I received a phone call from a young man who had gone out from our congregation to pastor a church less than two hundred miles from us. He asked what had been happening in the church about 11:15 that morning. I told him of the beautiful high level of praise we had reached, and asked him why he had asked about it. He explained that at 11:15 one of his deacons stood to his feet in the midst of the meeting and began walking down the center aisle of the church with anger in his eyes. As the treasurer of the church and its most moneyed member, he had for years assumed the leadership in matters of policy and managed to have his own way. Before the entire congregation he said, "Pastor, I demand your resignation. I'm sick and tired of this emphasis on praise and your constant calls to prayer."

I was familiar with the history of that church, and knew that deacon had successfully demanded and received the resignation of other pastors. This young pastor did not know what to do. He looked at the deacon, looked at his own wife, and began to quake with an inner fear. The deacon advanced further and repeated his demand for a resignation. When he got to about the second row of pews he suddenly stopped, his eyes opened wide as though he saw something, and he turned white with fear. He reached into his pocket, pulled out pen and paper, and began to write a note. He handed it to the pastor behind the pulpit and hastily walked out the front door of the church. The note was his resignation as deacon.

As soon as the man left the church, the glory of the Lord filled the building, and the congregation came into a beautiful level of praise and worship, and people began to make things right one with another. The pastor still had not made any movement; he was dumbfounded. During the time of praise and worship, he asked the Lord what had happened. The Lord told him that the home church had gone into high praises which enabled God Himself to deal with the rebel directly. "[With] the high praises of God ... in their mouth ... [they] execute punishments upon the people."

This, however, is not the end of the story. Some time later, I received a letter from a South American country where a young man from our congregation was laboring. He asked what had happened on that very same Sunday. Then he told me that three of the town officials had determined to close their church, using some technicality of a previous violation of building codes in the construction of the building. The word had gone out that anyone who attended the church would be arrested, and not many people were taking a chance on that. At the time our congregation was in praise, this young man went to his late afternoon service, which they had instead of an evening service, only to find an empty building. He went in, picked up his accordion, and began to have a one-man song service. The blessing of the Lord began to fill his soul, so he had a testimony service—both leading and participating in it. He then felt led to go ahead and preach the message he had prepared for his people, even to giving an altar call, as usual. To his utter amazement, two members of the city council walked through the doors of the church and came to the altar. These men had been standing outside, watching through the window, having come to arrest anyone attending the services. They were so over-awed at the sight of a preacher conducting a service with nobody there, that they had remained to watch. The Lord came in His convicting power upon them, and they were persuaded to answer His call. As a result, the church now has the official

113

blessing of the city. They have had to enlarge the building twice since then. The praising of one congregation reached out many thousands of miles and did the impossible.

Praise not only works as a foil for men, whether heathen or Christians, it is also a most effective weapon against the evil-spirit world. This passage promises that with "the high praises of God ... in their mouth ... [they] bind their kings with chains, and their nobles with fetters of iron." We've already determined that this is the Satanic kingdom. Jesus clearly stated that we are not going to be successful in taking out of the strong man's house that which we think is ours, unless we first bind the strong man (Mark 3:27). The time has come for the church of Jesus Christ to come back to the position where we bind the strong man with chains and his lesser emissaries with fetters of iron: then we can go in and totally spoil him of everything that he has taken from the church.

The church needs the faith that we let the enemy take away from us. We need the ministries that we have let the enemy steal. We need our children back, our love returned, our authorities in the Word restored. We can have them, if we will bind the "strong man" with "chains and fetters of iron." It is when we come into the high praises of God that God will bind the Satanic, put bondages upon it, put limitations on it, so that you and I have true deliverance and freedom. It is done with praise, not pleading. God wants His people to learn the lesson that if we will praise God with the high praises, He'll take care of any Satanic and demonic forces that are around, and bring forth a binding upon them, instead of letting them bring forth a binding upon us.

With the high praises of God in our mouth, balanced with the two-edged sword in our hand, we bind, put in chains, execute vengeance, bring forth Divine victory, transcend the miles, and bring unto God that which He has determined— "the judgment written"—whether deliverance or destruction.

114

Second Corinthians 10:3-5 tells us something about our weapons: "We do not war after the flesh: (For the weapons of our warfare are not carnal, but mighty through God to the pulling down of strong holds;) Casting down imaginations, and every high thing that exalteth itself against the knowledge of God, and bringing into captivity every thought to the obedience of Christ."

This passage was made very much alive to me some years ago. God was moving our church into a more vital relationship with Him through worship and praise, and one of the men of my board was very much against this moving. He and I had been good friends, but he now felt that I was absolutely wrong, and no amount of my seeking to communicate my vision could reach him. Levels of immaturity in me matched the levels of immaturity in him, and between the two of us, there arose a clash.

This man was a man of power, and he used his power against me. We were in a building program at the time, and he was the only man in my congregation who really understood construction. At one board meeting he declared, "Either Cornwall resigns as pastor and gets out, or I resign as being in charge of the building program, and I get out." After prayer, there was a short delay; then he took the key to the church out of his pocket and spoke directly to me. "Either your key is on the floor in ten seconds or mine is." I called what I thought was a bluff and found he was not bluffing. He threw his key down and that was that.

For months we were at opposite poles from each other. I felt I had done everything that could be done. I had pled with him, prayed for him, and finally, in my mind, written him off as hopeless. Then I began to read Ken Taylor's paraphrase, *The Living Letters*, and found he had translated the above passage in this way: "It is true that I am an ordinary, weak human being, but I don't use human plans and methods to win my battles. I

use God's mighty weapons, not those made by men, to knock down the devil's strongholds. These weapons can break down every proud argument against God and every wall that can be built to keep men from finding him. With these weapons I can capture rebels and bring them back to God, and change them into men whose hearts' desire is obedience to Christ. I will use these weapons against every rebel who remains after I have first used them on you yourselves, and you surrender to Christ."

God spoke to me, telling me that here was the solution to my longstanding problem. But I could not see it until He finally said, "My son, if you will use My weapon, you can drag that man back to captivity—to a man whose heart's desire is to serve Me. You can win him to Me, and to yourself, if you use My weapon. Praise Me for this man."

For a while, this was beyond my comprehension. But after finding no encouragement from other members of my staff, who, with me, had written this brother off as hopeless, I tried reading the verses aloud and said, "Lord, I praise You for this man and for everything he has done to me. And I praise You for this verse."

At first, the response on my part was very empty, but again God spoke. "If you can break through to *genuinely* praise Me for what that man has done and for what that man means to Me, I will make that verse come to pass in his life."

I praised for six hours—without success. I paused in the praising only long enough to minister in the evening service, then, sending my wife home alone, stayed in the office praising until the early hours of the morning. Finally God sparked faith to believe what I had been saying all those long hours. I was able to say with real genuineness, "I thank You, I praise You, I praise You for these two years. They have been glorious years, and I praise You for rescuing this man, as You have rescued me."

Naturally I expected to see this man be the first one at the altar call the following Sunday, but not so. He continued as belligerent and as antagonistic as before. But there was a change in me.

It was two full years later when we were having a teaching session on loving one another, that praise swung open the door of victory. Following the teaching, we were putting our love into action by greeting one another with a hug (men with men, women with women). As I was moving among the men, I noticed my still-resentful brother trapped in a corner, an observer, not a participant. I approached him and said, "For two years I have had nothing but love for you. I have never had a chance to tell you this, but I am going to tell you now. You have blessed me more than all my friends, because you have sent me to my knees. You have made me double-check everything twice in the Word. You have caused me to worship God as no one that loves me has caused me to worship God. Because of you, I have grown in God. My brother, I love you in the Lord." With this I embraced him and kissed him on the cheek. Later that evening, during the regular service, I had the feeling that I had failed again, but I felt good in my own spirit because it had been honest. God had brought me to a place where I really did love that man.

When the service was over, a friend came and told me that this brother wanted to see me. As I stepped toward him, he turned, and I saw that tears were streaming down his face. Calling me by a nickname of former years, he said, "Little Buddy, I can't take any more of it. I am sorry it happened. Can we just bury the hatchet and be friends in Jesus again?" God welded our spirits together and gave us years of warm relationship that continues to this day.

Saints, praise is a fabulous weapon! With it we can claim and conquer and bring men to a change of heart's desire. I think it would be good if we stopped worrying about our loved ones

and start praising God for their deliverance. I wonder if a lot of what we call intercession is not just an anxious mouthing of our unbelief. We do not think He heard us, so we are going to say it again. This is like the prayer wheels of China, or the water wheels of Japan, where prayers are written and attached in the belief that the prayer is prayed to the gods every time the wheel is given a spin. Once you know you have touched God in your requests, stop the petitioning and get involved in praising.

You may say, "If God has really heard, why do I not see the results?" That is because He has to answer without violating the will of the other person involved. He is having to bring him into submission through gentle channels of persuasion, and the greatest weapon you have is praise.

Do we always know whether the real enemy is men or demons? No! But God knows! If we will simply praise against all opposition, God will know against whom to move and with what level of force. "The battle is not yours, but God's" (2 Chron. 20:15). As we continue to praise, it affords heaven legal permission to engage in the conflict on our behalf. It is equivalent to signing a complaint or warrant against a law-breaker. Praise starts the whole legal process in motion. God is our defense. Praise Him with the highest praise you can produce, and then allow the Holy Spirit to begin a higher level of praise, that may very well lift you into the heavenlies to join the praisers up there. This will always produce a victory!

10

Preventives to Praise

In the light of all that we have seen thus far, you may well wonder why more people do not praise the Lord. I wonder if the answer, at least in part, isn't found in Romans 7:18-19, 21: "For I know that nothing good dwells within me, that is, in my flesh. I can will what is right, but I cannot perform it.—I have the intention and urge to do what is right, but no power to carry it out; For I fail to practice the good deeds I desire to do, but the evil deeds that I do not desire to do are what I am [ever] doing....So I find it to be a law [of my being] that when I want to do what is right and good, evil is ever present with me and I am subject to its insistent demands" (TAB).

Here is the great struggle and inner conflict that surfaces the moment we start to become a participant in praise. People who have been comfortable in their religion for years suddenly find themselves engaged in dissension, contention, and altercation. Even after the facts of praise are well known, the act of praise is painfully difficult. There are preventives to praise. Just what are these forces, or "laws [of my being]" (TAB), that work so possessively to prevent me from praising?

In my years of seeking to bring others into a life of praise, I have found at least seven major preventives to praise. There are undoubtedly others, but these seven seem to be the most deadly deterrents.

The first great preventive to praise, not necessarily because of its importance, but because Christians usually blame it for all negatives, is the interference of the Satanic kingdom. Having spent so many eons in service to the Kingdom of Heaven, Satan understands the value, purpose, and power of praise far better than do the people. Inasmuch as his basic purpose is to frustrate the workings of God's kingdom, he certainly will do his utmost to restrict the flow of praise from the children to the Father. Because he knows our "high praises" can put him in bondage and immobilize his demonic forces, his first line of defense is to attack our praise before it begins and certainly before it can join the heavenly praises.

The New Testament, however, teaches that the saints are not subject to Satan, but that Satan is subject to the saints! Romans 16:20 assures us, "And the God of peace shall bruise Satan under your feet shortly." Jesus gave His disciples power and authority, over "all devils" (Luke 9:1), and assured the believers that, "In my name shall they cast out devils" (Mark 16:17).

By His life, death, resurrection, and ascension, Jesus stripped the devil of all the power, authority, position, and rank that he had usurped and displayed before mankind. Hebrews 2:14, speaking of Jesus, says: "That through death he might destroy him that had the power of death, that is, the devil."

The Greek word translated here as "destroy," literally means to "reduce to a zero." Jesus reduced Satan to a nothing! He is a has-been. Our wonderful Lord Jesus Christ cut Satan down to the area of extremely limited power and authority he possessed in the Garden of Eden—the power of persuasion. He can only talk, entice, advertise, suggest, argue, or lie.

When Ephesians 4:27 says, "Neither give place to the devil," it sets it in a context that is discussing communication. Don't give place in your thought patterns to him. Don't talk to him, don't listen to him. Unless he has access to your mind, he is powerless to deter you from praise. He could surround you with ten thousand demons, and your praise would burn a pathway right through them. His only chance of preventing you from praising the Lord is to be able to talk you out of it, or to keep your mind so full of negative thoughts that you are unable to positively praise. Once you are fully aware of his impotence, Satan is probably the least forceful of the preventives to praise. He has no more power against you than you are willing to give him by your mental assent. "Submit yourselves therefore to God. Resist the devil, and he will flee from you" (James 4:7).

Perhaps the simple philosophy of a convert from deep sin would help those who feel the devil's intrusion into their thought patterns makes praise impossible. When asked how she could remain so victorious, she replied, "When Satan rings the doorbell, I just ask Jesus to answer the door."

A second, equally obvious preventive to praise is sin. As David so succinctly put it, "If I regard iniquity in my heart, the Lord will not hear me" (Ps. 66:18). The prophet Isaiah expressed it, "Your iniquities have separated between you and your God, and your sins have hid his face from you, that he will not hear" (Isa. 59:2). Praise is almost impossible if the recipient rejects it, refuses it, or won't even listen to it. We are unable to handle the rejection of silence for very long. If we try to express praise to God, and the heavens seem to be "as brass," don't rebuke the devil, repent from sin. Only sin can close God's ear to your praise. We are told to "lift up holy hands" unto the Lord, not defiled hands. It is the "voice of the redeemed," that gets an audience with God, not the voice of the rebel. God wants us to "call on the Lord out of a pure heart" (2 Tim. 2:22).

Of course, we do not praise the Lord out of our own righteousness, which, in His sight, is as "filthy rags," but out of the humble righteousness of Christ, which has been conferred upon us. Sin need be no more than confessed, and it is cleansed (1 John 1:9). Sin is no problem for God, only for religion. "The blood of Jesus Christ his Son cleanseth us from all sin" (1 John 1:7). "For by one offering He hath perfected for ever them that are sanctified ... And their sins and iniquities will I remember no more" (Heb. 10:14, 17). God dealt with sin, conclusively and eternally, at Calvary. No person need live in sin. Sin can be handled by confession and cleansing.

The cross of Jesus deals with sin as to its penalty, its power, its presence, and its guilt.

As to sin's penalty: "Much more then, being now justified by his blood, we shall be saved from wrath through him" (Rom. 5:9). "Justified," simply means just-as-if-I'd never sinned.

As to sin's power, Romans 6:14 declares, "Sin shall not have dominion over you: for ye are not under the law, but under grace." The Wesley brothers wrote and sang, "He broke the power of cancelled sin, and set the prisoner free. His blood can make the vilest clean, His blood availed for me."

As to sin's presence, God not only takes you out of "Egypt," He takes "Egypt" out of you. Immediately after Passover is the Red Sea, which will both totally destroy the enemy's power over you, and separate you forever from returning to the land from which you were delivered. 2 Peter 2:9 states "that ye should shew forth the praises of him who hath called you out of darkness into his marvellous light."

As to sin's guilt: "There is therefore now no condemnation to them which are in Christ Jesus, who walk not after the flesh, but after the Spirit" (Rom. 8:1). Looking at it from God's side, confessed sin becomes remitted guilt.

None need be hindered from praise because of sin. Deal with the sin first. Don't try to cover it; expose it to God. Confess it. Let Him cleanse it and remove every trace of it from you. Then you can praise the Lord out of purity. And you will have fresh motivation to praise!

A third preventive to praise, and one that is very strong in many Christians' lives, is guilt. If sin has not been handled, then the guilt is actual, but all too frequently, even after we have confessed the sin, we allow the guilt to linger in our consciousness. Sometimes this is the result of a weakness of faith. Instead of believing what the Word says, that we are forgiven, we believe what we feel, and we don't feel forgiven.

All of us feel the need to "do something" to remit guilt, yet the Bible declares that Jesus has already done everything necessary for the remission of sin. Once we have confessed our sin to Christ, anything further we attempt to do to remit that sin and its guilt is only a religious response. Since it produces nothing, we find it necessary to repeat it, or replace it with another act, that is even more penalizing than the first. And Satan, the accuser of the brethren, will use every argument to get us and keep us under condemnation. Every time we wring our hands over what wretched sinners we are, Satan certainly agrees, and if we are really mired in self-condemnation, we will agree with his agreeing. But finish the sentence: we are all wretched sinners, *saved by grace.* And who did Jesus come to save? *Sinners!* Praise God He did!

Not all sense of guilt is the result of a weakness of faith, however. Often it is the result of an unwillingness to forgive ourselves. We accept the truth of the Word that God has forgiven, but add, "I can never forgive myself." Are you greater than God? If He has forgiven you, why do you refuse to forgive yourself? Haven't you yet learned the great danger of an unforgiving spirit—even if you are the object of that unforgiveness? Ephesians 4:32 says, "And be ye kind one to

another, tenderhearted, forgiving one another, even as God for Christ's sake hath forgiven you." Have you lost sight of the fact that you are part of this brotherhood, this body?

Don't let your knowledge of your motivations, thought life, and dreams keep you from accepting His forgiveness, or from forgiving yourself. He knew all these inner workings when He said, "Neither do I condemn thee: go and sin no more" (John 8:11). You weren't forgiven because He didn't have all the facts. He knew, and forgave anyway. Walk out of guilt, let the shackles fall from your hands, so those hands may be lifted in praise. Get your eyes off your failures, and back onto your forgiving God, for this will motivate you to praise. Stop condemning your past; it is ruining your present, and destroying your chance for a praise-filled future.

When the Scripture promises, "if any man be in Christ, he is a new creature: old things are passed away; behold, all things are become new" (2 Cor. 5:17), that is exactly what it means. Dare to believe it. Conduct your life as a new person. The past is canceled and buried deep; there let it lie. Concern yourself with today; grasp it, and teach it to obey your will and plan. Praise is God's command for man. Don't let a false sense of guilt frustrate the will of God for your life.

A fourth, and possibly even stronger preventive to praise, is fear—fear of ourselves, fear of the opinion our peers, fear of God, fear to release inner feelings, fear of rejection, fear of ridicule, or just plain fear itself. There are few emotions in human experience that will immobilize and incapacitate a person faster than fear. Fear can stop sound reasoning, anesthetize the senses, and exercise a censorship over our will. So dangerous and so anti-God is fear that Revelation 21:8 lists "the fearful" among those who are cast into "the lake of fire." I do not believe it is so much that God is punishing them for their fear, as it is that their fear incapacitated them from entering into the

promises and provisions of God. That is why Jesus, after His resurrection, so often said, "Fear not."

I have seen people so controlled by fear that no amount of teaching on praise could move them to participate. I have watched them move all the way to the back walls of the room, withdrawing from all who were praising, as inner fear overcame conscious desire to participate in praise. Until the fear is conquered, praise is not possible. And Satan, who is the author of fear, uses it as his major weapon to counter our weapon of praise.

Like all things Satan corrupts, fear is not totally a bad thing. It is part of the defense mechanism God has built into each of us to protect us. However, it was intended to protect, not rule. There are times when we must move against our fear levels to do what we know must be done, and this is when God gives us the courage—moral, as well as physical—to overcome our natural fear and trembling. Hemingway once defined courage as "grace under stress," without ever realizing the spiritual truth he spoke.

The man who claims never to know fear is a liar. Fear is common to all of us. Often the only difference between a coward and a courageous man is the way each handled his fear. One was ruled by it, the other insisted on ruling the fear. "Lord, I know this fear is not from You. Forgive my unbelief, for doubting for an instant that You were in control of this situation, and grant me Your peace. And now, Holy Spirit, give me the words with which to praise my Maker, Defender, Redeemer, and Friend."

There is a perfect scriptural antidote to fear. "There is no fear in love; but perfect love casteth out fear: because fear hath torment. He that feareth is not made perfect in love" (1 John 4:18). The little child cries out during the night, terrorized by the thunder and lightning. The father answers, "It's all right

dear; daddy's here." What kind of answer is that? It is an offering of "perfect love that casts out fear." If that answer isn't sufficient, the child is put in the bed of the parents, and feeling the warmth of love, lying next to them, he falls back to sleep in the midst of the storm.

How our Heavenly Father wants to comfort the terror-stricken heart with the simple words, "It's all right now, I'm here." How His arms are outstretched to comfort and assure us of His great love! How can we fear, when so totally surrounded by His love? When a Christian gets his eyes off Satan, himself and others, and focuses the eye of his spirit upon the loving Heavenly Father, his fears melt within him; he can ignore the storm that fear has produced, and respond, child-like, to a loving God whose love for him is totally perfect.

The saints of the ages, who have moved into the things of God, have learned to handle their fear by submitting it and themselves to the magnificent love of God. In the midst of the love flow, they could not be afraid.

How well I remember the deep fear levels I had to deal with in my own life, and in the lives of the people of our congregation, as we began to move into praise and worship responses to the Lord! It was during this time that a chorus, reportedly smuggled out of Communist China, came into my hands. It was said to be the "marching song of the Church in China." It had many verses, but the one I remember best is one we sang repeatedly:

"I will not be afraid. I will not be afraid,

With God beside me, His love to guide me,

I'll not be afraid!"

A fifth preventive to praise is our own ego, the attitude we have toward ourself—our self-image. Sometimes this image is extremely positive, and we see ourself as perfect, or nearly so.

This type person tends to be a braggart. He is self-righteous, proud, superior, boastful, haughty, very much enamored of himself. This person has great difficulty truly praising God, for he can never seem to get his eyes completely off himself. It is hard not to pray the prayer of the publican, "God, I thank thee, that I am not as other men ..." (Luke 18:11). When he does attempt to praise, he usually expresses it as, "I praise thee that I ..."

It is very difficult to praise God, when all you can see is yourself and your accomplishments. There is a shallow form of compliment or praise that demands a response of a higher degree, but this is not acceptable praise to God. Romans 12:3 says, "For I say...to every man that is among you, not to think of himself more highly than he ought to think."

The core, the heart of praise, must be the Lord Jesus Christ. My mind *must* be centered upon God, not myself. My desire must be to call attention to Him, not me.

It is not only the self-exalting person, however, who has difficulty in praising. The self-abasing person has equal difficulty. Whether your attitude and expression is "How great I am" or "How worthless I am," the heart of the expression is still "I."

Some Christians never seem to get over this self-debasement. They think it is humility. They constantly speak ill of themselves, deprecate their talents and abilities, shun any service by saying they are so unworthy, and "Others can do so much better than I" The truth is, they have developed a form of self-righteousness that is far more hideous than the religious self-righteousness Paul confesses. Because it is self-deceptive, the individual is utterly, unshakably convinced of the purity of his humility. So convincing is this sham humility that the naive even point to them as examples of piety.

Nonsense! They're just as "I" centered as the braggart. In their obsequious, retiring manner, they're calling attention to themselves as surely as the person who demands the spot light. Their pride in their failures is as great as another's pride in his successes.

The same verse that warns us not to think of ourselves more highly than we ought to think, concludes, "but to think soberly, according as God hath dealt to every man the measure of faith" (Rom. 12:3). We neither exalt nor abase self; we think according to what God has done for, in, and through us. What we were is not important. What we are becoming is! None among us is worthless, because the same price was paid to ransom each of us. We are to deal exclusively with God: *His* person, *His* doings, *His* graces, *His* promises, and *His* provisions.

Still a sixth preventive to praise involves wrong concepts of God. If we see God as harsh, tyrannical, exacting, unfeeling, or even austere, it is most difficult to release happy emotions of praise to Him. Or, if our concepts of Him are so lofty and elevated that He becomes impersonal, unapproachable, uninvolved, we again will have great difficulty worshiping with praise.

We have all picked up many of our concepts outside the Bible. We've been influenced by the way Bible stories were told to us in our childhood. We've gained many concepts from the hymns and gospel songs we have sung. The pastors under whose preaching we were taught have had a tremendous influence in molding our concepts of God. Religious art, books, movies, and dramas have determined much of our thought patterns concerning God. Our relationships with our earthly fathers obviously have an enormous influence on us.

I found it necessary to return to the Bible and find how God has revealed Himself to us before my praise could be much more than an act of obedience. I needed a total new picture of

the love of God, His mercy, His tender compassions, and His unfailing forgiveness. I needed to see how much He really cared, and that praise ministered to Him as well as to me.

When I began to see Him in a bridegroom relationship, as in the Song of Solomon, I found responding to Him became far more natural, and thereby, more enjoyable. I found I could respond to love, and eventually learned to respond *with* love. But I discovered it necessary in my case to have a "change of mind" about God, before I could accept or give Him love.

There are so many other concepts of God that will limit our praising. If we have a mental image of a God of permissiveness where everything goes because of great mercy, it will be hard to praise; all of us need and desire guidelines. Unless we see God as just, it will be difficult to praise when facing man's injustice. Unless we can see the faithfulness of God, the unfaithfulness of men may very well overwhelm us to a praiseless existence.

All we will ever know about God must come by His revelation. But that revelation has already been given to us in His Word. It is imperative that a praiser acquaint himself with the Scriptures, to increasingly enlarge his comprehension of God, that his praises unto God may abound more and more.

Perhaps a seventh preventive to praise can best be understood by reading Isaiah 61:3: "To appoint unto them that mourn in Zion, to give unto them ... the garment of praise for the spirit of heaviness; that they might be called trees of righteousness, the planting of the Lord, that he might be glorified." This seems to picture a Divine exchange. He offers a "garment of praise *for* the spirit of heaviness." In order to be clothed with praise, we must be willing to relinquish the spirit of heaviness which has surrounded us. We must give up our self-pity, our enjoyment of our misery, and our mournful, negative attitude. Praise cannot be an addition to a negative

life; it is a replacement for it! The joy replaces the sorrow. Triumphing replaces the tears. Shouting replaces the sobbing, and praise replaces the heaviness. If we have learned to be comfortable with the negatives, it may take a while to get comfortable with praise. But if you have had all of that negative, gloomy, mournful way of life you want, just hand it to the Lord, and receive, in exchange, a glorious garment of praise!

I would not presume to suggest that this list of hindrances is all inclusive. There is the problem of the undisciplined mind that just cannot seem to keep itself focused on the Lord. Or the problem of being so out of relationship in our home that praise seems to be a mockery. But I believe these seven I have listed are major, and it is rather likely that you have seen yourself in one or more of them.

Don't bypass praise because you have something in your life that resists it. Use praise to conquer that area of your life. You'll be stronger for it, praise will flow through you like a river, God will be glorified, and the saints will, through your praise, be edified.

"Who shall separate us from the love of Christ? [Or from expressing that love?] shall tribulation, or distress, or persecution, or famine, or nakedness, or peril, or sword? ... Nay, in all these things we are more than conquerors through him that loved us. For I am persuaded, that neither death, nor life, nor angels, nor principalities, nor powers, nor things present, nor things to come, Nor height, nor depth, nor any other creature, shall be able to separate us from the love of God [or its expression], which is in Christ Jesus our Lord" (Rom. 8:35, 37-39).

11

The Permanence of Praise

How wisely does the Psalmist declare, "As for man, his days are as grass: as a flower of the field, so he flourisheth. For the wind passeth over it, and it is gone; and the place thereof shall know it no more" (Ps. 103:15-16).

In our youth, our life stretched out before us as an endless pattern of opportunity, but as years advance, we become increasingly aware of the shortness of our life span. Try as we will to immortalize ourselves, life is very impermanent. Names that are in the headlines today are all but forgotten within the year. Today's heroes are often tomorrow's strangers. We are flowering grass today and fodder tomorrow. "So teach us to number our days, that we may apply our hearts unto wisdom" (Ps. 90:12).

Even the things in life over which we *have* control, seem to have a built-in obsolescence. The housing development, which was the pride of yesterday's generation, is demolished to make room for a freeway for this generation. Our cars, which were lauded as wonders in engineering technology

when we purchased them, are often obsolete when the new model comes out.

Consider the tremendous advancement made in transportation within the life-span of some of you older readers. From horse-and-wagon to the horseless carriage, the automobile, the train, the airplane, the jet aircraft, and now rockets to the moon and back. If that isn't almost "instant obsolescence," what is?

While all of this has brought an improvement in life-style, it has also brought with it a tremendous sense of impermanence, of temporization, of transience. It is difficult for the younger generation to develop any sense of permanence.

Unfortunately, religion seems to have lost much of its steadfast qualities. In the past two decades we have seen many "religious fads" come and go. There has been unbalanced emphasis upon one thing, and then another. Often the Bible has been set aside, so an "experience" could be emphasized, or a "philosophy of life" taught. In the struggle for survival, there have been many mergings that have produced conflicting compromises, leaving communicants greatly confused. There have been few authoritative declarations of "Thus saith the Lord." Whereas men used to anchor their lives to the church, now many fear that the church is sinking in the sea of change, and are loath to tie themselves to it.

We are surrounded with the carnage of death. We slaughter the population of a small city on our highways annually. We seem to be constantly engaged in a war action of one sort or another, and television has brought the horror and massacre of war into our living rooms. We hear so much of the rising tide of crimes of violence, that we have become almost hardened to it. It was recently reported that of the ten things Americans worry about the most, the first five things concern death. This report also indicated that the average American youth thinks of death once every ten minutes.

Is there anything of value that is immutable, unchangeable, enduring, or permanent to be found in our society? Is there anything we can become involved in that will not perish soon?

Yes, praise God, worship and praise are eternal and enduring by their very nature! Revelation 4:11 tells us, "Thou art worthy, O Lord, to receive glory and honour and power: for thou hast created all things, and for thy pleasure they are and were created."

This verse reveals that worship demands recognition of two things: (1) that all things come from God, and (2) all must return to God. When speaking of man, Isaiah 43:7 says, "I have created him for my glory." The man who worships and praises enters into the flow of eternity while still locked in the dimension of time. We have been created unto His pleasure, and we have already learned that it is praise that gives Him that pleasure. God's purposes for man are not temporary or limited to time, but are eternal and timeless. We are now in training for a timeless ministry! We are already engaged in eternity's highest function when we praise God. Man was made to praise the Lord, and through the work of Christ's cross has been re-made into a creature that dares to approach a Holy God in praise.

You will remember that the shouting praise, that produced such a signal victory at Jericho, was just across the borders into the Promised Land. Far from being obsolete, praise is only the beginning revelation of what God has in store for His Church on the earth. We are just commencing to enter into the "high praises," just at the threshold of the Divine worship. This is not another religious fad that will soon pass away; praise is entering into that which God has ordained to be eternal.

In two passages in the book of Revelation (5:8; 8:3), we see the worshipers holding vials, or censers, filled with incense which is defined as, "the prayers of the saints." The Greek word, translated here as "prayers," is also translatable as "worship."

It is not simply the petitions of the saints, but their praises and worship that have ascended up before God over the ages, and have been put into incense form, and preserved in the Divine presence. When the great worshipers, who stand before God's presence, begin to worship, they also present the worship of the saints on earth. Imagine! Your praise and worship is preserved in the heavens, throughout eternity! There is something in life that is permanent, for God has chosen to preserve your praise.

Revelation 7:11-12 speaks clearly of the eternity of praising: "And all the angels stood round about the throne, and about the elders and the four beasts, and fell before the throne on their faces, and worshipped God, Saying, Amen: Blessing, and glory, and wisdom, and thanksgiving, and honour, and power, and might, be unto our God *for ever and ever.*"

Perhaps the most arresting argument for the permanence of praise is rooted in the nature of the object of our praise. It is God we are praising. It is Jesus Christ we are worshiping, and over and over in the book of Revelation, it speaks of "Him that sitteth upon the throne ... for ever and ever" (Rev. 5:13). As long as the object of our praises exists, He will continue to excite our praise.

When we are released from the planet earth, and ushered into God's great heavens, what an inspiration to praise will meet us. When we stand with "ten thousand times ten thousand, and thousands of thousands" of angels (Rev. 5:11), and multitudes of people, "which no man could number, of all nations, and kindreds, and people, and tongues" (Rev. 7:9), how electrifying will be our praise motivation! When all the angels of God's creating stand around God's throne, and the four living creatures (RSV) begin to lead the praise, while the twenty-four elders fall on their faces before the throne (Rev. 7:11), how could we help but be carried away in the vast spirit of worship and praise of that very hour!

And so we are able to insert a parenthesis in the midst of the eternity and interpolate our human, weak, fragile praise and know it will be incorporated forever into the worship of our heavenly Father. And since praise *is* eternal, it will likely take much of eternity to teach us all the truths about it. This book is just a small part of the beginning.

Some Examples of Methods of Praise in Scripture

Using the mouth in praise:

I heard a great voice of much people in heaven, *saying, Alleluia,* Salvation, and glory, and honour, and power, unto the Lord our God. (Rev. 19:1)

0 sing unto the Lord a new song, for he hath done marvellous things. (Ps. 98:1)

I will worship toward thy holy temple, *and praise thy name* for thy lovingkindness and for thy truth. (Ps. 138:2)

Give unto the Lord the glory due unto his name. (Ps. 96:8)

I will give thee thanks in the great congregation. *I will praise thee* among much people (Ps. 35:18)

I will pray with the spirit, and I will pray with the understanding also; I will sing with the spirit, and I will sing with the understanding also. (1 Cor. 14:15)

Bless the Lord. (Ps. 103:20)

0 magnify the Lord with me, and *let us exalt his name* together. (Ps. 34:3)

Speaking to yourselves *in psalms and hymns and spiritual songs,*

singing and making melody in your heart to the Lord. (Eph. 5:19)

And cried with a loud voice, saying, Salvation to our God which sitteth upon the throne, and unto the Lamb. (Rev. 7:10)

Then was our mouth filled with laughter, and our tongue with singing. (Ps. 126:2)

Let them exalt him also in the congregation of the people, *and praise him* in the assembly of the elders. *(Ps. 107:32)*

And let them sacrifice the sacrifices of thanksgiving, and declare his works with rejoicing. (Ps. 107:22)

Make a joyful noise unto the Lord, all the earth: *make a loud noise,* and *rejoice,* and *sing praise.* (Ps. 98:4)

Let them ever *shout for joy,* because thou defendest them: let them also that love thy name *be joyful* in thee. (Ps. 5:11)

Be glad in the Lord, and *rejoice,* ye righteous: and *shout for* joy, all ye that are upright in heart. (Ps. 32:11)

I will extol thee, O Lord. (Ps. 30:1).

Let my mouth be filled with thy praise and with thy honour all the day. (Ps. 71:8)

Using the Hands in Praise

Lifting the hands:

I will lift up my hands in thy name. (Ps. 63:4)

My hands also will I lift up unto thy commandments. (Ps. 119:48)

Lift up your hands in the sanctuary, and bless the Lord. (Ps. 134:2)

The lifting up of my hands as the evening sacrifice. (Ps. 141:2)

Clapping the hands:

O clap your hands, all ye people. (Ps. 47:1)

Let the floods clap their hands. (Ps. 98:8)

All the trees of the field shall clap their hands. (Isa. 55:12)

Playing musical instruments:

Praise the Lord with harp. (Ps. 33:2)

Awake up, my glory; awake psaltery and harp. (Ps. 57:8)

Upon a psaltery and an instrument of ten strings will I sing praises unto thee. (Ps. 144:9)

Sing praise upon the harp unto our God. (Ps. 147:7)

Praise him with the sound of the trumpet: praise him with the psaltery and harp. Praise him with the timbrel ... praise him with stringed instruments and organs. Praise him upon the loud cymbals: praise him upon the high sounding cymbals. (Ps. 150:3-5)

Using the Posture or Motion of the Body in Praise

Dancing:

Thou hast turned for me my mourning into dancing. (Ps. 30:11)

Let them praise his name in the dance. (Ps. 149:3)

Praise him with the ... dance. (Ps. 150:4)

And David danced before the Lord with all his might. (2Sam. 6:14)

Walking and leaping:

And he leaped up, stood, and walked, and he entered with them into the temple, walking, and leaping, and praising God. (Acts 3:8)

David leaping and dancing before the Lord. (2 Sam. 6:16)

Standing:

Ye that stand in the house of the Lord. (Ps. 135:2)

Bless ye the Lord, all ye servants of the Lord, which by night stand in the house of the Lord. (Ps. 134:1)

Bowing and kneeling:

O come, let us worship and bow down: let us kneel before the Lord our maker. (Ps. 95:6)

I bow my knees unto the Father of our Lord Jesus Christ. (Eph. 3:14)

Some Scriptures on Praise, Book by Book, through the Bible

Genesis 14:20: The praise of Melchizedek: "Blessed be the most high God, which hath delivered thine enemies into thy hand."

Genesis 29:35: The praise of Leah: "And she said, Now will I Praise the Lord: therefore she called his name Judah."

Exodus 15:1-19: The Song of Moses which will be sung in heaven: "I will sing unto the Lord, for he hath triumphed gloriously....The Lord is my strength and song, and he is become my salvation: he is my God, and I will prepare him an habitation; my father's God, and I will exalt him.

... Thy right hand, O Lord, is become glorious in power.

... And in the greatness of thine excellency thou hast overthrown them that rose up against thee.

... Who is like unto thee, O Lord, among the gods? who is like thee, glorious in holiness, fearful in praises, doing wonders?

... The Lord shall reign for ever and ever."

Leviticus 19:24: "The fruit ... shall be holy to praise the Lord withal."

Numbers 21:16-17: "The Lord spake unto Moses, Gather the people together, and I will give them water. Then Israel sang this song, Spring up, O well; sing ye unto it."

Deuteronomy 10:21: "He is thy praise, and he is thy God ... "

Joshua 6:20: The praiseful shouting at Jericho's walls: "When the people heard the sound of the trumpet, and the people shouted with a great shout, ... the wall fell down flat."

Judges 5:2-3: The praise of Deborah and Barak: "Praise ye the Lord for the avenging of Israel, when the people willingly offered themselves. Hear, O ye kings; give ear, O ye princes; I, even I will sing unto the Lord; I will sing praise to the Lord God of Israel."

Ruth 4:14: "And the women said unto Naomi, Blessed be the Lord, which hath not left thee this day without a kinsman, that his name may be famous in Israel."

1 Samuel 2:1-2: "And Hannah prayed, and said, My heart rejoiceth in the Lord, mine horn is exalted in the Lord.

... There is none holy as the Lord: for there is none beside thee: neither is there any rock like our God."

2 Samuel 22:4: The praise of David after his deliverance from Saul: "I will call on the Lord who is worthy to be praised."

1 Kings 8:15: Solomon's praise of God at the dedication of the Temple: "Blessed be the Lord God of Israel, which spake with his mouth unto David my father, and hath with his hand fulfilled it."

2 Kings 3:15-16: The singing praise of a minstrel stirred the prophetic gift in Elisha: "And it came to pass, when the minstrel played, that the hand of the Lord came upon him. And he said, Thus saith the Lord ..."

1 Chronicles 16:4: "And he [David] appointed certain of the Levites ... to thank and praise the Lord God of Israel."

2 Chronicles 20:21: Tells of Jehoshaphat's praising choir: "He appointed singers unto the Lord ... that should praise the beauty of holiness ... and ... say, Praise the Lord; for his mercy endureth forever."

Ezra 3:11: Speaks of the loud shouting praise at the foundation

laying of the Temple: "And they sang together by course in praising and giving thanks unto the Lord; because he is good, and his mercy endureth forever toward Israel. And all the people shouted with a great shout, when they praised the Lord, because the foundation of the house of the Lord was laid."

Nehemiah 12:24: Tells of praisers being re-appointed to the service of the Lord: "And the chief of the Levites: Hashabiah, Sherebiah, and Jeshua the son of Kadmiel, with their brethren over against them, to praise and to give thanks, according to the commandment of David, the man of God."

Esther 8:15-16: Gives the praise of the Jews at Shushan after divine intervention had saved Mordecai: "And the city of Shushan rejoiced and was glad. The Jews had light, and gladness, and joy, and honour."

Job 13:15: Praises in the midst of negatives: "Though He slay me, yet will I trust in him."

Psalms lists the praises of David, Solomon, Asaph, Sons of Korah, and others.

Proverbs 8:30-31: "I was daily his delight, rejoicing always before him; Rejoicing in the habitable part of his earth."

Ecclesiastes 2:26; 3:12, 22: "God giveth to a man ... joy." "But for a man to rejoice." "A man should rejoice."

Song of Solomon 1:4: "Draw me, we will run after thee: the king hath brought me into his chambers: we will be glad and rejoice in thee."

Isaiah 43:21: "This people have I formed for myself; they shall shew forth my praise:"

Jeremiah 33:11: "The voice of joy, and the voice of gladness ... the voice of them that shall say, Praise the Lord of hosts ... and of them that shall bring the sacrifice of praise into the house of the Lord."

Lamentations 3:41: "Let us lift up our heart with our hands unto God in the heavens."

Ezekiel 44:15: Shows the specified priests who shall minister directly to the Lord: "But the priests the Levites, the sons of Zadok, that kept the charge of my sanctuary when the children of Israel went

astray from me, they shall come near to me to minister unto me, and they shall stand before me to offer unto me the fat and the blood, saith the Lord God."

Daniel 2:20: "Blessed be the name of God for ever and ever: for wisdom and might are his."

Hosea 12:6: "Wait on thy God continually." (Compare with Psalm 65:1: "Praise waiteth for thee, O God.")

Joel 2:23: "Be glad then, ye children of Zion, and rejoice in the Lord your God."

Amos 9:11: "In that day will I raise up the tabernacle of David that is fallen."

Obadiah 1:17: "But upon mount Zion shall be deliverance, and there shall be holiness." (As we see this last day "revival" being fulfilled, we find praise as its keynote.)

Jonah 2:9: "I will sacrifice unto thee with the voice of thanksgiving."

Micah 7:7-9: "Therefore I will look unto the Lord; I will wait for the God of my salvation: my God will hear me." (Read the next two verses.)

Nahum 1:15: "Behold upon the mountains the feet of him that bringeth good tidings, that publisheth peace! O Judah [which means Praise], keep thy solemn feasts, perform thy vows."

Habakkuk 3:18: "Yet I will rejoice in the Lord, I will joy in the God of my salvation."

Zephaniah 3:14: "Sing, O daughter of Zion; shout, O Israel; be glad and rejoice with all the heart, O daughter of Jerusalem."

Haggai 2:7, 9: God promises to give greater glory to the second Temple: "I will fill this house with glory, saith the Lord of hosts ... The glory of this latter house shall be greater than of the former."

Zechariah 9:9: The "Palm Sunday" prophecy, "Rejoice greatly, O daughter of Zion; shout O daughter of Jerusalem: behold, thy King cometh unto thee: he is just, and having salvation; lowly, and riding upon an ass."

Malachi 1:5: "And your eyes shall see, and ye shall say, The Lord will be magnified."

Matthew 26:30: Jesus and the disciples at the time of His passion: "And when they had sung an hymn, they went out into the mount of Olives."

Mark 11:8-10: Describes Palm Sunday with the rejoicing of the people: "And many spread their garments in the way: and others cut down branches off the trees, and strawed them in the way. And they that went before, and they that followed, cried, saying, Hosanna; Blessed is he that cometh in the name of the Lord: Blessed be the kingdom of our father David, that cometh in the name of the Lord."

Luke 1:46-55: Gives Mary's glorious Magnificat of praise: "My soul doth magnify the Lord, And my spirit hath rejoiced in God my Saviour ...

John 1:49: Nathanael praises Jesus, saying, "Rabbi, thou art the Son of God; thou art the King of Israel."

John 7:37-39: Tells of the flow of the Holy Spirit that produces praise: "Jesus stood and cried, saying, If any man thirst, let him come to me, and drink. He that believeth on me, as the scripture hath said, out of his belly shall flow rivers of living water. (But this spake he of the Spirit, which they that believe on him should receive.)

Acts 16:25: In prison, "At midnight Paul and Silas prayed, and sang praises unto God."

Romans 15:11: "Praise the Lord, all ye Gentiles; and laud him, all ye people."

1 Corinthians 14:15: "I will pray with the spirit ... I will sing with the spirit."

2 Corinthians 8:18: "Whose praise is in the gospel throughout all the churches."

Galatians 4:27: "For it is written, Rejoice, thou barren that bearest not; break forth and cry."

Ephesians 1:12: "That we should be to the praise of his glory, who first trusted in Christ."

Philippians 4:20: "Now unto God and our Father be glory for

ever and ever. Amen."

Colossians 1:3: "We give thanks to God and the Father of our Lord Jesus Christ."

1 Thessalonians 5:16: "Rejoice evermore."

2 Thessalonians 1:3: "We are bound to thank God always for you."

1 Timothy 2:8: "I will therefore that men pray everywhere, lifting up holy hands."

2 Timothy 4:18: "And the Lord shall deliver me ... to whom be glory for ever and ever."

Titus makes no mention of praise, but abundant reasons for praise are given, and we know the author was a praiser.

Philemon 4: "I thank my God, making mention of thee always in my prayers."

Hebrews 2:12: "Saying, I will declare thy name unto my brethren, in the midst of the church will I sing praise unto thee.

James 5:13: "Is any merry? let him sing psalms."

1 Peter 1:7: "That the trial of your faith ... might be found unto praise and honour and glory at the appearing of Jesus Christ."

2 Peter 1:5: "Add to your faith virtue" (Greek *arete*, translated in 1 Peter 2:9 as "praises").

1 John 4:17: "Because as He is, so are we in this world." Jesus was a praiser—so are we.

2 John 4: "I rejoiced greatly that I found of thy children walking in truth."

3 John 3: "I rejoiced greatly, when the brethren came and testified of the truth that is in thee, even as thou walkest in the truth."

Jude 24:25: "Now unto Him that is able to keep you from falling, and to present you faultless before the presence of his glory with exceeding joy, To the only wise God our Saviour, be glory and majesty, dominion and power, both now and ever. Amen."

Revelation 19:5: "And a voice came out of the throne, saying,

Praise our God, all ye his servants, and ye that fear him, both small and great."

Scriptures Concerning Praising in the Congregation

Psalm 22:22: "I will declare thy name unto my brethren: in the midst of the congregation will I praise thee."

Psalm 22:25: "My praise shall be of thee in the great congregation: I will pay my vows before them that fear him."

Psalm 111:1: "Praise ye the Lord. I will praise the Lord with my whole heart, in the assembly of the upright, and in the congregation."

Psalm 149:1: "Praise ye the Lord. Sing unto the Lord a new song, and his praise in the congregation of saints."

1Chronicles 29:20: "And all the congregation blessed the Lord God of their fathers, and bowed down their heads, and worshipped the Lord."

2 Chronicles 29:28: "And all the congregation worshipped, and the singers sang, and the trumpeters sounded: and all this continued until the burnt offering was finished."

Psalm 35:18: "I will give thee thanks in the great congregation: I will praise thee among much people."

Psalm 26:12: "My foot standeth in an even place: in the congregations will I bless the Lord."

Psalm 68:26: "Bless ye God in the congregations, even the Lord."

1 Peter 2:9: "But ye are a chosen generation, a royal priesthood, an holy nation, a peculiar people; that ye should shew forth the praises of him who hath called you out of darkness into his marvellous light."

Devil-Demons

The following is quoted from the *Expository Dictionary of New Testament Words* by W.E. Vine, published by Fleming H. Revell Company:

Devil, devilish (from page 306)

Diabolos, an accuser, a slanderer, is one of the names of Satan. From it the English word "Devil" is derived, and should be applied only to Satan, as a proper name. *Diamön, a* demon, is frequently, but wrongly, translated "devil," it should always be translated "demon," as in the R.V. margin. There is one Devil, there are many demons. Being the malignant enemy of God and man, he accuses man to God, Job 1:6-11; 2:1-5; Rev. 12:9, 10, and God to man, Gen. 3. Being himself sinful, 1 John 3:8, he instigated man to sin, Gen. 3, and tempts man to do evil, Eph. 4:27; 6:11 encouraging him thereto by deception, Eph. 2:2.

Demon, demoniac (from page 291)

Daimön, a demon ... In the N.T. it denotes an evil spirit. It is used in Matt. 8:31, mistranslated "devils."

*Daimonion,. . .*the neuter of the adjective *daimonios,* pertaining to a demon, is also mistranslated "devil," "devils." ...Demons are the spiritual agents acting in all idolatry. The idol itself is nothing, but every idol has a demon associated with it who introduces idolatry, with its worship and sacrifices, 1 Cor. 10:20, 21; Rev. 9:20; cp. Deut. 32:17; Isa. 13:21; 34:14; 65:3, 11. They disseminate errors among men, and seek to seduce believers, 1 Tim. 4:1. As seducing spirits they deceive men into the supposition that through mediums (those who have "familiar spirits," Lev. 20:6, 27 e.g.) they can converse with deceased human beings. Hence the destructive deception of Spiritism, forbidden in Scripture, Lev. 19:31; Deut. 18:11; Isa. 8:19. Demons tremble before God, Jas. 2:19; they recognized Christ as Lord and as their future Judge, Matt. 8:29; Luke 4:41. Christ cast them out of

human beings by His own power. His disciples did so in His Name, and by exercising faith, e.g. Matt. 17:20.

Acting under Satan (cp. Rev. 16:13, 14) demons are permitted to afflict with bodily disease, Luke 13:16. Being unclean they tempt human beings with unclean thoughts, Matt. 10: 1; Mark 5:2, 7:25; Luke 8:27-29; Rev. 16:13; 18:2, e.g. They differ in degrees of wickedness, Matt. 12:45. They will instigate the rulers of the nations at the end of this age to make war against God and His Christ, Rev. 16:14.